Representing Conflicts in Games

This book offers an overview of how conflicts are represented and enacted in games, in a variety of genres and game systems. Games are a cultural form apt at representing real-world conflicts, and this edited volume highlights the intrinsic connection between games and conflict through a set of theoretical and empirical studies. It interrogates the nature and use of conflicts as a fundamental aspect of game design, and how a wide variety of conflicts can be represented in digital and analogue games.

The book asks what we can learn from conflicts in games, how our understanding of conflicts change when we turn them into playful objects, and what types of conflicts are still not represented in games. It queries the way games make us think about armed conflict, and how games can help us understand such conflicts in new ways.

Offering a deeper understanding of how games can serve political, pedagogical, or persuasive purposes, this volume will interest scholars and students working in fields such as game studies, media studies, and war studies.

Björn Sjöblom is Senior Lecturer at the Department of War Studies and Military History at the Swedish Defence University.

Jonas Linderoth is Professor in the Department of Education, Communication and Learning at the University of Gothenburg, and Visiting Professor at the Department of War Studies and Military History at the Swedish Defence University.

Anders Frank is Senior Lecturer at the Department of War Studies and Military History at the Swedish Defence University.

Routledge Advances in Game Studies

Evolutionary Psychology and Digital Games
Digital Hunter-Gatherers
Edited by Johannes Breuer, Daniel Pietschmann, Benny Liebold, and Benjamin P. Lange

The Playful Undead and Video Games
Critical Analyses of Zombies and Gameplay
Edited by Stephen J. Webley and Peter Zackariasson

Hybrid spaces
Crossing Boundaries in Game Design, Players Identities and Play Spaces
Edited by Adriana de Souza e Silva and Ragan Glover-Rijkse

Forms and Functions of Endings in Narrative Digital Games
Michelle Herte

Independent Videogames
Cultures, Networks, Techniques and Politics
Edited by Paolo Ruffino

Comics and Videogames
From Hybrid Medialities to Transmedia Expansions
Edited by Edited by Andreas Rauscher, Daniel Stein, and Jan-Noël Thon

Immersion, Narrative, and Gender Crisis in Survival Horror Video Games
Andrei Nae

Videogames and the Gothic
Ewan Kirkland

Longing, Ruin, and Connection in Hideo Kojima's Death Stranding
Amy M. Green

Manifestations of Queerness in Video Games
Gaspard Pelurson

Representing Conflicts in Games
Antagonism, Rivalry, and Competition
Edited by Björn Sjöblom, Jonas Linderoth, and Anders Frank

Videogames and Agency
Bettina Bódi

Representing Conflicts in Games

Antagonism, Rivalry, and Competition

Edited by Björn Sjöblom, Jonas Linderoth, and Anders Frank

LONDON AND NEW YORK

First published 2023
by Routledge
4 Park Square, Milton Park, Abingdon, Oxon OX14 4RN

and by Routledge
605 Third Avenue, New York, NY 10158

Routledge is an imprint of the Taylor & Francis Group, an informa business

© 2023 selection and editorial matter, Björn Sjöblom, Jonas Linderoth, and Anders Frank; individual chapters, the contributors

The right of Björn Sjöblom, Jonas Linderoth, and Anders Frank to be identified as the authors of the editorial material, and of the authors for their individual chapters, has been asserted in accordance with sections 77 and 78 of the Copyright, Designs and Patents Act 1988.

All rights reserved. No part of this book may be reprinted or reproduced or utilised in any form or by any electronic, mechanical, or other means, now known or hereafter invented, including photocopying and recording, or in any information storage or retrieval system, without permission in writing from the publishers.

Trademark notice: Product or corporate names may be trademarks or registered trademarks, and are used only for identification and explanation without intent to infringe.

British Library Cataloguing-in-Publication Data
A catalogue record for this book is available from the British Library

Library of Congress Cataloging-in-Publication Data
Names: Sjöblom, Björn, editor. | Linderoth, Jonas, 1970– editor. | Frank, Anders, editor.
Title: Representing conflicts in games : antagonism, rivalry, and competition / Edited by Björn Sjöblom, Jonas Linderoth, and Anders Frank.
Description: Abingdon, Oxon ; New York, NY : Routledge, 2023. | Series: Routledge advances in game studies | Includes bibliographical references and index.
Identifiers: LCCN 2022042258 (print) | LCCN 2022042259 (ebook) | ISBN 9781032278278 (hardback) | ISBN 9781032285597 (paperback) | ISBN 9781003297406 (ebook)
Subjects: LCSH: Video games—Social aspects. | Interpersonal conflict. | Two-person zero-sum games. | Video games—Psychological aspects.
Classification: LCC GV1469.3 .R45 2023 (print) | LCC GV1469.3 (ebook) | DDC 794.8—dc23/eng/20220917
LC record available at https://lccn.loc.gov/2022042258
LC ebook record available at https://lccn.loc.gov/2022042259

ISBN: 9781032278278 (hbk)
ISBN: 9781032285597 (pbk)
ISBN: 9781003297406 (ebk)

DOI: 10.4324/9781003297406

Typeset in NewBaskerville
by Apex CoVantage, LLC

Contents

List of Contributors viii
Acknowledgements xiii

The Inevitable Relation between Games and Conflict:
An Introduction 1
JONAS LINDEROTH AND BJÖRN SJÖBLOM

PART I
Game Systems, Transformation, and Learning 11

1 **Red in Bits and Bytes: Evolutionary Conflicts in Biological**
 God Games 13
 PÉTER KRISTÓF MAKAI

2 **On Bikers at War: Transformations of Non-Fictional and**
 Fictional Conflicts from *Hamlet* to *Sons of Anarchy: Men of*
 Mayhem 30
 ULF WILHELMSSON

3 **From Zero-Sum Business Games to Coopetitive Simulation** 46
 J. TUOMAS HARVIAINEN

4 **The Limits of 'Serious' Play: Frame Disputes around**
 Educational Games 58
 JONAS LINDEROTH, ADAM CHAPMAN AND SEBASTIAN DETERDING

PART II
Representing War and Armed Conflicts   73

5 On Wargames and War: Modeling Carl von Clausewitz's
  Theory of War   75
  VILLE KANKAINEN AND LLMARI KÄIHKÖ

6 Wargames as Reenactment: An Ecological Framework for
  the Development of Military Games for Education   97
  ADAM CHAPMAN AND JONAS LINDEROTH

7 The Grasping Eye: Wargames and the Ideal-Typical Field
  Commander's Inner Vision   116
  TOMAS KARLSSON

PART III
Critical Perspectives on Conflicts in Games   133

8 War Never Changes? Creating an American Victimology in
  Fallout 4   135
  RYAN SCHEIDING

9 Are the Bullets Going over Our Head? Designed
  Ambivalence in the Representation of Armed Conflict in Games   153
  PATRICK PRAX

10 Where Are the White Perpetrators in All the Colonial Board
   Games? A Case Study on *Afrikan Tähti*   171
   SABINE HARRER AND J. TUOMAS HARVIAINEN

PART IV
Alternative Ways of Representing Conflicts in Games   189

11 Narrative and Mechanical Integration: Playing with
   Interpersonal Conflicts in *Life Is Strange*   191
   FATIMA JONSSON AND LINA EKLUND

12 **The Most Intimate Conflict of All: Marriage as Conflict in Digital Games** 208
JAKUB MAJEWSKI AND PIOTR SIUDA

13 **All Smoke, No Fire: The Post-mortem of Conflicts in the 'Walking Simulator' Genre** 226
JAKUB MAJEWSKI AND PIOTR SIUDA

Index 241

Contributors

Adam Chapman
Independent Scholar
United Kingdom

Adam Chapman's research focuses on historical games, i.e. those games that in some way represent, or relate to, discourses about the past. He is the author of *Digital Games as History: How Videogames Represent the Past and Offer Access to Historical Practice* (Routledge 2016), alongside a number of other publications exploring games as a historical form. Adam is also the co-founder and a current convener of the Historical Games Network. A former Senior Lecturer at the University of Gothenburg, Sweden, he is currently working as an independent scholar.

Sebastian Deterding
Imperial College London
United Kingdom

Professor Sebastian Deterding is Chair of Design Engineering at the Dyson School of Design Engineering, Imperial College London, UK, co-editor of *Role-Playing Game Studies* (Routledge, 2018) and *The Gameful World* (2015), as well as founding editor-in-chief of *ACM Games: Research and Practice*. His work focuses motivational and game-inspired design for human flourishing.

Lina Eklund
Uppsala University
Sweden

Lina Eklund's work focuses on how game settings and stories together and in opposition with mechanics create certain gameplay experiences. She is also researching the evolution of video games to heritage and how games are exhibited in museums. Her interests are social interaction and gender in relation to games and digital technologies.

Anders Frank
Swedish Defence University
Sweden

Anders Frank is Senior Lecturer at the Swedish Defence University. His research is focused on how wargames can be used for education and training of military tactics and operations. His dissertation is titled *Gamer mode: Identifying and managing unwanted behaviour in military educational wargaming*.

Sabine Harrer
University of Vienna & Uppsala University
Austria & Sweden

Sabine Harrer (PhD, Mmag.) is a Hertha Firnberg scholar at University of Vienna, Austria, and Senior Lecturer at the Game Design Department, Uppsala University, Sweden. Alumna of the Centre of Excellence in Game Culture Studies in Tampere, Finland, Sabine has taught games and culture at BTK Berlin, ITU Copenhagen, and University Vienna. They are the author of Games and Bereavement (transcript 2018), and the satire board game Kyoto (2020).

J. Tuomas Harviainen
Tampere University
Finland

J. Tuomas Harviainen (PhD, MBA) works as Associate Professor of Information Practices at Tampere University, Finland. He is a former editor of *Simulation & Gaming*, and has published in venues such as *Organization Studies*, *Journal of Business Ethics*, *Games and Culture* and *Journal of Documentation*.

Fatima Jonsson
Södertörn University
Sweden

Fatima Jonsson's current work focuses on uses and practices of social media, gameplay experiences, the impact of anonymity on digital sociality as well as social presence in online education. Her areas of interest are design justice, critical design and activism in relation to digital technologies and design.

Ilmari Käihkö
Swedish Defence University
Sweden

Ilmari Käihkö is Associate Professor at the Swedish Defence University, and a veteran of the Finnish Defence Forces. He is interested in strategic theory and thinks Twilight Struggle is the best board game ever made. His research focuses on creation, control, and use of force.

Ville Kankainen
Tampere University
Finland

Ville Kankainen is a PhD researcher and game designer, working in the Centre of Excellence in Game Culture Studies at Tampere University. In his dissertation he studies the hybridization of digital media and material tabletop gaming. He also enjoys reflecting history by moving cardboard armies around the table.

Tomas Karlsson
Independent scholar
Sweden

Tomas Karlsson holds a PhD in History Didactics. In 2018 he successfully defended his PhD thesis *Låtsaskrigen: föreställningar om krig, maskulinitet och historia i krigsspel under 200 år* (eng. *Pretend Wars, Notions of War, Masculinity and History in 200 Years of Wargames*) at Umeå University, Sweden. He is currently an employee of The Swedish Schools Inspectorate.

Jonas Linderoth
Swedish Defence University & University of Gothenburg
Sweden

Jonas Linderoth is appointed as Professor in two subjects, Education and MEB (Media, Aesthetics, and Narration). He has worked as Professor at the School of Informatics at University of Skövde, Sweden, the Department of Education, Communication and Learning at the University of Gothenburg, and at the Department of War studies at the Swedish Defense University. Linderoth's research is mainly about the educational usage of games in various settings.

Jakub Majewski
Kazimierz Wielki University in Bydgoszcz
Poland

Jakub Majewski (PhD) is Assistant Professor at Kazimierz Wielki University in Bydgoszcz, Poland. His research interests include role-playing games and cultural heritage, game storytelling techniques, game industry history, among others. He is also a game developer with two decades' worth of experience and a portfolio of about forty diverse games.

Péter Kristóf Makai
Ludwig-Maximilians-Universität, München
Germany

Péter Kristóf Makai is a Landhaus Fellow at the Rachel Carson Center, Munich, Germany, researching how games portray climate change. He worked as a KWI International Fellow in Essen, Germany, focusing on how computer games mediate theme parks. He was a Crafoord Postdoctoral Research Fellow in Intermedial and Multimodal Studies at Linnaeus University, Sweden.

Patrick Prax
Uppsala University
Sweden

Patrick Prax is Associate Professor in Game Design. His work centers around critical perspectives on games in society. He is writing about critical game literacy, games and sustainability, and games as civic culture, but also works with miniature war gaming. Patrick is a climate activist and anti-fascist.

Ryan Scheiding
Georgia Institute of Technology
United States

Ryan Scheiding is Assistant Professor of Digital Media (Game Design and Game Studies) at the Georgia Institute of Technology, USA. He is the founder of TUBBA Games Manufacturing Concern, a game-design academic artist collective. His research is primarily focused on collective memory, video games, and the atomic bombings of Japan.

Piotr Siuda
Kazimierz Wielki University in Bydgoszcz
Poland

Piotr Siuda (PhD) is a media and game studies scholar, Associate Professor at the Institute of Social Communication and Media at the Kazimierz Wielki University in Bydgoszcz, Poland. His research interests include gamer communities, esports, media sports, and dark web communities.

Björn Sjöblom
Swedish Defence University
Sweden

Björn Sjöblom is Senior Lecturer at the Swedish Defence University. His current research focuses on the educational use of wargames in military education, examining interaction in pedagogical practices. He has published research on learning, identity and interaction in a wide variety of contexts, including internet cafés, museums, online forums, and military tactics education.

Ulf Wilhelmsson
University of Skövde
Sweden

Ulf Wilhelmsson is currently Associate Professor at the School of Informatics, Division of Game Development at the University of Skövde, Sweden. His research focus is on games, game audio, player agency, inclusive game design, and serious games. He is a member of the GAME Research Group at the University of Skövde.

Acknowledgements

The editorial work with this volume was done within the research and development project *Games for Conflict Management and War*, funded by the Swedish Armed forces and hosted at the Swedish Defence University. We gratefully acknowledge this financial support and productive collaboration.

We would also like to thank the department of Education, Communication, and Learning at the University of Gothenburg as well as the School of Informatics at the University of Skövde which in part supported professor Linderoth's work with the volume.

A special thanks to university librarian Camilla Olsson for her invaluable contributions and help with the manuscript.

Finally, we are of course grateful to all the authors who have contributed their hard work and analytical insights to this book

Björn Sjöblom, Jonas Linderoth, and Anders Frank

The Inevitable Relation between Games and Conflict
An Introduction

Jonas Linderoth and Björn Sjöblom

The Playful Conflict

The playful opposition either between players or between players and game environments is a significant characteristic of games. To overcome challenges provided either by opponents or by a game's rule system is one of the traits that make games interesting. In other words, games and conflict are intrinsically linked. Conflict is at the heart of games, where artificial challenges are designed to test some aspects of the players (see Linderoth, 2013). While many such designed challenges lack a representational layer, such as many sports and games without a theme, games are a cultural form that often combines designed challenges with media and representation (Juul, 2003). As a cultural form, games seem to be apt at representing real-world conflicts. Numerous games portray clashes between opposing agents, most obviously in wargames and other games about armed conflict.

Wargames are perhaps the quintessential game about conflict – players taking on the role of military commanders, controlling real-world or fantastical forces and competing for tactical or strategical victory in war. From *Kriegsspeil* (Reisswits, 1824/2019) to *Little Wars* (Wells, 1913/2002) to *Command* (Warfare Sims, 2013), wargames have been used in everything from military education to operations planning and analysis to pure entertainment. In modern 3D shooters, the player is placed in the midst of a variety of martial conflicts, taking the perspective of the individual combatant, managing opposition through armed violence.

However, games also depict such conflicts as political conflicts, economic competition, legal conflicts, conflicts in social hierarchies and within an individual's psyche. To mention a couple of examples, *The Sims* series portray numerous everyday conflicts between different needs of family members, their resources and their domestic environment. Other games such as *Democracy 3* (Positech Games, 2013) are about political struggles between ideologies and the interests of different voter groups. Even though gaming culture to a large degree is associated with the representation of violence (Kirkpatrick, 2012), conflict in games is not necessarily a matter of armed conflicts or war.

This volume investigates the relation between conflict as a phenomenon and the way it is represented and adapted in both analogue and digital games. The volume explores the cultural significance of representing real-world conflicts in games. The overall question that guides this exploration is what happens when conflicts are turned into playful objects?

Conflicts can be said to be an unstated undercurrent to our knowledge of games – almost ubiquitously present but much more seldomly highlighted as a significant aspect of both game design and gameplay. Given that the concept of *conflict* covers several different natural and sociocultural phenomena it is hardly surprising that it eludes game scholars as being a topic in itself. Yet other academic fields have attempted to outline and explore the similarities and differences of conflicts.

What Is a Conflict?

Drawing upon reviews from conflict management literature Wall and Callister (1995) define *conflict* as 'a process in which one party perceives that its interests are being opposed or negatively affected by another party' (p. 517). A conflict, for Wall and Callister, is a process that lies between cause and effect. Differences in values and goals, desire for autonomy, distrust, misunderstandings, power imbalances, distributive relationships and status differences are some examples of causes that can start the conflict process. The effects, results or outcome of the conflict process in turn feed back to the causes in a cycle that can take several iterations (Wall & Callister, 1995, p. 516). This definition contains some elements that make it suitable as a starting point for exploring the relation between conflicts, as an ever-present part of life, and games as a cultural form. Firstly, we are dealing with a *process*; that is events that take place over time and will have outcomes. Secondly, conflicts are *goal-driven processes* where actors have *stakes and interests*. However, many processes are goal driven without being conflicts. The defining trait that turns the goal-driven process into a conflict is *the perception that another actor poses an obstacle to our goals and needs*. This definition works as a template for several sociocultural and sociopsychological processes on different levels and with different degrees of intensity. Everything from children quarrelling over whose turn it is to go on the swing to war between nations constitutes conflict.

Not only do conflicts differ regarding their seriousness, but they can be found on different levels where the involved individuals have different social relations. Rahim and Bonoma (1979) classify organizational conflicts as originating from their sociopsychological locus. Firstly, there are *intrapersonal* conflicts, which originate from a single individual, that is, when an individual must choose between mutually exclusive options or when the individual's different social roles and identities conflict with each other (e.g. religious identity and sexual orientation, see Subhi & Geelan, 2012). Then there are *interpersonal* conflicts, that is, conflicts that take place between two or more persons. Interpersonal conflicts can have different group dynamics. They can either take place within a group (*intragroup*) or between groups (*intergroup*). Intragroup and intergroup conflicts influence each other in different forms of social dynamics (Orian Harel et al., 2020). For instance, intergroup conflicts can reduce intragroup conflicts, a social dynamic that is not only found among humans but has also been observed among birds (Radford, 2011). Hence, it is important to note that conflict is not exclusive to the human world, but also a central part of animals' life conditions. As such it cannot solely be perceived as a sociocultural phenomenon.

Conflicts, Storytelling, and Classical (Ortho)games

Given that conflicts are such an abiding part of life it is not surprising that they play a central role in the stories mankind tells. In classical drama and storytelling, conflict is a fundamental ingredient. Something is at stake that sets the protagonist and antagonist of the drama on their collision course. As Roberts and Jacobs (1986) put it: 'The reason that conflict is the major ingredient in plot is that once two forces are in opposition there may be doubt about the outcome' (p. 103). In general conflicts will, over time, come to some form of conclusion. Conflicts in stories, just as any event with some form of uncertainty combined with stakes, make us interested in the outcome. It can make us, as Goffman (1961) puts it, 'engrossed' that is absorbed in the situation here and now and interested in what is going to happen as events unfold. For Goffman, games are clear examples of activities that potentially have such a structure.

It should be clarified that Goffman is referring to classical games such as chess. Goffman seems to be discussing what game designers later has described as *orthogames*, a concept coined by Elias et al. (2012). They state that an orthogame is 'a game for two or more players, with rules that result in a ranking or weighting of the players and done for entertainment.' (p. 8). Their definition is done for the purpose of finding a concept that includes classical games where players compete against each other without discussing games with more complex structures such as many storytelling games and roleplaying games without clear rules that demark a winner. That does not mean that conflict is not part of these games as well. The orthogame and the classical *protagonist – conflict – antagonist* storytelling structure are both cultural forms that rely heavily upon interpersonal conflicts (be it in the form of intragroup or intergroup conflicts). However, any game where the player, in accordance with star game designer Sid Meier's classical saying, makes 'a series of interesting decisions' (Meier, 2012), can potentially put the player in an intrapersonal conflict. The defining trait of an interesting choice is that there, for the player, cannot be any optimal choices. If a certain choice is obviously better than others, than there is no choice at all. Hence an interesting choice can potentially put the player in a situation where different possible paths forward conflict with each other.

As a cultural form, games seem to be designed to set off conflicts. One could say that games (or at least orthogames) in a sense *are* conflicts. To play a game means to engage in an activity that is filled with decisions and tension as the outcome unfolds over time.

At the same time games can represent and tell stories about conflicts. The game form both presents and represents conflict, sometimes simultaneously. Linderoth (2015) has argued that digital games with stats and leveling are activities that empower the player, that is the player becomes empowered with new capabilities in the digital/virtual realm. At the same time this empowering structure can tell stories about empowerment. This means, according to Linderoth, that the game form fits specific themes and settings. The form lends itself to certain stories better than others. The player is engaged in both the thematic representation and the story of the game at the same time as they interact with the rules of the game and gain new opportunities in the virtual realm (through leveling and gearing up). Hence, games draw upon rather different experiences to engage the player. The emotions of the players come from these different forms (or frameworks) but blend into one coherent experience. Linderoth argues that games hence are a 'composite form':

> I find the metaphor of composites particularly useful for thinking and theorizing about video games. A composite material, such as fiberglass, is a material made up of at least two independent materials with clearly different properties, that when combined (without being mixed, hence maintaining their original chemical properties) create a material that has clearly different properties than its components. I therefore suggest the metaphor composite form as a way of approaching video games.
>
> (pp. 281–282)

Conflict is an even more present design element in games than empowerment. Conflict is perhaps one of the clearest examples of the composite structure Linderoth suggests. Game themes that lack natural conflicts can sometimes, in their story, be framed in such a way that the conflict in the rules make sense in relation to the thematic layer of the game. For instance, the board game *Reykholt* (Rosenberg, 2018) is about growing vegetables in Iceland using geothermal energy. A peaceful theme that does not seem to lend itself to any representation of conflict. Yet the game frames vegetable farming as competition for the attention of tourists and in the introduction to the game one can read: 'with all the tourism around the natural wonders, competition to have the best vegetables is fierce!' (Rosenberg, 2018).

Through their rules, games can orchestrate both interpersonal (social) and intrapersonal (psychological) conflicts. At the same time, they, as cultural form, can represent and portray different forms of conflict. This is a rather unique condition where the process of consuming a cultural form partly resembles the thematic representations of the form. It raises questions about how to intellectually frame and describe it, and raises questions about possibilities and limitations. Does the composite nature offer some unique ways of portraying conflicts? If so, what aspects of conflicts are games good at depicting and what aspects do they, because of their composite structure, exclude? What do these affordances and constraints mean for the use of games for educational purposes, for example wargames in military training? And what are the ideological and moral entailments when a conflict is being represented in a composite form?

In this volume, scholars explore these and similar issues. The book is structured in four parts. The first part of the book considers how rules and game mechanics influence the portrayal of various types of conflicts in games. The second part of the book focuses specifically on portrayals of armed conflict and wargames. The third part of the book collects chapters with a critical perspective on how particular conflicts or types of conflicts are portrayed in games. The chapters in the fourth and final part of the book concern games that handle conflicts in novel, non-traditional and innovative ways and games with mechanics that potentially can push the medium forward. The four parts of the book should be seen as complementary and overlapping, where many similar themes and lines of argumentations are developed in relation to the analyses of a wide range of games and theoretical approaches.

In the first chapter in part I of the book, *Red in Bits and Bytes: Evolutionary Conflicts in Biological God Games*, Péter Kristóf Makai investigates how games portray the conflicts in evolutionary processes. Makai's chapter demonstrates how games, through their game mechanics and aesthetic conditions, present simplified versions of evolutionary theory that overemphasize the importance of competition over cooperation. The following chapter, *On Bikers at War – Transformations of Non-Fictional and Fictional Conflicts from Hamlet to Sons of Anarchy: Men of Mayhem*, written by Ulf Wilhelmsson, deals with literary adaptations of conflicts. Wilhelmsson's chapter explores how real-life conflicts from biker wars as well as the narrative conflicts of *Hamlet* are first transformed into the TV-series *Sons of Anarchy* and then from the series into a board game. This analysis shows that while the series is mainly driven by interpersonal conflicts, the game focuses on intragroup conflicts. Both Makai's and Wilhelmsson's chapters illustrate limitations of the game form – alterations and simplifications are made in complex subject matters in order to fit them into more conventional game mechanical molds. These shortcomings of the game form are also discussed in relation to the use of games in educational settings.

In his chapter *From Zero-Sum Business Games to Coopetitive Simulation*, J. Tuomas Harviainen demonstrates how business simulations often represent the market as a zero-sum competition between companies, which is a problematic way of portraying more recent business models where companies instead form 'coopetitive networks'. The chapter concludes that these simulations could be developed further. By harnessing mechanics from recreational games, mainly allowing students to modify the simulated systems, more complex, less conflict-oriented business models could be taught.

Educational games are also the focus of Jonas Linderoth, Adam Chapman and Sebastian Deterding's chapter *The Limits of 'Serious' Play: Frame Disputes around Educational Games*. By exploring the controversies surrounding two game portrayals of historical atrocities, they conclude that games, unlike other media, seem to be a representational form that fails to produce socially legitimate representations that are in line with respectful use of themes and credibly signal moral regard for the victims of various conflicts. Games seem to be inherently trivializing, expecting players to detach themselves from the game's thematic layer. Even the educational games that encourage players to reflect upon real horrific events try to utilize this trivializing ability. The players are expected to first detach themselves from the represented events, to then reattach themselves, an expectation that is highly vulnerable to individual readings and interpretations of the game. This chapter connects to the second part of the book which deals with the *representation of war and armed conflicts* in games.

In the book's fifth chapter, *On Wargames and War: Modeling Carl von Clausewitz's Theory of War*, Ville Kankainen and Ilmari Käihkö explore how aspects of Clausewitz's conception of war are incorporated in two different wargames. Their analysis shows that some important aspects are hard to represent in games or left out for other reasons. Hence, wargames tend to contain conventional, and somewhat limited, portrayals of war. In accordance with previous chapters, Kankainen and Käihkö's work highlights the mechanical aspects that limit the representation of conflicts. This means that educational wargames, designed for the purpose of training officers, rarely consider important aspects such as the ethics and morality of war. In the subsequent chapter, *Wargames as Reenactment: An Ecological Framework for the Development of Military Games for Education*, Adam Chapman and Jonas Linderoth seek to develop a framework that in part could address some issues regarding the design that is brought up in Chapter 5. Chapman and Linderoth stress that all wargames are, in the broadest sense, historical in some way, inevitably based on some previous instance(s) of activity deemed useful for future concerns. In their chapter they conceptualize educational wargames as systems offering opportunities for learning through *reenactment*. They suggest that the content of an educational wargame (what it models) is less important than its presentation to the player (the experience it gives). This is an approach that has implications for how armed conflicts ought to be approached in educational wargames and as part of military education.

Tomas Karlsson's chapter, *The Grasping Eye: Wargames and the Ideal-Typical Field Commander's Inner Vision* discusses the reciprocity between the 'ideal-typical field commander' (as presented in historical accounts) and wargamers when they are positioned to play as military commanders. For wargamers, representations of field commanders in game rules are resources for 'playful identification', and at the same time military theory positions the field commander in a privileged position of agency, with a game-like vantage point over the battlefield. Karlsson's perspective sheds light over the rarely discussed issue regarding the potential mutuality between representation and represented. It shows not only how games portray conflicts but also the potential for armed conflict to contain elements from games.

The next part of the book deals with critical perspectives on how games represent conflict. Ryan Scheiding's chapter, *War Never Changes? Creating an American Victimology in Fallout 4*, is a critical reading of the commercial role-playing game *Fallout 4*. Scheiding focuses on how the game portrays the consequences of nuclear war and discusses how the game is mainly concerned with potential nuclear war in the USA. This portrayal will, according to Scheiding, contribute together with other mediums to an American victimhood that disregards real historical victims. Hence, Scheiding's analysis supplements Chapter 4 (Linderoth, Chapman, & Deterding) by highlighting how the portrayal of conflicts in games also is part of a larger media ecology.

The next chapter in this section is Patrick Prax's *Are the Bullets Going over Our Head? Designed Ambivalence in the Representation of Armed Conflict in Games*. In this chapter, Patrick Prax engages in a critical reflection of representations of armed conflicts using his concept of *designed ambivalence*. This designates game design that is simultaneously militaristic, and, superficially critical of war. An engaging military shooter or tabletop wargame can at the same time provide grounds for critical analyses of the military, war, and fascism, while at the same time draw liberally on militaristic sentiments and entertainment. Prax connects this double sidedness to the political economy of game production, where designed ambivalence allows for freedom of interpretation among players, and plausible deniability from producers, coupled with greater profits associated with a bigger and more diverse player base. In another critical study, *Where Are the White Perpetrators in All the Colonial Board Games?* Sabine Harrer and J. Tuomas Harviainen analyze the popular Finnish board game, *Afrikan Tähti* ('The Star of Africa'). The authors raise the question of the absence of the colonial atrocities and its perpetrators in European, colonial-themed board games. The analysis exemplifies how this game fails to approach its setting respectfully and with historical accuracy. Instead, the game opts for a racist and colonial worldview materialized in rules and thematic representations. Their chapter shows how also the *absence* of conflict in a game can be a conveyor of ideological discourse.

The final section of the book discusses novel and innovative ways of representing conflicts in games. These are mostly ordinary life situations that do not involve direct violence or physical aggression. The first chapter in this section, *Narrative and Mechanical Integration: Playing with Interpersonal Conflicts in Life Is Strange* by Fatima Jonsson and Lina Eklund, is a study where a narrative adventure game has been analyzed through close playing. Jonsson and Eklund show how the combination of specific game mechanics allows the player to explore the position of others in the conflict. Hence, the game offers an experience where the player can reflect upon different outcomes of a conflict, opening up the perspectives of empathy instead of adversity. While Jonsson and Eklund's analysis shows a case where the game form offers some unique possibilities regarding conflict representation and resolution, the subsequent chapter, *The Most Intimate Conflict of All: Marriage as Conflict in Digital Games* by Piotr Siuda and Jakub Majewski, highlights a missed opportunity in how games represent the complex nature of conflicts in long-term relationships. Even though many games have a preoccupation with conflict, they rarely represent more nuanced aspects of romantic partnership. The authors argue that the complexity and small scale of martial conflicts is hard to fit into the commercial expectations surrounding the game medium. Any attempt in doing so will have to rely on more unusual/experimental game mechanics. Siuda and Majewski expands upon this topic in the book's final chapter, *All Smoke, No Fire: The Post-Mortem of Conflicts in the 'Walking Simulator' Genre*. This genre relies mainly upon exploration of virtual worlds and refrain from gameplay with overt conflicts. This does not mean that walking simulators do not portray conflicts at all. On the contrary, the authors show that these games provide other ways of representing conflict. Using environmental storytelling, they place the audience in the aftermath of conflicts that have already taken place. Ironically, the lack of gameplay mechanics that pitch forces against each other make walking simulators well suited for the examination of more complex and nuanced perspectives on conflicts.

The Relation between Games and Conflicts

Taken together, the chapters in this volume illustrate how the representation of conflict in games are intertwined with specific ways of designing game challenges. As a cultural form, games lend themselves to represent specific aspects of conflicts, yet limits other. Several of the chapters show that nuanced or novel portrayals of conflict presupposes innovative and new game mechanics. A paradox with these conditions is that for games, as a media for both entertainment and education, innovation does not start by simply asking for other media content.

At the same time, games are embedded in a social, political, and economic landscape. As with any medium, representations will inevitably be shaped by these factors, both regarding their design and their interpretations. These external aspects are therefore conditions for how conflicts can be part of games and of how they are understood by players.

It makes sense to regard the representation of conflict in games as being shaped by both internal factors (the unique duality of rules and thematic representation) and the external factors, such as those mentioned above. In this volume, the authors explore different perspectives on what this means for the possibilities of the game form. It seems as if games are proficient at representing certain kinds of conflicts, or at least certain aspects of certain kinds of conflicts. Where a wargame can represent armed struggle across a battlefield with regards to the movement and actions of military units, it may omit, reduce, and/or simplify moral, ideological, and emotional aspects of war. The same goes for representations of other kinds of conflicts, where parts suitable for representation using conventional game mechanics can more easily be included. Aspects that are not readily captured in a game format will be omitted or transformed altogether, leading to conflict representations that are limited and biased. Certainly, selections of the design of representations of conflicts in games, through rules and narrative, serve ideological, political, and economical purposes (see for instance Bogost, 2007). Game mechanics might have to be stretched to the point where it can be discussed if it is a game at all – the game as a representational form might eventually have to be dissolved in order to successfully accommodate representations of certain kinds of conflicts.

As Linderoth's composite theory suggests, innovation is dependent upon the craft of designing challenges, that is, creating new game mechanics as well as finding novel ways of combing existing mechanics. The watershed here is whether any kind, nuance, or aspect of a conflict is possible to capture, even with future developments of game mechanics or new sensibilities towards external factors, or if games as a cultural form has limits with regards to what they can successfully represent. The chapters in this volume explore these limits of conflict representation in games – how games both exist within them and may attempt to transgress them.

References

Bogost, I. (2007). *Persuasive games: The expressive power of videogames*. MIT Press.
Elias, G. S., Garfield, R., & Gutschera, K. R. (2012). *Characteristics of games*. MIT Press.
Goffman, E. (1961). *Encounters: Two studies in the sociology of interaction*. Bobbs-Merrill.
Juul, J. (2003). *Half-real: Video games between real rules and fictional worlds*. [Dissertation, IT-University of Copenhagen].
Kirkpatrick, G. (2012). Constitutive tensions of gaming's field: UK gaming magazines and the formation of gaming culture 1981–1995. *Game Studies, 12*(1).
Linderoth, J. (2013). Beyond the digital divide: An ecological approach to gameplay. *Transactions of the Digital Games Research Association, 1*(1). https://doi.org/10.26503/todigra.v1i1.9
Linderoth, J. (2015). Creating stories for a composite form: Video game design as frame orchestration. *Journal of Gaming & Virtual Worlds, 7*(3), 279–298.
Meier, S. (2012, March 5–9). Interesting decisions [Video]. *2012 Game Developers Conference*. www.gdcvault.com/play/1015756/Interesting
Orian Harel, T., Maoz, I., & Halperin, E. (2020). A conflict within a conflict: Intragroup ideological polarization and intergroup intractable conflict. *Current Opinion in Behavioral Sciences, 34*, 52–57. https://doi.org/10.1016/j.cobeha.2019.11.013

Positech Games. (2013). *Democracy 3* [PC]. Positech Games.
Radford, A. N. (2011). Preparing for battle? Potential intergroup conflict promotes current intragroup affiliation. *Biology Letters*, 7(1), 26–29. https://doi.org/10.1098/rsbl.2010.0507
Rahim, A., & Bonoma, T. V. (1979). Managing organizational conflict: A model for diagnosis and intervention. *Psychological Reports*, 44(3, Pt 2), 1323–1344. https://doi.org/10.2466/pr0.1979.44.3c.1323
Reisswits, B. von. (2019). *Kriegsspiel: Instructions for the representations of military manoeuvres with the kriegsspiel apparatus.* Publ. by Bill Leeson. (Original work from 1824). www.scribd.com/document/201901872/B-Von-Reisswitz-1824-Wargames-Rules-of-the-Prussian-Army
Roberts, E. V., & Jacobs, H. E. (1986). *Literature: An introduction to reading and writing.* Prentice-Hall.
Rosenberg, U. (2018). *Reykholt* [Board game]. Renegade Game Studios.
Subhi, N., & Geelan, D. (2012). When Christianity and homosexuality collide: Understanding the potential intrapersonal conflict. *Journal of Homosexuality*, 59(10), 1382–1402. https://doi.org/10.1080/00918369.2012.724638
Wall, J. A., & Callister, R. R. (1995). Conflict and its management. *Journal of Management*, 21(3), 515–558. https://doi.org/10.1177/014920639502100306
Warfare Sims. (2013). *Command: Modern air/naval operations* [PC]. Matrix Games.
Wells, H. G. (2002). *Little wars: A game for boys from twelve years of age to one hundred and fifty and for that more intelligent sort of girl who likes boys' games and books.* Project Gutenberg. (Original work from 1913). www.gutenberg.org/files/3691/3691-h/3691-h.htm

Part I
Game Systems, Transformation, and Learning

1 Red in Bits and Bytes
Evolutionary Conflicts in Biological God Games

Péter Kristóf Makai

Life is often metaphorically called a game (Ching, 1993; Gozzi, 1990).[1] Yet, for many, life is anything but a game: tedious, repetitive, full of conflict and suffering, and, above all, nonnegotiable – there is no *outside* to experience life from. All meaning and lived experience is created in our brains, mediated by bodies, and sustained by biological life. Therefore, understanding how life came about has been a perennial subject of human speculation. Evolution by natural selection is the single most coherent framework for explaining the diversity of life on Earth, as well as humankind's place in it. Even so, there have been numerous misconceptions among educated laypeople (and sometimes even among undergraduate biology students) about the basic facts of evolution, which suggests that the evolved human mind struggles to comprehend its own condition (Abbott, 2003; Nelson, 2012; Shtulman, 2017; Shtulman & Calabi, 2012).

This chapter investigates how digital games imitate biological life and, more specifically, how they portray the conflicts inherent in evolution. As an explanation of how the variety of life came to be, evolutionary theory interprets the diversity of species as a result of competition and cooperation between and among organisms of various levels of complexity. However, as this chapter illustrates, conflict often gets overrepresented in games. One reason for this is that combat tends to require more and quicker player input than other, more strategic forms of gameplay. Conflict in biological *god games* is also more likely to take shape according to a gross misconception of evolutionary conflict called *vulgar Darwinism* (see Lewontin, 1977). Vulgar Darwinism holds that nature is always rife with strife, or red in tooth and claw: the strong shall conquer the weak in a struggle for life. However, this is a simplified image of a more complex process, since evolution fosters cooperation just as much as competition. In this chapter, I demonstrate that games mostly reinforce these conflict-driven narratives of vulgar Darwinism instead of challenging them.

To better understand how video games represent conflicts in evolution, I analyze three games: Maxis' *Spore* (2008), *Niche: A Genetic Survival Game* by Stray Fawn Studios (2016), and Panache Digital's *Ancestors: The Humankind Odyssey* (2019). These games showcase different aspects of evolutionary conflict: *Spore* is a botched and scientifically shaky attempt at presenting a form of *universal Darwinism* (see the following text); *Niche* is a more rigorous simulation of evolutionary game mechanics of fictitious mammals; and ancestors is a game deeply rooted in the scientific account of hominin development. I look at how in-game conflicts are presented and whether the game mechanics reflect the tenets of vulgar Darwinism. The analysis looks at the strategies these computer games use to incorporate player agency into their simulation of what is essentially a non-agentive, non-teleological process: the unfolding of life.

I start by defining vulgar Darwinism and then proceed to investigate to what degree these games adhere to a vulgar Darwinist conception of life. My analysis seeks to answer a set of questions: How do the game mechanics incorporate evolutionary principles of conflict and cooperation? Do they reinforce or challenge vulgar Darwinism? How does the tension between player agency and the non-agentive nature of evolution influence our understanding of these games?

I pay specific attention to how the generic history of god games, which are inspired by strategy and *4X games*, utilize the potential of game conflicts and how game systems place you, the player[2] in a conflict with in-game AI characters.

Vulgar Darwinism

Evolution has been debated for more than one and a half century. Ideologically motivated misrepresentations of evolution have led to some grossly caricatured versions of its key tenets. I will here use Richard Lewontin's term vulgar Darwinism (1977) for referring to such simplified understandings of evolution. In a vulgar Darwinist conception of evolution (as described by their detractors, Carroll, 2010, pp. 59–60; Edelman, 2004, p. 2; Lewontin, 2001, p. 52), conflict is central and all-encompassing: a literal free-for-all deathmatch. Therefore, I define vulgar Darwinism as a set of misrepresentations of evolutionary theory which overemphasize its competitive character. Vulgar Darwinism holds that:

- The struggle for life in nature is a vicious, pitched battle in which violence and avoiding it is the key to survival (inter-specific aggression).
- Reproductive success is directly linked to violence against competitors (intraspecific aggression).
- Aggression beats cooperation hands down.
- Successful reproduction means that all inherited traits or behaviors of the winning organism are beneficial or adaptive to an organism (as opposed to being a by-product or a result of genetic drift).

In contrast to vulgar Darwinism, the evolution of cooperation and altruism has been a key theoretical focus of sociobiology and evolutionary game theory (Axelrod, 2006; Axelrod & Hamilton, 1981; Bahar, 2018; Lindenfors, 2017; Nowak & Coakley, 2013; Trivers, 1971; Wilson, 2002). This framework has been used to make sense of rising levels of social and organismic complexity among living beings, especially human cooperation. Evolutionarily stable strategies of survival foster a degree of cooperation among conspecifics and even among distant species, as has been widely documented in naturalists' and biologists' research under the label "symbiosis."

In game scholarship, conflict and contests have been emphasized. Huizinga writes of the cross-pollinating metaphors of play as war and war as play, and interprets "fighting as a cultural function," and *agōn* (ἀγών, meaning contest) as a "ludic function" (1950/2014, pp. 89–90). Caillois understands *agōn* as a "rivalry which hinges on a single quality" that is found in "other cultural phenomena conforming to the game code," namely duels, tournaments, and courtly war (2001, pp. 15–16). While conflict cannot be reduced to war and violence, it is certainly the most cherished form of conflict represented in computer games. International studies scholars trace the making of the military-industrial-media-entertainment complex, with video games thoroughly implicated in preparing war for consumption (Der Derian, 2009), while game studies contests the position of military-funded and strategy games in the gaming ecosystem (Huntemann & Payne, 2009; Schulzke, 2013). This goes to show that – as the present book also attests – conflict, contests, and games are close kin indeed.

Playing God – A Working Definition of God Games

Like most game genre labels, the term god game is ill-defined; it masks a bewildering diversity of game mechanics and forms of presenting the game world. As a specific genre at the intersection of building, *4X* strategy and action-adventure games, god games offer players the ability to step into the shoes of a species or a tribe's leader, and to make momentous decisions on how a civilization should develop. Not all god games encompass the whole of human history, but most are informed by a Whiggish view of progress and technological determinism (Ghys, 2012). Progress is represented by the unlocking of skill and technological trees that resemble evolutionary cladograms. The games selected for the analysis in this chapter mix elements from different game genres: *Spore* (Maxis, 2008) has rudimentary aspects of browser-based games, role-playing games (RPGs), city builders, and real-time strategy games cobbled together. *Niche* (Stray Fawn, 2016), meanwhile, is a turn-based strategy game with RPG elements as well as a more Sims-like focus on genealogy. Ancestors (Panache Digital, 2019) fuses action-adventure gameplay over the course of millennia with an RPG-like neural development chart and realistic survival mechanics.

All of them represent biological conflict as a challenge for your species to overcome, often by enhancing your species' cooperative capabilities. Players progress through these games by securing food, coordinating tasks with their AI-controlled tribe members, staving off predators by giving commands to these AI characters, and successfully mating with other members of their species to provide offspring that are more capable of facing the challenges of the environment. Experience or gene points are collected by repeating tasks (most often by winning combat encounters), which then can be used to unlock new abilities that organize your tribe better. However, there is a lot of healthy innovation and a unique flavor to each game, so, for the purposes of defining them, I focus on their commonalities.

I suggest that a *god game* should be defined as a digital entertainment software that includes the following features:

- It grants the player simulated powers that ordinary living organisms cannot exert over their lifeworlds.
- These powers are exercised over a group of living beings whose interactions and social organization are modeled with a degree of computer-controlled autonomy.
- This group's betterment or continued survival is the overarching goal of the player.
- This is served by dedicated game mechanisms that quantify the group's adaptive traits or quality of life, and the player's impact on the game-world.
- The player draws its power from the belief and well-being of this group, often quantified as "mana" or "creator points," which can be spent on divine interventions.
- The represented game time spans whole historical or geological periods.
- The game pits the player-controlled group against out-groups controlled by an artificial intelligence or a competing human player.
- The death of an individual member of the controlled group does not constitute a fail state for the player and control is then given over another group member.

Even though god games can implement mechanics from its sister genres, this definition is intended to exclude pure strategy games, historically delimited city-building and business management games, RPGs (role-playing games) and ARPGs (action role-playing games), individual survival games, and story-focused adventure games.

God Games as Life Simulators

Games are tamed, designed conflicts. This complicates any straightforward understanding of conflict as triumph over adversaries in the struggle for resources, since video games are designed to be eventually overcome with effort, even in notably difficult video games (Sirlin, 2006, but see Newheiser, 2009 for fairness in seeking to win and Juul, 2013, for a counterargument to Sirlin). If a challenge is designed to be beaten with effort, the threat of radical powerlessness inherent in real-life challenges is eliminated in favor of flipping back and forth between frustration and the fun of progress. Competition is simulated to provide challenge to the player, to force them to master game systems, and to display proficient performance. Mandating the mastery of mechanics grants games the power to persuade through procedural rhetoric (Bogost, 2008) and thus to impart practical know-how, or even scientific knowledge.

As products of Euroatlantic game designers, god games bear their ideological marks on them, sometimes with pride: they have been templated on modern, Western, technocentric assumptions about historical progress and social cohesion (Caldwell, 1998; Ghys, 2012). They adhere to a model of gameplay progression that was developed in strategy games, known as the 4Xs: *explore* a discrete and knowable terrain, *exploit* (and exhaust) its natural resources using technological means, *expand* your tribe's borders as well as its political power by settling new lands, and *exterminate* other AI- or player-controlled tribes who are trying to do the same. Thus, being direct descendants of tabletop wargaming and the Prussian tradition of Kriegsspiel (Peterson, 2014; Schuurman, 2017), direct conflict is embedded in the cultural history of god games. Meanwhile, its tech trees celebrate inventions leading up to the microchip, the Internet, and space-faring as ultimate benchmarks of civilization. And even in literal god games where there is no tech tree, as in *Black and White* (Lionhead Studios, 2001), instrumental rationality guides mission/quest structure: Belief in you is quantified as mana points or similar units, which are used to cast spells that help your tribe and enable them to attack their enemies. It could thus be said that belief is weaponized in God games, as rival believers are to be defeated by superior magic, technology, and organization.

God games differ from strategy games by a degree of autonomy present in the tribe, civilization, clan, or species you influence – this is a defining feature of the genre, as is a focus on the simulation of artificial life. Other computer programs might hold a better claim to simulate evolution. However, unlike Conway's Game of Life or other cellular automata, which do not represent life mimetically, but only as the development of abstract mathematical patterns, biological god games build a living, breathing world with recognizably biological organisms that need sustenance to live and behave like animals, dying because of old age, starvation, or conflict. Cellular automata are said to simulate life insofar as they operate on relatively simple algorithms of generating the next state of the simulation, and complex patterns emerge as a result of these rules autonomously and without further human intervention. In this respect they are more evolutionary than God games, which need player interaction to guide a species along the long road of designed evolution.

Some form of autonomous life simulation is still present, though, in the games under discussion here. Believers (and species) need food, shelter, and a purpose in life to survive, and in most god games, they produce these resources at a bare subsistence level. But the player-god provides them with a *telos*, such as generational survival or creating wonders and other symbols of technological development that outlive individuals. God games reify (or deify) the power imbalance inherent between computer users and simulated lifeforms, as non-player characters demand solutions to their problems from a – to them – omnipotent god, and they merrily sacrifice themselves for the common good. Thus, in-group conflict is toned down to focus on out-group conflict. For example, your tribe in *Spore, Niche*, or Ancestors are programmed not to initiate fights with you, and AI tribe members do not compete with you for their choice of mate. The only pushback you get for imposing your will on the game world in these games is from members of other species.

Digital Theomachy: Conflicts in God Games

In general, conflicts in God games can occur on several levels. When I speak of conflict in these examples, I mean that at least two goal-driven intentions meet, and action needs to be taken to resolve the situation for the benefit of either party or both. By and large, a competitive digital game is a challenge posed to the player by the designer where obstacles of the game world will hinder your goals to be fulfilled until the right kind of resources and effort are spent to overcome them. A subset of this is a conflict between your character and an AI enemy over resources, which usually ends in combat with a single victor. Negotiation and alliance-making are also featured. However, mechanically speaking, combat systems tend to be more deeply designed than diplomatic systems, since game artificial intelligence is still not sophisticated enough to create believable semblances of psychological behavior. Some games also simulate AI vs. AI conflicts to more accurately reflect their autonomy and to provide a fairer challenge than all AI opponents ganging up on you.

Prima facie, biological god games are thematically ideal for open-ended, sandbox play: grow your species, shape the world to your liking, tinker with variables to see what grows, express yourself by making your tribe flourish or flounder. But conflicts generate emergent narratives even without the presence of a developed storyline. Therefore, even in biological God games with a sandbox design, there will be storylines to discover, and in most, a clear antagonist emerges. Narrative also serves as a cognitive bridge between gameplay segments as it condenses the imperceptible deep time of evolution into a highly salient series of events that mark out the evolution of biological complexity. Finally, narrative may serve as a justification of how and when evolutionary mechanics are introduced to the player.

The central drama of evolution, both in the games and in real life, is the competition for scarce resources. In the vulgar Darwinist conception, the primary means for securing them is by fighting. Combat mechanics owe much to the penchant of wargamers and role-playing games for quantifying basic statistical traits and pitting these traits against one another (Peterson, 2014). In many God games, organisms have a body plan whose various body parts and internal organs get given numerical advantages in dealing or withstanding damage. Improving these, either as rewards for player accomplishments or random mutation is part of the primary gameplay loop and is an important measure of progress.

Another marker of success is the continued survival of the player-controlled species by way of reproduction. Reproductive mechanics offer you a choice of conspecific to mate with (which assumes that your animal is of the dominant sex, regardless of biological reality). The choice might in turn translate to additional traits or a new combination of traits in the offspring. Mating is another aspect of biological life that is not simulated in graphic detail, and largely for the same reasons as excretion. Nonetheless, select titles introduce an element of randomness, or even a schematic system of genetic inheritance as part of the reproductive mechanics, while others allow you to interfere with random inheritance and to selectively breed for desired traits. Speciation and reproductive isolation are most conveniently implemented as tree-like cladograms which grant additional abilities to your creatures. Tool use is modeled for "more advanced" species, supplying canny creatures with complementary bonuses in the competition for resources. The constant improvement of in-game species might emergently model a genuine biological phenomenon known as the Red Queen's race, which describes the evolutionary arms race of various species to gain a reproductive advantage against other competitors (Benton, 2010; Brockhurst, 2011).

These mechanics are meaningful elements of a heavily abstracted, but still illuminating simulation of life that are found in biological God games. As I demonstrate with the case studies, such mechanics are complemented by more complex ones to nuance the forms of challenge and competition players face in the games. Regrettably, an exhaustive survey is beyond the boundaries of this chapter, but they are meant to represent different design solutions to the representation of conflict in biological God games.

Spore: Darwinism as Window-Dressing

Spore is one of those games that was sold on concept alone, and the execution lagged far behind. Touted by its lead designer, Will Wright, as a "SimEverything," *Spore* was meant to be a paean to *universal Darwinism*, the idea that everything can and will evolve (Dawkins, 1983; Dennett, 1995; Plotkin, 2010). Inspired by the Eames brothers' *Powers of Ten* and the Drake Equation (Garst, 2018), it was a game project that was supposed to revolutionize the industry. Procedural generation would supply character animation, create infinite numbers of planets with a dizzying number of random creatures, and write a soundtrack. Players would be able to design everything from animals to buildings to spacecraft and share their creations in an online Sporepedia. To top it off, in the epic story of the game, players would lead a single-celled organism through biological and cultural evolution to conquering the galaxy.

The development process was a struggle between a scientifically faithful faction of the development team and a so-called cute team that championed simplifications of the scientific content and visual appearance for the sake of accessibility to the general public (Gingold, 2011; Grossman, 2008). The results were inevitable: while still a pleasure to play, the purported evolution-simulation aspect ended up in shambles. Writing in *Science,* John Bohannon summarized: "Spore clearly has little in common with science, especially evolution" (2008). His co-investigator, T. Ryan Gregory explained: "The problem is that the game features virtually none of the key ingredients of evolution as we understand it" (Bohannon, 2008). For one thing, speciation does not occur. Instead, you can shape any creature into any other creature in a generation if you can afford it, and all conspecifics immediately shift to the new body plan. Still, although not representative of evolution in the slightest, it does represent biological conflict as a key driving force of progress.

In *Spore,* you control a member of your species – who are all virtually identical – until you decide to reproduce (even as a cell, this is done "sexually"). The game is structured into five distinct stages: *the cell stage, the creature stage, the tribal stage, the civilization stage,* and finally, *the space stage.* Each stage prompts you to collect DNA points to arm your protagonist with unique powers, and the stage is passed when sufficient organism complexity is achieved, or rival social structures are subsumed under your symbolic control. Notably, the latter three stages are templated after strategy and 4X games, heavily leaning toward economic exploitation and warfare.

However, brutal conflict is not the only way to beat *Spore.* The game features a tripartite morality system, representing the three different strategies you can use to progress through a stage: an aggressive (red) strategy that hinges on hunting other species to extinction, a pacifist (green) strategy that relies on cooperation, appeasement, and alliances, and an adaptable (blue) strategy that mixes the red and green strategies depending on what suits the situation best. All are equally viable to pursue at each stage, and competition and cooperation confer different bonuses upon entering the *space stage.*

In terms of what kind of conflicts the game represents, we have a range of different situations. You compete with conspecifics for food (albeit food is plentiful on any planet), but there is no intraspecific competition for mates (and mates are identical in every respect, as there is no sexual dimorphism). The bulk of the game is devoted to the simulation of interspecific conflict: The aggressive route to victory has players hunt other species to extinction, scoring DNA points in the process, and at later stages, perform genocide on rival species/tribes/cultures to unite the planet in one monoculture. Depending on the appendages you affix to the creature, it can engage in four hostile behaviors: biting, charging, striking, and spitting, graded Level 1–5, which deal increasing amounts of damage in a simplistic combat system with a minor random element. Rival creatures' nests have AI creatures, which form groups that can either be friendly, cautious, or hostile to you, sometimes initiating conflict to scare you away from the nest, but they largely leave you alone and do not engage in feeding or reproductive behavior.

The pacifist route to victory (and indeed, the defeat of tougher enemies) requires performing a friendly minigame of social mimicry. Successfully imitating your conspecifics in the *creature* and *tribal stage* will make the AI and the player form a hunting/diplomatic pack, which can go to other nests to suppress or impress the creatures therein, meaning another round of mimicking. Curiously, in the civilization stage, the pacifist route is functionally equivalent to the aggressive route, as purpose-built vehicles are produced and positioned to siege down or convert enemy cities with propaganda. (The economic unification of a planet is simply to buy cities in a global merger.) Thereby, the game rehashes the colonialist assumptions of the 4X genre, positing assimilation and/or destruction as the only acceptable conditions of "victory."

Conflict in the *space stage* takes the form of giant spaceship battles, with the player leading the way, in a manner not unlike the first hunting pack you form. There is an archenemy, called the Grox, who are machinic lifeforms owning about 5000 planets generated for the game universe – as such, violent destruction is close to impossible. However, there is another very tedious way to remove them from the game: since the Grox can only live on uninhabitable planets (with a T0 terraforming score), players can establish a functioning ecosystem on each and every T0 planet and remove the Grox's habitat. In a small victory for evolution, this way of handling conflict resolution does suggest that biological life triumphs over "pure" technology.

To summarize, *Spore* holds a vulgar Darwinistic view of conflict: it bastardizes evolution, and it often outright flaunts the accepted principles of biology altogether. In terms of the vulgar Darwinism checklist at the beginning of the chapter, *Spore* exhibits several characteristics that fit with the definition used in this analysis: (a) survival is based on interspecific aggression and assimilation, although (b) there is no sexual selection and thus no measure of reproductive success, (c) cooperation is only used to establish physical, social, or economic domination over rival species, and (d) all appendages confer some quantified benefit or skill to your species (and since it is wholly designed by you, there are no by-products or deleterious traits). Because the game does such a poor job of simulating biological life, these features will be thrown into sharp contrast with the other two case studies.

Niche: A Life Simulator That Rhymes with Quiche

Stray Fawn Studio's endearing *Niche: A Genetics Survival Game* (2016) hews much closer to orthodox evolutionary theory than *Spore*. In *Niche*, you control a fictitious mammalian species, called *nichelings*, who look like a cat-fox hybrid. The goal of the game is to give nichelings food, shelter, and protection from rival species to survive and flourish, traveling from island to island across different biomes to find Home Island, where your starting pair of nichelings originated from. Nichelings are omnivores and can be ordered to prey and feed on other creatures. The game features a working genetic system with random mutations, as well as dominant and recessive alleles which express phenotypically but do not radically alter the animal's body (some grow wings, but without losing their four legs).

Your job is to grow your nicheling tribe to withstand changes in the environment, fend off predators, and maintain a robust gene pool that protects nichelings from inbreeding. Some genes provide statistical bonuses in fighting, or allow flight, others affect the development of sensory organs, or grant fur patterns that suit particular biomes as camouflage. They may also bear twelve genes for different immunities: when a new nicheling is born with two copies of the same immunity allele, they suffer a genetic defect that halves their life expectancy, thus urging you to breed your nichelings strategically. This way of representing genetics is forward-thinking and more accurate than in rival games.

Nichelings do have natural predators and rival species, all of them fictional hybrids, and include aerial predators, which prey on the young of the species, while others are biome-specific and hunt adults. The presence of predators can trigger an evolutionary arms race as players desperately try to breed their nichelings to neutralize environmental threats. Wandering nichelings who are not part of the player-controlled tribe act as rivals, so, unlike *Spore*, intraspecific competition is present, and even parasites are included. The purpose of biological diversity, it seems, is to serve as AI foils to you rather than to interact with each other. And since they are generated randomly rather than as a result of biological competition, they do not form organic communities like your nichelings.

Unlike *Spore*, which has plant food in abundance, the islands of *Niche* have only few vegetable sources of nourishment, so at some point, conflict becomes inevitable, as a number of species compete for scarce resources. Berry bushes are harvested by nichelings, but there are other options for foraging, too. In an instance of direct intraspecies cooperation, food is collected in a community food bank that is distributed at the end of each game round in the order of the tribe's hierarchy. Players can specify the pecking order by setting Alpha, Beta, and Omega creatures, thereby deciding which creatures get to survive, and if they think strategically, which traits are bred out of the population – an example of direct intraspecies competition.

In particular, the presence of a functioning gene pool marks *Niche* as a thoughtful simulation of evolutionary principles.

The game compares favorably to *Spore* in terms of scientific accuracy, but also retains some key traits of vulgar Darwinism. Although interspecific aggression is unavoidable in the long run, cooperation within and without the circle of nichelings is essential to survival, and pacifist players can put off bloodshed for extended periods of time. Nichelings' reproductive success is solely dependent on your choice of whom to mate with whom, so there is no reproduction-based aggression, albeit it is worth noting that some nichelings are naturally infertile, so multiple copulations with various tribe members might be necessary for conception. Unlike *Spore*, not all traits are adaptive, as genetic defects and deleterious traits, such as sensitivity to heat or cold, or distasteful appearance are simulated in *Niche*'s gene pool. Finally, aggressive behavior is natural to predators, and your nicheling tribe can be played in a hostile fashion, but in contrast to the easy fights in *Spore*, it is self-defeating for all but the most overpowered tribes, therefore it promotes a largely foraging lifestyle for your tribe.

Ancestors: The Humankind Odyssey – Evolution's Tedium

Ancestors: The Humankind Odyssey (2019), a meticulous simulation of the development of human beings, is the game most faithful to the actual evolution of a species among the case studies. However, it still misses the mark on trait selection because you, rather than nature, selects new traits to evolve. The brainchild of Patrice Désilets, the lead designer of the original *Assassin's Creed*, *Ancestors* is an action-adventure game encompassing 8 million years of human evolution in which you control members of a hominin clan. Through breeding and cultural inheritance you lead them through successive stages of humanity's origin story. From *Sahelanthropus Tchadensis* through *Australopithecus Ramidus*, better known as "Lucy," all the way to *Homo Ergaster*, you experience the evolutionary leaps as you make your ape person stronger and smarter.

The game is notable for the very involved skill tree representing the growth of connections in the human brain, *the neuronal development map*: if a skill is practiced often enough, you can choose to pass it on to the next generation of proto-humans. Because you can switch between all members of the clan, mating is always by player choice and there is no sexual competition.

The tough business of survival is hallmarked by the 25 species of NPC animals you may encounter. Some are passive prey species, like bass or giant African snails, which can be caught and serve as food, or wildlife animals that only attack when cornered, such as the Dorcas gazelle or the "Miocene African horse" (conceptually, it is supposed to be of the genus *Hipparion*, but in appearance, it resembles the quagga); but the bulk of animals are deadly threats that the hominin clan must mitigate by avoiding or defeating them. Irascible threats, for example, hippopotami or giant warthogs, will try to intimidate you and can be fierce enemies due to their high health. Crawling threats, for example, Megarian banded centipedes or black mambas will also attack if cornered or approached too closely, but they can be easily avoided. Flying predators, like the Miocene pelican, are fiercely territorial, and will attack any unwary hominin approaching their habitat. Finally, defeating land predators, for example, Thorbjarnarson's crocodile or the white *Machairodus* (saber-toothed cat) requires the crafting of weapons, such as basalt choppers.

Conflict resolution is more elaborate than in the other two games. Although steering clear of an animal is always an option if you can detect it in time, there is also a possibility of avoiding conflict by passing an Intimidation check: if successful, the animal flees, if not, combat ensues. The game considers the tools you brandish and the company you keep – players may recruit conspecifics into a hunting party, and the larger your team, the greater the chance of scaring threats into submission. Thus, ancestors represents a crucial form of in-group cooperation. Whenever a fight is inevitable, hominins damage their opponent using a counterattack system familiar from the *Assassin's Creed* series. Failure to dodge or counterattack results in death or injuries sustained that will plague the player beyond the encounter. The injury mechanics are interesting because they have greater consequences than in most games, thus making you think twice before initiating combat.

Ancestors is arguably the scientifically most sophisticated of the games examined here, but it still bears some hallmarks of vulgar Darwinism. In-group cooperation is essential to survival and takes many forms: from hunting parties to grooming, healing other members of the tribe, and child-rearing, working together provides many benefits. In-group competition is minimal, and a clear hierarchy is established by age: babies, young ones, mature males or females, and elders of both sexes have different functions and capabilities (although unlike *Niche*, they can fend for themselves, so seniority does not determine who gets to eat). As discussed above, out-group competition is nuanced and varied, with many different species contributing to the challenges of survival. Finally, out-group intraspecies cooperation is the way you grow your clan, by finding outsider apes and solving their problems, such as healing injuries or sharing food, while out-group interspecies cooperation is not simulated in the game. Even so, the neuronal development skills and the random mutations are invariably beneficial, which is less nuanced than *Niche*'s take on genetics, which also includes deleterious traits. Violence is a major threat and a key conflict resolution strategy, but the intimidation mechanics provide a way to successfully get past predators without engaging in combat, and due to the size of the game world, avoidance is easier than on a heavily populated *Spore* planet or the crowded islands of *Niche*.

Conclusion: The Evolution of Conflict in Biological God Games – with No End in Sight

Even such a cursory overview of a select few god games can testify to the wealth and breadth of innovation by game designers to bring the counter-intuitive concept of evolution to their player base. My main purpose was to show that although commercial gaming is continuing to be fascinated by biological evolution, the computer game as a medium faces several challenges in portraying key tenets of evolution by natural selection, especially when it comes to the role of conflict in biological God games. I have set out to inquire: How do game mechanics incorporate evolutionary principles of conflict and cooperation? Do they reinforce or challenge vulgar Darwinism?

In my analysis of *Spore*, *Niche*, and *Ancestors*, I have looked at the degree to which there is a bias in the representation of cooperation and conflict. These games overwhelmingly promote in-group cooperation and out-group competition with their game mechanics: from banding together in order to gather resources to beating other species in combat, players are positioned as interested participants in their tribe's survival, and they have a determining role in the unfolding of the game narrative, usually through gaining victory through violent means. In the analyzed games, cooperation, while present, tends to play second fiddle to competition, which tends to drive gameplay. It is also presented in a more rudimentary format, with fewer mechanics dedicated to it, although in *Niche* we see a somewhat more elaborate version, which might be due to the fact that in *Niche*, you control all members of your tribe. Because of the biological god game's genre roots in strategy and 4X games, which themselves are descendants of wargaming, they reinforce conflict-driven narratives of vulgar Darwinism rather than challenge it. Success in all the games under consideration here depend on presenting a credible threat to AI-driven NPCs, and combat is simulated in detail, directly tied to group survival.

I have also sought to understand how the conflict between player agency and the non-agentive nature of evolution shape our understanding of these games. In this regard, the God game genre's aesthetic pleasure depend upon granting you an outsized, demiurgic power to shape the game-world to your liking, which needs to be kept in check by AI-driven conflict. In real life, this principle is not the sole driving force of the evolution of biological complexity. Even though conflicts extend to direct violence, they are often far more abstract. For instance, adaptation to one's habitat can prove to be a much more indirect form of conflict, an evolutionary arms race that might simply mean being better at finding nourishment or a suitable niche to be protected from predators. Evolution in games like *Spore*, *Niche*, or *Ancestors* is *always* at least partially, but sometimes fully directed by the player, who may act as a divine breeder to select for traits that they foresee to be advantageous when then evaluate the game state.

As life simulators, the biological god games surveyed here are all nominally evolutionary: They simulate biomes with food chains, animals with survival and reproduction mechanics (i.e., herbivory and carnivory, mating, inheritance), and allow for phenotypic and behavioral changes in the organisms you control. For these traits alone, they capture something essential in biological evolution. However, natural selection is a crucial facet that is misrepresented: player choice trumps the role of the environment. Granted, few games can hope to strive for a complete fidelity to the principles of evolution, but even small steps towards the curtailing of human agency would constitute genuine improvements over player-driven selection.

Since video games are entertainment media, they are designed to appeal to human minds and tastes. As such, their mediality helps explain why they fail to portray evolutionary conflicts accurately. First, the game relies on player interaction, and players fulfill goals they or the designers have set, which is in stark contract with the purposelessness of evolutionary development. Second, there is a definite progression along different stages of complexity on a designed timeline (represented by skill and technological trees or migration from level to level) that drives the narrative of the game, which is antithetical to the fundamental indeterminism of evolution. Although conflicts are inherent in competing for scarce resources and mating, species are not purpose-driven to "get more evolved." Complexity arises as a result of gradual change of traits, as byproducts of genetic transfer, or even due to constructive neutral evolution. Third, god games are games of emergence that are meant to be replayed time and again with different starting parameters, whereas evolution has only been observed on one planet (so far), therefore we cannot speculate as to what would happen if it began again from scratch. Fourth, these simulations are objects of human design, meaning they are different interpretations of evolution focusing on different aspects of the theory as they are meant to convey different play experiences. Despite these limitations, sound biological principles *can* be modelled into games without sacrificing player agency and fun, as exemplified by the likes of *Niche*.

In conclusion, one must note that there is a diversity of game mechanics that purport to present playful evolution to gaming audiences, which themselves are meaningful and unique to the genre. Still, many of the attempts to incorporate player agency belie the actual mechanisms that drive real biological evolution. Although deadly duels and waging warfare are not the only sources of conflict in evolutionary god games, they remain the main one. Curiously, this genre of game is explicitly biased toward the single-player mode. One reason why that might be the case is that designers of single-player games have greater control over narrative and temporal progression, so they may campaign for particular visions of society and biology more effectively. Another could be that multiplayer games require more real-life technical support from the developers or increasing the amount of screen time to properly simulate evolutionary conflicts. Multiplayer games favor actual combat and warfare even more than single-player games, and the more nuanced forms of competition in evolutionary biology are deemed to be less engaging.

Although we cannot fully gauge the reasoning behind every design choice, it is the case that the designers of evolutionary god games distil evolution to its more caricatured, vulgar Darwinist format because it is more congenial to the agonistic play for which the genre's ancestors (such as 4X and strategy games) have laid the foundations. In that case, I would even claim that the cultural evolution of this video game genre deliberately overrode the principles of biological evolution, because we have evolved to be cultured organisms. In the survival of cultural artifacts, the real competition is no longer for biological resources but for activating the evolved mechanisms of the brain with its biases towards agency-driven representations of life. Whether or not playful simulations that can portray biological evolution more accurately may become successful as new, innovative titles revolutionize the genre still remains to be seen. Until then, fights go on as long as they have to.

Notes

1 This research began at Linnaeus University and benefitted from the generous support of the Crafoord Stiftelska, and was honed during my time at the KWI in Essen, as well as at the Rachel Carson Center's Landhaus in Glonn-Herrmannsdorf. It could not have seen the light of the day without these institutions.
2 Throughout this chapter, the player will be frequently referred to as a general 'you' to save space.

References

Abbott, H. P. (2003). Unnarratable knowledge: The difficulty of understanding evolution by natural selection. In D. Herman (Ed.), *Narrative theory and the cognitive sciences* (pp. 143–162). CSLI Publications.
Axelrod, R. M. (2006). *The evolution of cooperation.* Basic Books.
Axelrod, R. M., & Hamilton, W. D. (1981). The evolution of cooperation. *Science, 211*(4489), 1390–1396. https://doi.org/10.1126/science.7466396
Bahar, S. (2018). *The essential tension: Competition, cooperation and multilevel selection in evolution* (pp. 271–307). Springer. https://doi.org/10.1007/978-94-024-1054-9_13
Benton, M. (2010). New take on the Red Queen. *Nature, 463*(7279), 306–307. https://doi.org/10.1038/463306a
Bogost, I. (2008). *Unit operations: An approach to videogame criticism.* MIT Press.
Bohannon, J. (2008). Flunking Spore. *Science, 322*(5901), 531. www.science.org/doi/10.1126/science.322.5901.531b
Brockhurst, M. A. (2011). Evolution: Sex, death, and the Red Queen. *Science, 333*(6039), 166–167. https://doi.org/10.1126/science.1209420
Caillois, R. (2001). *Man, play and games.* University of Illinois Press.
Caldwell, N. (1998). Games R US – And most of the western world as well: The hegemony of the strategic computer game. *M/C Journal, 1*(5). https://doi.org/10.5204/mcj.1734

Carroll, J. (2010). Three scenarios for literary Darwinism. *New Literary History*, *41*(1), 53–67. www.jstor.org/stable/40666484

Ching, M. K. L. (1993). Games and play: Pervasive metaphors in American life. *Metaphor and Symbolic Activity*, *8*(1), 43–65. https://doi.org/10.1207/s15327868ms0801_3

Dawkins, R. (1983). Universal Darwinism. In D. S. Bendell (Ed.), *Evolution from molecules to man* (pp. 403–25). Cambridge University Press.

Dennett, D. C. (1995). *Darwin's dangerous idea: Evolution and the meanings of life*. Simon & Schuster.

Derian, J. D. (2009). *Virtuous war: Mapping the military-industrial-media-entertainment network*. Routledge.

Edelman, G. M. (2004). *Wider than the sky: The phenomenal gift of consciousness*. Yale University Press.

Garst, A. (2018, September 11). Developing Spore: An oral ("Sporal"?) history 10 years on. *Game Developer*. www.gamedeveloper.com/audio/developing-i-spore-i-an-oral-sporal-history-10-years-on

Ghys, T. (2012). Technology trees: Freedom and determinism in historical strategy games. *Game Studies*, *12*(1). http://gamestudies.org/1201/articles/tuur_ghys

Gingold, C. (2011). *A brief history of Spore* [Blog post]. www.levitylab.com/blog/2011/02/brief-history-of-spore/

Gozzi, R. (1990). Is life a game? Notes on a master metaphor. *ETC: A Review of General Semantics*, *47*(3), 291–293. www.jstor.org/stable/42577234

Grossman, L. (2008, September 5). Will Wright on Spore: Cute vs. science. *Time*. https://techland.time.com/2008/09/05/will_wright_and_spore_cute_vs/

Huizinga, J. (2014). *Homo ludens: A study of the play-element in culture*. Martino Publishing. (Original work published 1950)

Huntemann, N. B., & Payne, M. T. (Eds.). (2009). *Joystick soldiers: The politics of play in military video games*. Routledge.

Johnson, S. (2013, September 30). *Spore: My view of the elephant* [Blog post]. www.designer-notes.com/?p=654

Juul, J. (2013). *The art of failure: An essay on the pain of playing video games*. MIT Press.

Lewontin, R. C. (1977). Caricature of Darwinism. *Nature*, *266*(5599), 283–284. https://doi.org/10.1038/266283a0

Lewontin, R. C. (2001). *It ain't necessarily so: The dream of the human genome and other illusions*. Granta.

Lindenfors, P. (2017). *For whose benefit? The biological and cultural evolution of human cooperation*. Springer.

Lionhead Studios. (2001). *Black and white* [PC]. Electronic Arts.

Maxis. (2008). *Spore* [PC]. Electronic Arts.

Nelson, C. E. (2012). Why don't undergraduates really "get" evolution? What can faculty do? In K. S. Rosengren, S. K. Brem, E. M. Evans, & G. M. Sinatra (Eds.), *Evolution challenges: Integrating research and practice in teaching and learning about evolution* (pp. 311–347). Oxford University Press.

Newheiser, M. (2009, March 9). Playing fair: A look at competition in gaming. *Strange Horizons*. http://strangehorizons.com/non-fiction/articles/playing-fair-a-look-at-competition-in-gaming/

Nowak, M. A., & Coakley, S. (2013). *Evolution, games, and God: The principle of cooperation*. Harvard University Press.

Panache Digital. (2019). *Ancestors: The humankind odyssey* [PC]. Private Division.

Peterson, J. (2014). *Playing at the world: A history of simulating wars, people and fantastic adventures, from chess to role-playing games.* Unreason Press.

Plotkin, H. C. (2010). *Evolutionary worlds without end.* Oxford University Press.

Schulzke, M. (2013). Rethinking military gaming: America's army and its critics. *Games and Culture, 8*(2), 59–76. https://doi.org/10.1177/1555412013478686.

Schuurman, P. (2017). Models of war 1770–1830: The birth of wargames and the trade-off between realism and simplicity. *History of European Ideas, 43*(5), 442–455. https://doi.org/10.1080/01916599.2017.1366928

Shtulman, A. (2017). *Scienceblind: Why our intuitive theories about the world are so often wrong.* Basic Books.

Shtulman, A., & Calabi, P. (2012). Cognitive constraints on the understanding and acceptance of evolution. In K. S. Rosengren, S. K. Brem, E. M. Evans, & G. M. Sinatra (Eds.), *Evolution challenges: Integrating research and practice in teaching and learning about evolution* (pp. 47–65). Oxford University Press. https://doi.org/10.1093/acprof:oso/9780199730421.003.0003

Sirlin, D. (2006). *Playing to win: Becoming the champion.* Lulu.com.

Stray Fawn Studios. (2016). *Niche: A genetic survival game* [PC]. Electronic Arts.

Trivers, R. L. (1971). The evolution of reciprocal altruism. *The Quarterly Review of Biology, 46*(1), 35–57. www.jstor.org/stable/2822435

Ubisoft. (2008). *Assassin's Creed* [PC]. Ubisoft.

Wilson, E. O. (2002). *Sociobiology: The new synthesis.* Belknap Press of Harvard University Press.

2 On Bikers at War

Transformations of Non-Fictional and Fictional Conflicts from *Hamlet* to *Sons of Anarchy: Men of Mayhem*

Ulf Wilhelmsson

Introduction

This is a study of how conflicts are transformed from real life, via narratives, into a game. The chapter explores four types of conflicts: intergroup, intragroup, interpersonal and intrapersonal derived from a material consisting of three cultural artefacts that are interconnected: *The Tragedy of Hamlet* (*Hamlet*) (Shakespeare, 2021), *Sons of Anarchy* (*SoA*) (Sutter, 2008–2014) and *Sons of Anarchy: Men of Mayhem* (*MoM*) (Dill et al., 2014). *Hamlet* explicitly has been used as a template for *SoA* which in turn has been the basis for *MoM*. The fundamental and underlining question in this chapter is what the board game medium can preserve from a Shakespearean drama and real-life conflicts. Can games, a cultural form built upon conflict and competition, capture and reenact elements from beloved dramas and real-life conflicts? What transformations are involved in creating a narrative based both on real life and another prototypical narrative and what transformations occur when such a narrative is *ludified* (Gunder, 2007), that is transformed into a game?

Theoretical Points of Departure

Aarseth's (2012) *narrative theory of games* is used in this study in a slightly altered form. At the basis for Aarseth's theory, or model rather, lies his question 'What do games and stories have in common?' (p. 130). The common denominators suggested by Aarseth are: *world, objects, agents* and *events*. Aarseth views these as four independent ontic dimensions. He argues that the common denominators are 'ordered by games and narratives order them' (p. 131). The four dimensions suggested are relevant and make an adequate list of basic elements for narratives and games. However, the dimensions may gain from not being understood as independent. On the contrary, the dimensions world, objects, agents and events are interdependent (Wilhelmsson, 2007) and as the analyses will show, may be distributed through various expressions in narratives and games. The world dimension

DOI: 10.4324/9781003297406-4

of Aarseth's model describes agency and accessibility in relation to geometry and/or topology. Aarseth's model (2012, p. 131) defines world in terms of 'linear corridor', the 'multicursal' or 'hub-shaped labyrinth' and 'the open world', 'the one room game' and 'the separate hub'. For defining game worlds in relation to possible agency patterns these distinctions make sense. However, Aarseth's concepts are limited in their focus on a specific kind of geometrical and topological system and hence miss other qualities. His model does not consider how a world is construed with regards to social relations between the agents of the world. This chapter puts emphasis to how a fictional game world not only is a matter of functional geometry and topology or whether it is accessible in one way or another to the audience, but how social structures may function as fuel for conflicts. Aarseth's model is also revised as the four ontic dimensions are regarded as highly dependent on each other in contrast to how Aarseth originally proposed.

Anna Gunder's (2007) study on the ludification of J. K. Rowling's *Harry Potter and the Philosopher's Stone* (1997) into the PC-game of the same name (KnowWonder, 2001) has also been an inspiration for this chapter. Gunder does not cover the relation between fiction and non-fiction and is not focused upon conflicts as the present chapter is. Gunder's focus lies on the specific literary adaptation she labels ludification, that is the process when a book, comic, movie or other media is turned into a game. Gunder concludes that much of the material from Rowling's book finds its way into the game and motivates the player to continue playing the game to its end by means of the same or very similar functions that motivates the reader. She finds that 'an important difference is that Harry Potter's personal development and inner life, which is a central theme in the novel, in essence have disappeared in the ludification process' (Gunder, 2007, p. 130, my translation). The two narratives analysed in this chapter, *Hamlet* and the graphically violent biker war TV-series *SoA* are at their very core narratives of personal development and the inner life of their respective protagonists. Hence Gunder's conclusions are of interest for this chapter.

The narratives and the game in this study reuse non-fictional conflicts as core material and transform real-life conflicts into structured experiences. The chapter comprises an introduction of core elements of Shakespeare's *Hamlet*, a close reading of *SoA* and a close reading through playing *MoM* as well as observations of players playing the game (Beasts of War, 2014; Tech Geek Gamers, 2019). The chapter contains a short contextualizing introduction to non-fictional biker wars which is mainly based on a literature study of governmental reports (FBI, 2011, 2015; Vesterhav & Korsell, 2016), TV-documentaries (History Channel, 2007–2010), biographical material (Dobyns & Johnson-Shelton, 2009) in addition to the authors own experience within the field. From this, a set of nine key elements are derived which serve as a platform to understand the conflicts of *SoA* and how some of these key elements constitutes the foundation of the game.

The following sections describe how the four ontic dimensions are building blocks of *MoM*, *SoA* and *Hamlet*. It highlights the interdependency of these dimensions and contributes to an understanding of how conflicts are transformed from real life, via narratives, to games.

Sons of Anarchy: Men of Mayhem

Men of Mayhem is a worker placement player versus player tabletop board game for three to four players. It makes use of the conflicts between different criminal organisations portrayed in *SoA*. The main objective of the game is to gather the largest sum of cash at the end of the game. To get cash the player will need to act as an outlaw: selling guns and *contraband* (i.e. drugs), fight other players in order to exploit locations and limit other player's incomes etc. Players may at any time create alliances with each other and are free to break such alliances any time they like. As the analysis will show the game can be understood from Aarseth's four ontic dimensions: world, objects, agents and events but first and foremost as a playground (Wilhelmsson, 2007) for conflicts based on social interplay between players. Before going into the details of the game it is necessary to understand the relation between *MoM*, *SoA*, *Hamlet* and non-fictional biker wars and what world, objects, agents and events they share.

The Origins of *Sons of Anarchy*

The main story (events) and some of the main characters (agents) of *SoA* are based on Shakespeare's *Hamlet*. Kurt Sutter, the creator of the TV-series has summarised the influence of *Hamlet* and real-life biker culture in an interview (Zoller Seitz, 2013). 'One of the recurring themes of Shakespeare is the idea that power doesn't just corrupt, but that the corruption continuously repeats itself' Sutter explains. He continues with his view on of how motorcycle clubs were started by bored adrenaline seeking WWII vets 'who'd get together and ride their bikes' and 'have a few too many beers and kick the shit out of each other'. He goes on to tell how these clubs became corrupted and classified as organised crime by the federal government. Sutter explains that he built his narrative around a character, John Teller, that sees how his clubs turns into something he did not envision. He continues 'What if that guy is the father in Hamlet? What if that guy is the ghost of John Teller? That archetype enabled me to establish the prince, our lead guy, Jax Teller. I loosely based all my characters on ones from Hamlet. I winked at it with Gemma as Gertrude and Clay as Claudius. Opie was Horatio. And the ongoing question was: Would the prince find out?' (Zoller Seitz, 2013).

As indicated in the interview, *SoA* is not solely to be understood as *Hamlet on Harleys*. Non-fictional conflicts between *Outlaw Motorcycle Gangs* (OMGs) also provide substantial material in forms of world, objects, agents and events for the TV-series (and the game). Conflicts involving OMGs are often called *war* (Dobyns & Johnson-Shelton, 2009; History Channel, 2007–2010). Such wars reportedly get very violent as a surveillance video capturing a fatal incident between Hells Angels MC (HA) and Mongols MC shows. The HA provoked the Mongols by going to their hotel. First a smaller group from HA scouted the place and they then called for backup. This resulted in a throwdown in which one member of the Mongols MC and two members of the HA were killed, 11 gang members were injured, 112 were detained. 14 guns and over 100 knives, of which ten were bloody, were seized (History Channel, 2007–2010). Fights like this are the templates used to create conflicts in *SoA* and *MoM*.

Real-life biker culture contains several key elements of importance. These elements are adapted and transformed into the narrative of *SoA* as a basis for the social structures in the series. They are also partly adapted and transformed into objects of play in *MoM* and substitute and supplement elements from *Hamlet*. This section is based on the author's experience within the field, *Gangland* (History Channel, 2007–2010), Dobyns and Johnson-Shelton (2009), FBI (2011, 2015), Dulaney (2005), and Vesterhav and Korsell (2016). From these sources nine key elements have been derived which are essential for the TV-series and the game.

Motorcycles: Objects. Predominantly large capacity Harley-Davidsons. Motorcycles are present in *SoA* and as part of a game piece in *MoM*.

Biker: Agent. A man devoted to Harley-Davidsons. A biker's life is focused on his interest in motorcycles and the fraternity surrounding it. *Sons of Anarchy* are bikers.

Club: Agent. Bikers often team up in clubs. Clubs enforce a very strict hierarchy. *Sons of Anarchy* is a club. In *MoM* the players are building clubs/gangs based on the TV-series. Not all gangs in the TV-series are OMGs but all players use game pieces that represents bikers in *MoM*. This is a transformation of social structures between *SoA* and *MoM*.

President/vice president: Agents. The leaders of a club. In *MoM* the players are the presidents of different gangs.

Cut: Object. A west onto which patches are attached. These shows which club the wearer belongs to and his position in the club. Cuts play a central role in the TV-series. In *MoM* the cut is combined with the full patch (see the following) and to claim the Patch is an important event in the game.

Patches: Objects. At the back of the cut there is a three-part patch (bottom rocker, top rocker and middle part) that tells what club and location a member belongs to. *SoA's* middle part is an image of 'the grim reaper' holding an automatic rifle with the blade of a scythe attached to its barrel. The font used on the rockers is very similar to the non-fictional HA and directly refers to a non-fictional club. Members' status within the club is displayed via patches such as President and Vice President. Other patches inform about services to the club. The *MoM*-patch from the TV-series means that the wearer has killed for the club. The phrase commonly used in *SoA* for a club decision to kill someone is 'Meeting Mr. Mayhem' from which the name of the game stems. This patch is fictional, but it does allegedly have counterparts in real OMGs. The full patch is an important part of *MoM*.

Prospect: Agent. A biker that is not a full member of a club but accepted as a possible future full patch member. A prospect is only to act on direct orders form a member. This is reflected in *MoM* as a player may not use a prospect game piece to initiate a throwdown.

Patched in: Event. This means to become a full member of a club and be honored to wear the full patch of the club. This is an important part of both the TV-series and *MoM*. To patch in prospects means that the player will be able to use guns in throwdowns.

Full patch member: Agent. If a prospect passes the prospect period, normally at least a year, he can be voted in as a full patch member. The time period of a year is not represented in *MoM*. Full patch members are important agents in both *SoA* and *MoM*.

Core Elements of Hamlet

Hamlet tells the story of how the crown prince of Denmark reluctantly revenges his father's murder by his uncle Claudius who overtakes the throne and marries his mother Gertrude and becomes Hamlet's stepfather. The marriage creates a conflict between Hamlet and his mother. The ghost of Hamlet's father appears before Hamlet and reveals that he has been murdered, asking Hamlet for revenge. Hamlet agonises over if he shall kill Claudius and in fear for his life, he pretends to be mad and hence poses no threat to Claudius' life. Eventually Hamlet kills Claudius but also dies himself.

This basic plot of *Hamlet* is not Shakespeare's own idea. Some of the more obvious sources for *Hamlet* are Saxo Grammaticus' *Gesta Danorum* (2013) and De Belleforest's *Histoires Tragiques* (ca 1570). Shakespeare might also have been inspired to recreate the genre of revenge tragedies and based *Hamlet* upon Kyd's (2013) *The Spanish Tragedy*, probably written between years 1582 and 1592, that is prior to *Hamlet* according to Ryan (2016). In a revenge tragedy the protagonist does not hesitate to kill the antagonist but in *Hamlet* this is the most important intrapersonal conflict portrayed in the play. In *Hamlet*, action is replaced by long soliloquies in which the psyche of Hamlet is put forth to the audience (Ryan, 2016). This feature added by Shakespeare allows for an in-depth character development of the protagonist resulting in a rich, deep and round character, which in turn is one of the key differences between agents in narratives versus games according to Aarseth (2012, p. 132).

There are four identified types of conflicts in *Hamlet*: *intergroup, intragroup, interpersonal and intrapersonal* (see Linderoth & Sjöblom, this volume).

The intergroup conflict in *Hamlet* is between the agents that are supportive of Hamlet, for example Horatio, versus those who supports King

Claudius, for example Hamlet's childhood friends Rosencrantz and Guildenstern who are hired by the king to spy on Hamlet pretending to be on his side. The intragroup conflict is exemplified by the relation between Horatio being a protestant and Hamlet being more ambiguous. Rosencrantz and Guildenstern are also an example of this, since they have been friends with Hamlet but have now chosen Claudius' side in the conflict. The interpersonal conflict in *Hamlet* stands between Hamlet, the ghost, his mother and King Claudius respectively.

The appearance of the ghost introduces a non-fictional contemporary religious conflict and transforms it into conflicts in the play. The ghost has been released from a state of being purged by fire and died without the last rites which implies that the murdered king was catholic. Purgatory and last rites are central concepts in Catholicism (the dominant religion in the era of the fictional world of the play) but during the Elizabethan era in which the play originally was performed, England was strictly Protestant why the concept of purgatory is not explicitly used (Goldman, 2001). This conflict is the key to understand why Hamlet hesitates to revenge his father, why he agonises over suicide, and the guilt he feels concerning stabbing his beloved Ophelia's father to death, leading to her suicide, etc. This sub theme in *Hamlet* creates a tension between Hamlet and his father's ghost, making Hamlet's relation to it complex. From a protestant perspective, the ghost might be a demon or an angel, but regardless of which is true, Protestantism in this early form forbade any contact with ghosts. It is also probable that Hamlet was brought up as a catholic and in that case, Hamlet should help the ghost to be cleansed and leave purgatory. The intrapersonal conflict is Hamlet's reluctance to revenge his father and his Oedipus-complex relation to his mother (Bergmann & Green, 2013).

Sons of Anarchy

Sons of Anarchy is a graphically violent TV-series which in 92 episodes tells the story of biker Jax Teller, his family and the gunrunning and drug dealing OMG *Sons of Anarchy Red Wood Original* (SAMCRO). The club acts an extension of Jax' family and his loyalties shift back and forth between his family and the club as a series of intrapersonal conflicts haunts him. Jax is the son of John Teller, the club's founder, and first president. John died in what appeared to be a motorcycle accident. In the series it is revealed that this accident was a murder initiated by John's friend (and vice president of the club) Clay who carried it out together with John's wife Gemma. Clay marries Gemma after the murder. By killing John, Clay becomes president (becomes king). When *SoA* begins Jax is the vice president of the club, that is the crown prince. Jax finds a manuscript written by his father which describes how the original values of the club have all deteriorated and become subject to corruption. John Teller reveals in the manuscript that his life is threatened by Clay and Gemma. The ghost of John Teller is hence introduced through this manuscript and the audience gets to hear him reading the script as a voice over. The core elements of *Hamlet* are thus integrated and transformed into the world and agents of the TV-series: a murder (event) of a father (agent), a murderous stepfather (agent), the marriage between the protagonist's mother and his father's killer (event), the ghost of the father (agent) and of course the crown prince himself in the shape of Jax Teller (agent). Jax does initially not act upon the information in the manuscript and does not realise that Clay and Gemma are behind the death of his father. Just as Hamlet, Jax agonises in deep intrapersonal conflict of what he should do.

The World of Sons of Anarchy

Aarseth's (2012) describes world in terms of accessibility, geometry and topology and disregards social relations between agents in the world. This aspect is of importance since social relations provide material for events, for example conflicts. A world contains objects that may be the material for conflict between agents. The four dimensions world, objects, agents and events are highly interdependent and regulate what is possible in the narrative or game in question. Social structures provide a set of rules that regulate what actions can be taken and what events can be set in scene or played out.

Frequently used locations are in or in close proximity of Charming, the fictional hometown of SAMCRO, which is a typical Californian small town (a 'hamlet'). Common locations are SAMCRO's original clubhouse, other gangs' clubhouses, a pornographic movie production studio, illegal gun warehouses, the docks into which guns are smuggled, the Stockton State Prison and of course different roads as roads constitute a natural habitat for an OMG.

An OMG's social structure is hierarchal. They live by rules set by themselves but do replicate a military structure which is in line with the background story of the series: most of the First Nine (the nine original members of the club) were Vietnam veterans. This back story in turn is a reference to how non-fictional clubs were founded by veterans from Second World War.

There are many different groups (agents) in *SoA*. The groups listed below are central for the narrative and constitute playable groups in *MoM*, that is they are common denominators of the TV-series and the game.

SAMCRO is the main group and from which perspective most of the story is told. They are primarily running guns, and do not initially deal heavy drugs. Through the efforts of Jax, they are at times trying to move away from illegal to legal businesses, for example their move into making pornographic videos at the Caracara Studio which in turn ends up in illegal business of prostitution.

Mayans is a Mexican OMGs that initially are SAMCRO's enemies. Mayans are mainly drug dealers.

One-Niners is an African American street gang that are into drug dealing. They buy guns from SAMCRO. They compete with Mayans over territory to sell their drugs.

Linn Syndicate is a Chinese street gang that are into drug dealing and gun-running. They compete with Mayans and One-Niners over territory.

Conflicts in Sons of Anarchy

In *SoA* conflicts between characters and different groups of people are portrayed as the normal state of things. Conflicts and alliances shift frequently, and groups initially rendered as long-term enemies unite and in other cases they will go into direct war with each other in a complex weave of deceitful behaviour. This complexity is established in the pilot episode as several ongoing and upcoming conflicts. SAMCRO are at war with Mayans. Mayans raid SAMCRO's illegal firearms storage, stealing the weapons and torch the place. This in turn puts SAMCRO in conflict with the local police force since they suspect that they have used the place for illegal business too close to or even inside the borders of the small town of Charming. Since they are running guns to other gangs their chain of distribution is now broken and they are in short supply of guns. This leads to a beginning conflict between SAMCRO and One-Niners. One-Niners need new guns to protect a big heroin delivery and consider SAMCRO to have broken a contract. At the same time a white supremacist gang, The Nords, are cooking methamphetamine in Charming which in turn affects the relations between SAMCRO and the local police.

The social structures of Charming provide material for conflicts between SAMCRO and some of the leading entrepreneurs of the town. SAMCRO is tolerated by the local chief of police but only if they keep theirs and others dirty business outside Charming. SAMCRO is obliged to keep order in town and act against other criminal activities such as the Nords' methamphetamine business. As SAMCRO are running guns they want to keep things downscaled in Charming and do not want the town to grow since growth would mean that it will be harder for them to keep order and hence they would attract more attention from a larger law enforcement presence. This is a strong basis for conflict between SAMCRO and those who promote any economic development and exemplifies how interpersonal relations relate to intergroup conflicts in the series. Also present in *SoA* are race-related conflicts between the different gangs. In *SoA* such conflicts are mainly subordinate to economic interests. While *SoA* portrays some extremely racist organisations as part of its narrative, there are also storylines about how the different gangs puts such conflicts aside if there is a profit to be made by collaborating.

There are conflicts between individual characters that sometimes will lead to intergroup and intragroup conflicts, for example a conflict between Jax and his ex-wife Wendy, pregnant with his child, stemming from her out of control drug abuse. Wendy overdose which nearly kills the baby. The conflict between Jax and Wendy, the fact that Jax has become a father of a child with a slim chance of survival, Mayans' attack and Jax finding the manuscript makes him disturbed over the state of things in general and the direction of SAMCRO. He consequently gets into a conflict with his stepfather at a club meeting. Acting as the vice president, he suggests that the club should leave the very lucrative but dangerous gunrunning business. Clay strongly opposes this, and a new conflict begins between fractions within SAMCRO (intragroup). Some become allies with Jax and his idea of going legit versus the ones that join Clay's direction. Gemma is informed by Clay of Jax' position and she becomes very concerned that Jax will destroy what she and Clay has achieved with the club. As Gemma and Clay both are responsible for killing Jax's father, there is a conflict here as well. Jax in turn is at this point unaware that his father was murdered and therefore has an interpersonal conflict with his dead and absent father.

Another level of conflict, the intrapersonal, will trouble several of the characters throughout the series. In the pilot episode the intrapersonal conflict of Jax slowly begins when he finds the manuscript and becomes a father. He faces not a religious problem as Hamlet does, but he does show signs of hesitation to act upon the information in the manuscript and needs better proof of the father being correct in his assumption that Clay is a deadly threat and will lead the club astray.[1]

Jax loves his club, he is the vice president and son of the founder, and in time he will be the president, but he does not see a future in continuing running guns given the pressure from other competing clubs leading to full blown war. This intrapersonal conflict escalates during the series as Jax makes numerous attempts to change the direction of the club, but it will for the most part only generate new interpersonal, intrapersonal, inter group and intragroup conflicts. In the concluding season Jax goes on a killing spree. When Jax realise who murdered his father, and that Gemma killed his new wife Tara, he kills both his own mother and Clay. At the end of the road Jax has run out of options and other *Sons of Anarchy* clubs demand that SAMCRO let him 'meet Mr. Mayhem', that is execute him for killing the president of *Sons of Anarchy*'s Indian Hills charter. SAMCRO, however, decides to let him meet his fate on his own and he deliberately crashes his father's Harley-Davidson into a truck.

To conclude this section, there are four identified types of conflicts in *SoA*.

Intergroup conflicts between groups that are often portrayed as conflicts of interest which often in turn manifest the conflict as being about some kind of resource. Resources come in a number of ways such as territory, guns, drugs etc. To some extent racism is also a source of conflict.

Then there are *intragroup conflicts* between members of a group which is often portrayed as a matter of choosing sides in an internal matter of conflicting interests such as going legit and stop running guns or continue to take care of business, that is continue to be criminals.

There are also *interpersonal conflicts* between individual persons which are often portrayed as someone doing something extremely harmful to someone else such as murdering a family member.

Finally, there are *intrapersonal conflicts*, that is conflicts in the mind of a person. These are mostly focused upon on Jax' struggles with the visions his father had about the club and later in the series how he copes with the realisation that his father was murdered.

Men of Mayhem Analysis

Men of Mayhem comes in a box decorated with a modified full patch of SAMCRO (where the bottom rocker's 'California' is replaced with Men of Meyhem) and photographs of some central characters from the series. These characters are not playable in the game. On the cards making up the world of the game, imagery from the TV-series is used to underscore the function of each card. That is to say, the narrative of the TV-series is not present in the board game by means of these images; they are transformed into backdrops to provide a visual illustration to locations and functions in the game and serve as possible references points for players acquainted with *SoA*. For a player with prior knowledge of the narrative, the images add a layer of connotative meaning in reference to the narrative, but the game will even without this layer still be comprehensible and fully playable. The same is true of the relation between *SoA* and *Hamlet*. The audience of the TV-series does not need to recognise the story of *Hamlet* to enjoy the narrative, but if they do, this added subtext may result in a different reading of the text. Equally true is the fact that players do not need any knowledge of real biker wars to play the game, but such knowledge enhances the experience.

Each player will control one of four gangs (i.e. be the president) of SAMCRO, Mayans, One-Niners or Linn syndicate. These are the superordinate agents of the game. A club consists of a number of game pieces, *dudes*, which are either full patch *members* or *prospects*. The figures representing members ride Harley-like motorcycles while the prospect figures are narrower and stand in a pose as being on their guard. These figures are the subordinate agents of the game which provides the material for the interpersonal (player versus player) conflicts that will take place during gameplay but at the same time simulate intergroup conflicts (gang versus gang).

The game contains two rulesets, *unleaded* and *high octane*. Depending on the rules used the game will be played differently. In unleaded, all players initially have the same starting assets (objects). In high-octane the players have asymmetrical starting conditions. The distribution of assets is made to mimic the profiles of the gangs in the series. For instance, SAMCRO starts with more weapons, while Mayans have more prospects.

The game world consists of four *club house* cards and nine *site tiles* (adequately resembling beer coasters). Each player has a club house where the specific club rules are printed. These rules vary between clubs if the game is played high-octane and in addition to different starting assets there are specific *gang rules* and *club orders* that mimic the profiles of the clubs in the TV-series. SAMCRO can use the club order *spend 1 cash to buy 1 gun*, and as a gang rule take one extra cash every time the player sells a gun. This reflects the profile of the gunrunning SAMCRO of the TV-series. Other gangs have similar features that are transformed from the TV-series.

All figures of dudes are located at the club house at the beginning of the game. Sites are dealt from a stack of 24 cards of which only five is in play when the game starts. During play new sites will be successively exposed, making the playable world larger. The world's topological and geometrical space is finite but allows substantial variation when played several times. The world is dynamic and undergoes changes between rounds of one game as well as between different sessions of games. Three sites are always in play when the game begins: *The St. James hospital*, *The emergency room* and *The Charming police department*. These sites are fixed points of the world that are at the very core of the gameplay. Since fighting between players (interpersonal conflict) is a substantial part of the game, an emergency room and hospital are necessary to host and cure injured dudes. The police department serves the purpose of dropping heat and claim the patch from another player. Additional sites may show up from a different stack of cards, called *anarchy cards* during gameplay. These sites are called *opportunities* and serve the same function as location cards, that is a player may exploit them (see the following text). At the beginning of the game, one player will be holding the patch, showing the full patch of *Sons of Anarchy*. Holding the patch gives a couple of advantages. The patch holder will always be the first to act, to perform an event of some kind in the game. In a throwdown (see the following text) it is therefore always the patch holder (if she is involved) that begin the turn taking during a fight between players. If the outcome of any event results in a tie, the patch holder always wins. The patch is much like a magic elixir (Vogler, 2007) that makes it a desirable object to hold as it empowers the player's social status.

The rules do not define who will be fighting who (events). Fans of *SoA* might prefer to mimic the TV-series intergroup conflicts and reuse the narrative while playing and in that process add elements that are not defined by the rules of the game. The *high-octane* rules mimic the different agendas of the playable clubs and is in that respect reusing the narrative conflicts of *SoA*, but it is nevertheless fully possible to play the game without any prior knowledge of the narrative.

Players may at any time in the game choose to become allies (events) for strategical reasons such as buying, selling and trading assets between each other. This makes *MoM* a game in which politics and even king making is encouraged to large extent. This serves as source for interpersonal conflicts between players acted out as an intergroup relation. The game instructions explicitly say that 'Talk is cheap! No deals are binding. Don't be an ass. We play games to have a good time. If you're being an ass, your friends aren't having any fun. Remember: it's only a game. Blood feuds end when the game does!' This means that any promises may be broken at any time by either part. It is part of the game. There is also a possibility that interpersonal conflicts from the game world seeps through what Goffman (2013) would call the *interaction membrane* of the game (the border between a specific activity realised here and now, and other contexts). When such things happen, a game session can lead to real-world conflicts after the game. Strategical decisions also provide incitements for intrapersonal conflicts as it is hard for players to know what strategy is best as the world changes between rounds and players can break any alliances.

Recruiting Members

Recruiting *members* mimics both the real world of OMGs and the fictional world of *SoA*. To recruit a full patch member the player either patch in a prospect or recruit a prospect that later can be patched in. Patching in costs one gun and one cash. Some non-fictional OMGs will allegedly test a prospects loyalty by ordering them to beat up or even kill someone to become a member. A gun used for murder or other criminal activates needs to be untraceable to the crime which might be the reason for this. A player might recruit new prospects for the cost of an *order token* (in form of a prepaid 'burner' cell phone). A possible reason for this lower cost is that OMGs generally does not have a problem to recruit prospects among men that serves time in prison or are outlaw wannabes (FBI, 2015, p. 23). In contrast to the TV-series (Patch Over, S1E4) and non-fictional OMGs (Vesterhav & Korsell, 2016) a player cannot do a complete patch over of another club. However, going into alliances with one or more players have a similar function but a complete patch over would mean that the patched over club would then follow the gang rules of the mother charter, which is not the case in alliances.

Exploits

To utilise a *site* (world) in the game, a player can use an order (event) to exploit it. In such cases the player has a couple of different options depending on the site, such as spend to buy guns or contraband, swap guns for contraband of sell guns or contraband in exchange for cash. The events that each site cards do have connections to the TV-series. At the pornographic film studio Caracara studios, a player may skim 3 cash and use a boost function spending an additional order to sell contraband and in return get 3 cash. This exemplifies how sites relate to the narrative world of the TV-series as they share the same functions.

Exploits create interpersonal and simulated intergroup conflicts. A player may only exploit a site if she is the sole occupant of it. To hinder a player to exploit a site another player may put an order to move some of his members or prospects to the site in question and later initiate a throwdown. Since the game board is dynamic and starts with only five of the nine sites visible and with the additional anarchy cards providing both new sites *(opportunities)* as well as other cards (obstacles, hazzles and last call) new material for conflicts will appear successively and randomly.

Changes in the world affect the social structures of the game. In the first round only one anarchy card is in play, in the second round two new cards and for the remaining four rounds three new ones will be in play. One possible exploit is the Charming police department where a player may *claim the patch* from the patch holder. In a non-fictional context, depriving an OMG-member of his cut and hence the patch is amongst the most offensive things that can be done. In the TV-series there are events that portray this, for instance in S1E5 in which a former member of the *SoA* that is considered to be an enemy of the club has his full patch tattoo burnt off his body with a welding torch. There are allegedly examples of this happening in the non-fictional world as well (Kent, 2009). The reason for such brutal and violent acts is simple: any form of insignia of a club is the property of the club and if someone no longer is a member, the club will claim it back, no matter what it takes. To claim the patch in the game has an important subtext and is to be understood as a major offense.

Throwdown

A *throwdown* is a fight between players' clubs performed in several sequential steps (player versus player simulating an intergroup conflict). If a player decides to exploit a site, she can be stopped short in the process if one or more players relocate members to this site. Any of the players may in the next turn issue the order throwdown and challenge the other player to fight for the right to exploit the site. Involved players may call for backup, spending one order token per other site from which they move dudes to participate. The next step is to pull guns. Guns are not always used, either because players do not have any to bring or because they do not want to since it attracts heat (attention) from the police. After the decision to use or not use guns is made, each player that is part of the throwdown secretly places a number of guns in their closed fist, hold them out and opens the hand to reveal the number. The last step is to *get bloody* which is a term often used in the TV-series as well as among non-fictional OMGs. Getting bloody in this game means that the players now roll a six-sided dice and add to the outcome a number of bonuses depending on the number of figures and guns they have present in the throwdown. Throwdowns transform the graphical violence of the TV-series to strategic mathematics. The player with the highest total wins. All guns used are discarded. If a player brought two guns to the throwdown two of the opponent's dudes are injured and must be relocated to the emergency room. All other dudes of the loosing player must be relocated to their clubhouse. The dice is then rolled to decide if the dudes in the emergency room survives and returns to the club house or if they die and return to the recruiting pool. If a player has no members after this stage she is eliminated from the game.

To summarise, *MoM* adapts and transforms elements from the TV-series and non-fictional biker wars. The game is not narrative in the sense that a specific plot is told during gameplay; however, the game includes some components of the TV-series. These adaptations and transformations of narrative elements omit characters and character development. Instead, it focuses on exploitation of sites and throwdowns as its core elements and transform non-fictional conflicts to strategic mathematical endeavours framed by real and fictional biker culture elements.

Conclusions

This study is a close reading of two narratives, Shakespeare's *Hamlet* and Sutter's *SoA*. It shows, in a condensed way, the origins of these two narratives and how they both build on other fictional narratives that include conflicts as a core subject matter as well as on non-fictional conflicts. Furthermore, it has shown similarities between the four ontic dimensions world, objects, events, agents suggested by Aarseth (2012) as the common denominators for narratives and games. This is of course not surprising since plot elements and characters of *SoA* are transformed from *Hamlet*. What is interesting, however, is how these elements are put in use in the TV-series in combination with the non-fictional contemporary conflicts and how parts of the conflicts are transformed into game mechanics in a worker placement board game?

Table 2.1 below formalise the different types of conflicts in the narratives and the game. It shows how different forms of structured experiences contribute to differences and shifting topics of the four types of conflicts.

Table 2.1 Conflict overview

	Hamlet	*Sons of Anarchy*	*Men of Mayhem*
Intergroup	Loyal to Hamlet versus loyal to the king	Gunrunning, drug running, prostitution, territory Outlaws versus law enforcement, race issues, etc.	Exploitation of Sites, getting most Cash at the end of the game
Intragroup	Choosing sides in the intergroup conflict	Go legit or not Choosing sides in go legit etc.	Not applicable
Interpersonal	Hamlet versus the king murdered Hamlet's father Hamlet versus the queen who married the murderer	Jax versus Clay murdered father Jax versus his mother married to Clay and part of the murdering of Jax' father	Being constantly attacked by players Politics including king making
Intrapersonal	Oedipus complex If to act or not on the ghost's information. Suicide versus Religious beliefs	Oedipus complex If to act or not on the 'ghosts' information. Go legit or not	Choosing strategies Handling rules of irrelevance

The results show that the game does not rely on narrative to be playable but to a certain degree it is part of the *SoA* world, objects, agents and events. Thematically *MoM* reuse and adapts elements (world, objects, agents and events) from the TV series as well as non-fictional biker wars. The narrative from the TV series does only supply a foundation for the game mechanics thematically by reusing imagery, names and characteristics of the different clubs and specific sites in which the narrative of the series is played out. The game is emphasizing only parts of the content of the TV-series. Whereas *SoA* allows in-depth character development and thus portrays intrapersonal conflicts based on Shakespeare's *Hamlet*, *MoM* centres on the intergroup conflicts and it is not necessary for a player to have even a basic knowledge of the TV-series or *Hamlet*. *MoM* reuse actual footage of actual settings (world), characters (agents), objects and events as part of the game design. The narratives have a set of central agents in common. Even though all but one type of conflict (event) can be clearly identified across all the material the variations in topic of the conflicts diversify narrative from game. For each step in the transformation from *Hamlet* to *MoM* the conflicts take on a slightly different form. The world, objects, agents and events undergo changes dependent on the social construction of and in the narrative and the game respectively. The analysis of *SoA* and *MoM* shows that they reuse elements from a non-fictional outlaw biker world and transform them into plot elements, events, characters, objects construing a similar but fictional world. Conflicts are presented in terms of motivation, how they are initiated and how they are turned into events such as direct war player versus player. What is happening in the stepwise transformation from *Hamlet* to *MoM* is different from Gunder's conclusion (2007) and goes even one or two steps further as the characters as such disappear and only function as emblematic objects rather than agents in *MoM*. The main finding of the chapter is that there is no room for intrapersonal and intragroup conflicts in the game. Social structures and social conflicts are the common denominators between non-fiction, narrative and game in this case.

'And the rest is silence.'
(Shakespeare, 1599–1602, *Hamlet*, Act 5, Scene 2)

Note

1 There are however conflicts based on religion in *SoA*. SAMCRO buy their guns from the Real IRA etc. but that lies beyond the limitations of this chapter.

References

Aarseth, E. (2012). A narrative theory of games. In M. S. El-Nasr (Ed.), *FDG '12: Proceedings of the international conference on the foundations of digital games* (pp. 129–133). ACM.

Beasts of War. (2014, September 17). How to play the Sons of Anarchy board game! [Video]. *YouTube*. www.youtube.com/watch?v=vDo1ss_yHGg
Bergmann, M. S., & Green, A. (2013). *The unconscious in Shakespeare's plays*. Routledge.
De Belleforest, F. (ca 1570). The history of Hamlet. In D. Bevington (Ed.), *Histoires tragique* (mod. ed., Internet Shakespeare ed.). University of Victoria.
Dill, A., Kovaleski, J., & Sweigart, S. (2014). *Sons of Anarchy: Men of Mayhem* [Tabletop]. Gale Force Nine.
Dobyns, J., & Johnson-Shelton, N. (2009). *No angel: My harrowing undercover journey to the inner circle of the Hells angels*. Thorndike Press.
Dulaney, W. L. (2005). A brief history of 'outlaw' motorcycle clubs. *International Journal of Motorcycle Studies*, *1*(2), 1–19.
FBI. (2011). National gang threat assessment: Emerging trends. *FBI*. www.fbi.gov/file-repository/stats-services-publications-2011-national-gang-threat-assessment-2011%20national%20gang%20threat%20assessment%20%20emerging%20trends.pdf
FBI. (2015). National gang report. *FBI*. www.fbi.gov/file-repository/stats-services-publications-national-gang-report-2015.pdf
Goffman, E. (2013). *Encounters: Two studies in the sociology of interaction*. Martino Fine Books.
Goldman, P. (2001). Hamlet's ghost: A review article, Greenblatt, Stephen. Hamlet in Purgatory. *Anthropoetics: The Journal of Generative Anthropology*, *VII*(1). http://anthropoetics.ucla.edu/ap0701/hamlet/
Gunder, A. (2007). Berättelse blir spel: Om ludiseringen av J. K. Rowlings Harry Potter and the Philosopher's Stone. In J. Linderoth (Ed.), *Datorspelandets dynamik: Lekar och roller i en digital kultur* (pp. 111–136). Studentlitteratur.
History Channel. (2007–2010). *Gangland: Behind enemy lines* [TV-series]. History Channel.
Kent, P. (2009, May 6). Hells Angels use welding torch used to remove gang tattoo. *The Advertiser*.
KnowWonder. (2001). *Harry Potter and the philosopher's stone* [PC]. Electronic Arts.
Kyd, T. (2013). *The Spanish tragedy*. (Original work from ca 1616). Project Gutenberg. https://www.gutenberg.org/files/6043/6043-h/6043-h.htm
Rowling, J. K. (1997). *Harry Potter and the philosopher's stone*. Bloomsbury.
Ryan, K. (2016). *Hamlet and revenge*. British Library. www.bl.uk/shakespeare/articles/hamlet-and-revenge
Saxo Grammaticus. (2013). *The Danish history, books I-IX*. Project Gutenberg. https://www.gutenberg.org/files/1150/1150-h/1150-h.htm
Shakespeare, W. (2021). *Hamlet*. (Original work from 1623). Project Gutenberg. https://www.gutenberg.org/files/1524/1524-h/1524-h.htm
Sutter, K. (Creator). (2008–2014). *Sons of anarchy* [TV series]. FX.
Tech Geek Gamers. (2019, May 6). Sons of Anarchy Men of Mayhem board game session [Video]. *Youtube*. www.youtube.com/watch?v=5Zpgu0SB4h4
Vesterhav, D., & Korsell, L. (2016). *Kriminella nätverk och grupperingar: Polisers bild av maktstrukturer och marknader*. Brottsförebyggande rådet.
Vogler, C. (2007). *The writer's journey: Mythic structure for writers* (3rd ed.). Michael Wiese Productions.
Wilhelmsson, U. (2007). Datorspel som lekplats och skådeplats: Rummets roll i lek och narration. In J. Linderoth (Ed.), *Datorspelandets dynamik: Lekar och roller i en digital kultur* (pp. 137–154). Studentlitteratur.
Zoller Seitz, M. (2013, September 8). Kurt Sutter explains his cultural influences. *Vulture*. www.vulture.com/2013/09/kurt-sutter-explains-his-cultural-influences.html

3 From Zero-Sum Business Games to Coopetitive Simulation

J. Tuomas Harviainen

Introduction

Business games are, right after wargames, one of the oldest uses of computers for gaming (Faria et al., 2009). In them, players learn how to run a business, or further refine their skills in running a business, in a safe, simulated environment that allows for experimentation (Harviainen et al., 2014; Tsuchiya & Tsuchiya, 1999). A typical business simulation[1] consists of controlling the various functions and decision processes of a fictional small to medium enterprise (SME), or a large corporation, in order to utilize the play for learning purposes (see Lainema, 2003, for an example). Some early versions of these games had people calculating the results of actions, as in the case of the game known alternatively as *The Andlinger game*, *The McKinsey game*, or *the Harvard Business Review Game*, presented by Andlinger (1958) in a *Harvard Business Review* article (Kibbee et al., 1961), but quickly moved on to using computerized calculations, starting with the *Top Management Decision Simulation* of Ricciardi, published by the American Management Association in 1957. Such games functioned first with turn-based batch processing and later, increasingly, by using continuous processing, which allowed for the simulation of different types of time (Lainema, 2010). This way such games may provide an efficient learning curve, by allowing the players to first practice their decisions and then accelerating to an approximation of real time (Lainema, 2003). While still rare in the early years of computing, computerized business games became commonplace by the early 1990s (Wolfe, 1993). A highly useful history of them, including phases of development and the move to internet-based delivery, can be found in the work of Faria et al. (2009).

As the games' ability to provide detail and address representational veracity of business practices grew, it became possible to go more and more into detail about companies and their supply chains (Faria et al., 2009). Yet in many cases, the games' depictions of business environments, networks and ecosystems did not evolve as realistically. In this chapter, I examine the ways in which business simulations, both historically (e.g., Keys & Wolfe, 1990) and still nowadays (e.g., Harviainen et al., 2014) too often treat the

DOI: 10.4324/9781003297406-5

market as a zero-sum competition against other companies, and not as the complex, often coopetitive, and most likely turbulent environment that it is. This has serious consequences. In effect, we are possibly teaching the wrong thing in business schools: an outdated remnant of an earlier time.

This attitude is tied to the ways in which the simulations' companies are placed in fictional supply chains, not in networks or ecosystems. For the purposes of learning how to run the basic, internal functions of a company, or to ground basic coursebooks' contents with simulated practice, this is fine, and demonstrably efficient. Learning to crawl before one can walk is usually necessary. The key challenge is that market realities do not function the same ways as the simulations do. As noted by for example in the *causal texture* theory of Emery and Trist (e.g., 1965; see also Baburoglu, 1988), only certain conditions allow an organization to control its own situation and position toward the market. If the surrounding business environment is turbulent (i.e., in situations where the environment defines everything for business possibilities), companies cannot function alone, or even in supply chains. Alliances are needed, even between competitors. In the current world, this is even more crucial, as most SMEs can no longer view their position as being between only their suppliers and their customers, adding their own value in between and gathering the resulting profit. They need networks to function, and engaging with the dark sides of behavior in networks, such as pressuring other companies in them based on one's prominent presence, rarely provides long-term advantages (Mele et al., 2018).

Companies have of course known the value of cooperation for a long time, and training simulations reflect this. Therefore, most simulations do not tend to feature sudden betrayals, but players may exploit the possibility to conduct them nevertheless (see Harviainen et al., 2014). Likewise, collaboration simulation/games have existed for a long time, but those tend to teach interpersonal or intergroup skills, not intercompany or ecosystemic ones (see, e.g., Oksanen, 2013; Palyga & Wardaszko, 2018). Computerized business simulations are always simplifications, in their systems, architecture, mechanics, and even their time and temporalities (Lainema, 2010; Thavikulwat, 2004). Otherwise, they would not function as simulations and training tools. Yet there is always a risk that one learns the wrong things from them, because of this simplification. This is a critique that has remained present as long as we have had business simulations (e.g., Neuhauser, 1976; Vesa et al., 2017). The question therefore becomes *what should be represented, why, and how?* The answers to these affects what can be learned from the game (Leigh & Tipton, 2014). In my view, it is time to put less emphasis on just running the business, and more on also learning how to read the environment, and how to take a proactive role within it. This is done by placing more design value on business games that can represent networks or entire ecosystems and enable players to interact with each other. To accomplish this, we need to look on one hand at theories of coopetition – cooperation by business competitors – and on the other, at recreational games that show how this can be accomplished.

Value Creation Networks and Coopetition

Knowledge of the surrounding, changing business environment (aka., environmental scanning; Choo, 2002) is a known success factor. This includes knowing what the competition is doing. Without environmental scanning, companies can quickly become complacent and stop to innovate. Yet, increasingly, this is only the start. As causal textures grow more and more uncontrollable by singular actors within them, it is important to also scout ahead and explore potential futures. This can be done by methods such as scenario work (Ramírez & Selsky, 2016), or by other forms of "playful" exploration. A playful mindset is necessary, because the future has yet to exist, and a purely goal-oriented mind-state does not combine well with making hypotheses, not even strategic ones. Goal-orientation, in turn, is needed to ground ideas eventually with facts, and turn them into actions instead of getting carried away by groupthink (Vesa et al., 2018). This balancing act between trying out strategic ideas and then applying them into strategies and actions would sound like a perfect match with business gaming, but for several reasons, games and strategizing rarely come together. A key reason so far has been the constrained nature of the simulation/games that are being used: They present technical and managerial aspects of business but are not (yet) able to allow for free ideation or radical innovation.

Research over the last two decades on markets, business networks, and competitive advantage (e.g., Normann, 2001; Lusch et al., 2010; Ramírez & Mannervik, 2016) points to key advantages in companies being able to work together, also over traditionally adverse lines. Firms are moving increasingly into forming alliances between multiple partners (Lavie et al., 2007). Turbulence – the uncontrollability of the business environment by the actors within it – is making this increasingly important. Examples of this can be seen in how, for example, multiple software producers create applications for smartphones. The smartphones, while providing the applications a platform, in turn gain more value from increasing amounts of content and applications made by others. Neither party would likely be able to remain competitive on its own. They need each other. Yet such alliances may not be enough. One must also find common ground with one's competitors, not just with natural allies like content and component producers. To extend on our phone example: alliances between competing application producers may be needed in order to keep the terms set by the smartphone manufacturer reasonable and the application producers' businesses viable. And it may be in the interests of the phone manufacturer too to ally with some of the key application producers, because without such third-party content, the phone itself is uninteresting to potential buyers. *When to ally and when to compete* and *in what functions to ally and in what to compete* are issues of increasing complexity, which is very difficult to model in the closed environment of a business game.

A key element that expands value-creating systems is therefore the formation of coopetitive (as per Bengtsson & Kock, 1999, 2000) networks, in which two or more business competitors also cooperate for mutual advantage and for market opportunity expansion. Some theorists have suggested that coopetition is a calculated, game theory approach by participating companies (e.g., Brandenburger & Nalebuff, 1996), but it appears that the phenomenon also contains relational aspects discussed by Bengtsson and Kock (2000). What is crucial to note is that for coopetition to take place, the companies are cooperating and competing at the same time, not in phases (Bengtsson & Kock, 2014). Intensity of competition and cooperation aspects between the companies may vary. They are not opposites, but rather form two independent axes, of "how much and where do we cooperate" and "how much and where do we compete" (Lado et al., 1997). The same companies may, for example, collaborate in marketing activities but be purely competitive in their research and development – or develop technologies together but compete on the end user market. Likewise, they can collaborate in one country but be fierce competitors in the next. The tension between the two conflicting aspects is a key element for a situation to be coopetitive (Czakon et al., 2020). Depicting that tension in a game is much more difficult than is showing cooperation or competition alone.

Central advantages that have been suggested from coopetition are better chances at seeing what the competition is doing (as per Choo, 2002) and the possibility to better position one's own presence in the business network (Gnyawali & Madhavan, 2001), as well as the shared innovation possibilities created by information sharing (see, e.g., Powell et al., 1996). Of particular value appears to be the possibility of widening the market together with the competition, so as to create more demand for the shared product or service type. An example of this would be two competing phone manufacturers working together to increase general market demand for more smartphones. Another advantage is coordination, so that the coopeting organizations do not create completely overlapping value propositions to their customers. Examples of this can be found in many industries but have recently been especially researched in the Finnish game development community (Harviainen et al., 2021). It is well known for its shared community spirit, information sharing, and joint work for breaking out to international markets in a coopetitive manner, which takes advantage of all the aforementioned opportunities (e.g., Komulainen & Sotamaa, 2020; Lehtonen et al., 2020).

What Is Wrong with Going Zero-Sum in a Game?

As business simulations to a large extent remain the hidden possessions of their service providers (one sees the advertisements but does not get to see the game, unless one is a client), the material for this chapter was collected by discussing aspects of current day and earlier business simulations/games with ten scholars who have been developing, analyzing, deploying, and evaluating business games for at least 20 years, in a convenience and snowball sample collected 2017–2020. The central question was whether the respondents had encountered any simulation/games that would or could support the exploration of any facet of coopetitive networking. Only one respondent provided a positive response, but several others reported significant problems with the current game models. Most essentially, the respondents' players had seen a problem in the games' isolation from wider contexts. This chapter summarizes that critique.

The central problem with isolated business simulations is that they do not show the true nature of the marketplace and the networks and alliances needed on it. The games thereby teach players to act in competitive manners and to perceive success as individual (or some cases, team) performance success, not as successfully navigating the complex market conditions (Harviainen et al., 2014). In the long run, unless expertly debriefed by a teacher, this may lead to false self-confidence and a way of seeing competitors purely as competitors, not also as potential partners.

As Bengtsson and Kock (2000) argue, coopetition may take place on multiple levels and at multiple strengths, ranging from almost pure competition to almost complete cooperation. Finding and negotiating that range is a skill that business experts need to master, if their companies are supposed to survive environmental turbulence. This is a skill learned over time (Lundgren-Henriksson & Kock, 2016). Learning should therefore start early enough and be present in also business simulations, which have been shown to anchor mental models well in business students, once they are past the novice stage (Palmunen et al., 2013).

Klabbers (2009) describes experiments toward this direction, from over a decade ago. These were *Perform*, *Perform-P*, and *Funo*. *Perform* represented a university's management processes, involving decisions on the university level as well as on the level of two faculties. These were multi-actor and based on data from a real university. Playing this computer-supported simulation took one day. In retrospect, *Perform* can be considered a rigid-rule business simulation involving representatives of multiple stakeholder groups and requiring coopetition between its represented parties. Of particular interest to this chapter is that players experienced it as a zero-sum game, despite this being an erroneous interpretation of the full possibilities of *Perform*. *Perform-P* (Klabbers, 2009, pp. 276–285) depicts a major corporation in a volatile market, consisting of five task-different teams. As the game develops, it is necessary for the teams to consider coopetitive functions if they want to succeed. This corresponds with studies on company-internal coopetition (e.g., Chiambaretto et al., 2019), and is therefore a step in the right direction.

There are also some positive examples of more recent games that are approaching networks in a positive and more accurate way (e.g., Kaneko et al., 2019), but they are still rare. It seems that scaling up from interpersonal team business games to an organizational level is needed. If we want to improve network and coopetition learning from business gaming, such games' design-in-the-small (veracity of game elements) must sufficiently resemble the intended design-in-the-large (corresponding elements in the real world, knowledge of and/or attitudes towards which the game is intended to change (as per Klabbers, 2003; Kriz, 2003). Klabbers (2000, 2009) has further discussed different types of simulation, based on their allowances for learning. Mode I simulations are closed, meaning that there is no influence from any actors during their run-time. Mode II simulations allow for step-based adjustments. An example of this would be a turn-based game or business simulation, but most real-time games would also fall into this category, due to their design constraints. The most complex (and still very rare, even 20 years later) is Mode III:

> [Mode III simulation/games are] learning environments in which the learners are given the opportunity to interactively build their own system of resources and rules [, and which provide] conditions for the interactive self-reproduction of social systems.
> (Klabbers, 2000, p. 400)

If we want to find examples of such games, currently, we need to look beyond business gaming, into recreational games.

Lessons from Recreational Gaming

While it seems that for business simulations and games it is difficult to create sufficiently open options – partially because of cost structures, partially because of player base scale, several well-known recreational games have been successful in this endeavor. Even social media games like *FarmVille* (Zynga, 2009) contain cooperative networks, while the players may also compete on whose farm looks best. Sid Meier's *Civilization* (e.g., Meier & Shelley, 1991) game series has, in all of its installments, featured alliances between competing cultures and countries, including the exchange of technology and resources. Yet underlying these alliances is always the threat of competition, which may lead to reneged treaties or a lack of military support at crucial times.

A particularly interesting example here is the Massively Multiplayer Online Role-Playing Game (MMORPG) *EVE Online*, launched by CCP Games (2003). The gameplay is based around resource production and acquisition, as well as colonialism and space conflict. Due to its structure as a laissez-faire capitalism environment where the game producers have stated that they will not intervene, the game has become a favorite of not just its some hundreds of thousands of players, but also game and organization scholars (e.g., Milik & Webber, 2020; Warmelink, 2014).

What makes EVE Online particularly interesting is that the game has featured many types of in-game transactions, from hostile to mutually beneficial. Oskar Milik (2016), for instance, has described a particularly fascinating case of coopetitive alliances, in which players from several countries and generally competing in-game organizations joined in an attack upon one particular competitor group for the purpose of exhausting their players' resources and endurance, not just in-game but also behind the screens.

EVE Online is of course a rare exception. It is a specifically tailored play environment that also makes itself very hostile to new players (Carter et al., 2016). At the end of the day, it offers its players an experience of *anything goes and might makes right*. Yet what the game excels at, in these situations, is the presentation of conflict and coopetion. With its nearly two decades of history, the game has functioned as a kind of laboratory of free market decisions, and – for the purposes of this chapter, more importantly – coopetitive activities. In many ways, it forms an example of what coopetitive, network-emphasizing business simulations could do, had they bigger budgets and wider player bases. The game environment of EVE Online and the way it extends to player forums and even communities and practices outside of play and vice versa (Page, 2016) is sufficiently wide to cater for various types of experimentation, and thereby simulation-based learning (Warmelink, 2014).

A word of caution is in order. It is easy to argue that such games provide direct benefits to actual business practices and foster management learning. Yet as Myers (2010) has shown, these kinds of *open world/sandbox* games do not provide direct, useful results either. Deployers of educational gaming cannot trust in stealth learning – indirect learning that takes place while playing – alone (e.g., Whitton, 2014). Too much player liberty often leads to limited, or even problematic, learning results (Harviainen et al., 2014; Myers, 2010). This is especially true of games that emphasize aggressive business behaviors, which EVE definitely does (Warmelink, 2014). Therefore, while *EVE Online* may offer certain ideas for more efficient business game designs, it is by no means unproblematic. Applying similar principles and possibilities to a business game would require thorough briefings and regular debriefings, to make sure the desired learning goals are met. Unless care is taken, we would be exchanging the games that now teach market dominance and zero-sum thinking, instead of cooperation and coopetition, to games that reward treachery and dark side network behaviors.

The key challenges here are twofold. The most prominent here is that games' design-in-the-small does not sufficiently resemble their potential design-in-the large, that is, real-world practices. Either the games are too competition-focused and insufficiently social, or they are undirected and open. Learning history from *Civilization* games without a facilitator or teacher will simply lead one astray, because their level of historical simulation is conceptual rather than realistic (see Chapman, 2016; Chapman & Linderoth, this volume). The same thing would happen if one would follow *EVE Online* as a business principle, because beneath the game's surface exist numerous practices and cultures that are outside of the play itself, but which influence the gameplay nevertheless. Examples of these include time requirements created by life outside of the play, logics adopted from image boards rather than the game's fiction, and so forth (see Milik, 2016, and Page, 2016, for details).

Furthermore, while these games and simulations (or their players) may take advantage of time and temporalities, they do not necessarily consider real time and the changes that it may bring to actual businesses (although Milik, 2016, presents a fascinating exception in which real time was used against rivals). As shown by researchers such as Enrico Gandolfi (2016), play-time gets distorted in games, and this causes challenges for learning. Coopetition is a practice and a negotiation process that needs the right timing (Lavie et al., 2007), so that both its inclusion in the play, and its optimal timing (as per Lainema, 2010), are necessary. Coopetition requires knowing when the time is right for forming partnerships and networks, and when to share what (e.g., Harviainen et al., 2021). This is difficult to model in a game, but for example the offers of alliances in *Civilization* games represent this issue to some extent. For coopetition to be realistic enough for proper learning, however, the game environment – again – needs to be sufficiently flexible so that there are no right/wrong decisions set by the system, but rather the whole flexibility of human affairs.

Conclusions

This chapter has not argued that learning to run a business by way of simulation is useless, but that the medium could offer much more. By embracing Klabbers' (2000) Mode III principles of adaptability and social actions, the next generation of business simulation/games might be able to transcend the current limitations of the form, and to create business professionals able to steer companies in turbulent times. It nevertheless appears that too many business simulations are inadequate for the task, and we need to look elsewhere. The inadequate games can still be highly useful, as they can teach key principles of management, accounting, finance and so forth, as well as function as solid grounding for trying out skills in those areas in a safe manner.

To teach coopetition requires more. For that to happen in a realistic manner, business games would require a level of flexibility and adaptability that they do not currently have. This is very much in line with Klabbers' suggestion that we did (do) not have real Mode III games yet. The example of *EVE Online* nevertheless shows us that such games are possible and that if permitted to do so by the game, players will form coopetive networks and utilize them on fictional markets, learning the necessary skills (Warmelink, 2014). Another option would be to take a step back: going back to the techniques of the human-tracked business games of old, it would be possible to create games that truly are flexible enough, because unconstrained by code, a player would be able to ask if a certain move were possible, and an umpire could say "yes." The analogue multi-player game *Funo* described by Klabbers (2009, ch. 11) is one such example, with its players representing various executives in an international furniture company while having the possibility to influence the game's communication patterns. Faria et al. (2009) have suggested a kind of mixture of these approaches, in the form of pervasive business games that would take advantage of multiple technologies. What we need in any case is complexity that is sufficient to represent market realities on also a social, intercompany level, and this should be the goal of future games of business simulations.

In the meantime, let us keep using the games that we have. They will just need to be grounded and debriefed the right way, so that players will understand that in them, they are only learning parts of the big picture. Important parts without which they cannot function in a turbulent business world either, but just parts nevertheless.

Acknowledgments

The author wishes to thank professor emeritus Jan H. G. Klabbers for his important assistance in locating business simulation/games that included coopetitive aspects in play, and professor Sören Kock, for inspiring the entire analysis here through discourses about the nature of coopetition and its market importance.

Note

1 Due to both the contested nature of whether these are business *games*, business *simulations*, or *simulation/games*, and for general text flow and readability, I use all three contexts interchangeably in this chapter.

References

Andlinger, G. R. (1958). Business games – Play one. *Harvard Business Review*, 36(2), 115–125.
Baburoglu, O. N. (1988). The vortical environment: The fifth in the Emery-Trist levels of organizational environments. *Human Relations*, 41(3), 181–210.
Bengtsson, M., & Kock, S. (1999). Cooperation and competition in relationships between competitors in business networks. *Journal of Business and Industrial Marketing*, 14(3), 178–193.
Bengtsson, M., & Kock, S. (2000). "Coopetition" in business networks – To cooperate and compete simultaneously. *Industrial Marketing Management*, 29(5), 411–426.

Bengtsson, M., & Kock, S. (2014). Coopetition – Quo vadis? Past accomplishments and future challenges. *Industrial Marketing Management, 43*(2), 180–188.

Brandenburger, A. M., & Nalebuff, B. J. (1996). *Co-opetition*. Currency/Doubleday.

Carter, M., Bergstrom, K., & Woodford, D. (Eds.). (2016). *Internet spaceships are serious business: An EVE Online reader*. University of Minnesota Press.

CCP Games. (2003). *EVE online* [PC]. CCP Games.

Chapman, A. (2016). *Digital games as history: How videogames represent the past and offer access to historical practice*. Routledge.

Chiambaretto, P., Masse, D., & Mirc, N. (2019). "All for one and one for all?" Knowledge broker roles in managing tensions of internal coopetition: The Ubisoft case. *Research Policy, 48*(3), 584–600.

Choo, C. W. (2002). *Information management for the intelligent organization: The art of scanning the environment*. Information Today.

Czakon, W., Srivastava, M. K., Le Roy, F., & Gnyawali, D. R. (2020). Coopetition strategies: Critical issues and research directions. *Long Range Planning, 53*(1), 101948.

Emery, F. E., & Trist, E. L. (1965). The causal texture of organizational environments. *Human Relations, 18*(1), 21–32.

Faria, A. J., Hutchinson, D., & Wellington, W. J. (2009). Developments in business gaming: A review of the past 40 years. *Simulation & Gaming, 40*(4), 464–487.

Gandolfi, E. (2016). Subjective temporalities at play: Temporality, subjectivity and gaming affordances in Cities: Skylines, Europa Universalis IV and Pillars of Eternity. *Simulation & Gaming, 47*(6), 720–750.

Gnyawali, D. R., & Madhavan, R. (2001). Cooperative networks and competitive dynamics: A structural embeddedness perspective. *Academy of Management Review, 26*(3), 431–445.

Harviainen, J. T., Lainema, T., & Saarinen, E. (2014). Player-reported impediments to game-based learning. *Transactions of the Digital Games Research Association, 1*(2), 55–83.

Harviainen, J. T., Lehtonen, M. J., & Kock, S. (2021). Timeliness in information sharing within creative industries. Case: Finnish game design. *Journal of Documentation, 78*(1), 83–95.

Kaneko, T., Hamada, R., & Hiji, M. (2019). Business game promoting supply chain collaboration education at universities. In R. Hamada, et al. (Eds.), *Neo-simulation and gaming toward active learning* (pp. 137–146). Springer.

Keys, B., & Wolfe, J. (1990). The role of management games and simulations in education and research. *Journal of Management, 16*(2), 307–336.

Kibbee, J. M., Craft, C. J., & Nanus, B. (1961). *Management games: A new technique for executive development*. Reinhold.

Klabbers, J. H. G. (2000). Learning as acquisition and learning as interaction. *Simulation & Gaming, 31*(3), 380–406.

Klabbers, J. H. G. (2003). Gaming and simulation: Principles of a science of design. *Simulation & Gaming, 34*(4), 569–591.

Klabbers, J. H. G. (2009). *The magic circle: Principles of gaming & simulation* (3rd rev. ed.). Sense.

Komulainen, L., & Sotamaa, O. (2020, January 29–30). IGDA Finland hubs and their role in local game development. In *Proceedings of Academic Mindtrek '20*, Tampere. ACM.

Kriz, W. C. (2003). Creating effective learning environments and learning organizations through gaming simulation design. *Simulation & Gaming, 34*(4), 495–511.

Lado, A. A., Boyd, N. G., & Hanlon, S. C. (1997). Competition, cooperation, and the search for economic rents: A syncretic model. *Academy of Management Review, 22*(1), 110–141.

Lainema, T. (2003). *Enhancing organizational business process perception – Experiences from constructing and applying a dynamic business simulation game*. Turku School of Economics and Business Administration.

Lainema, T. (2010). Theorizing on the treatment of time in simulation gaming. *Simulation & Gaming, 41*(2), 170–186.

Lavie, D., Lechner, C., & Sing, H. (2007). The performance implications of timing of entry and involvement in multipartner alliances. *Academy of Management Journal, 50*(3), 578–604.

Lehtonen, M. J., Ainamo, A., & Harviainen, J. T. (2020). The four faces of creative industries: Visualizing the game industry ecosystem in Helsinki and Tokyo. *Industry & Innovation, 27*(9), 1062–1087.

Leigh, E., & Tipton, E. (2014). What is being simulated. In W. C. Kriz (Ed.), *The shift from teaching to learning: Individual, collective and organizational learning through gaming simulation* (pp. 12–23). Bertelsmann.

Lundgren-Henriksson, E.-L., & Kock, S. (2016). A sensemaking perspective on coopetition. *Industrial Marketing Management, 57*, 97–108.

Lusch, R. F., Vargo, S. L., & Tanniru, M. (2010). Service, value networks and learning. *Journal of the Academy of Marketing Science, 38*(1), 19–31.

Meier, S., & Shelley B. (1991). *Sid Meier's Civilization* [PC]. MicroProse.

Mele, C., Nenonen, S., Pels, J., Storbacka, K., Nariswari, A., & Kaartemo, V. (2018). Shaping service ecosystems: Exploring the dark side of agency. *Journal of Service Management, 29*(4), 521–545.

Milik, O. (2016). The digital grind: Time and labor as resources of war in EVE online. In M. Carter, K. Bergström, & D. Woolford (Eds.), *Internet spaceships are serious business: An EVE online reader* (pp. 55–76). University of Minnesota Press.

Milik, O., & Webber, N. (2020). Feudal alliances in a hyper-capitalist world: Power and organization in EVE online. *Journal of Gaming & Virtual Worlds, 12*(2), 165–181.

Myers, D. (2010). *Play redux: The form of computer games*. University of Michigan Press.

Neuhauser, J. J. (1976). Business games have failed. *Academy of Management, 1*(4), 124–129.

Normann, R. (2001). *Reframing business: When the map changes the landscape*. Wiley.

Oksanen, K. (2013). Subjective experience and sociability in a collaborative serious game. *Simulation & Gaming, 44*(6), 767–793.

Page, R. (2016). We play something awful: Goon projects and pervasive practice on online games. In M. Carter, K. Bergström, & D. Woolford (Eds.), *Internet spaceships are serious business: An EVE online reader* (pp. 99–114). University of Minnesota Press.

Palmunen, L.-M., Pelto, E., Paalumäki, A., & Lainema, T. (2013). Formation of novice business students' mental models through simulation gaming. *Simulation & Gaming, 44*(6), 846–868.

Palyga, A., & Wardaszko, M. (2018). A management model for effective team communication in business simulation games. In A. Naweed, M. Wardaszko, E. Leigh, & S. Meijer (Eds.), *Intersections in simulation and gaming* (pp. 43–57). Springer.

Powell, W. W., Koput, K. W., & Smith-Doerr, L. (1996). Interorganizational collaboration and the locus of innovation: Networks of learning in biotechnology. *Administrative Science Quarterly, 41*(1), 116–141.

Ramírez, R., & Mannervik, U. (2016). *Strategy for a networked world.* Imperial College Press.

Ramírez, R., & Selsky, J. W. (2016). Strategic planning in turbulent environments: A social ecology approach to scenarios. *Long Range Planning, 49*(1), 90–102.

Ricciardi, F. M. (1957). *Top management decision simulation* [Univac]. American Management Association.

Thavikulwat, P. (2004). The architecture of computerized business gaming simulations. *Simulation & Gaming, 35*(2), 242–269.

Tsuchiya, T., & Tsuchiya, S. (1999). The unique contribution of gaming/simulation: Towards establishment of the discipline. In D. Saunders & J. Severn (Eds.), *The international simulation & gaming research yearbook: Simulations & games for strategy and policy planning* (pp. 46–57). Kogan Page.

Vesa, M., den Hond, F., & Harviainen, J. T. (2018). On the possibility of a paratelic initiation of organizational wrongdoing. *Journal of Business Ethics, 160*(1), 1–15.

Vesa, M., Hamari, J., Harviainen, J. T., & Warmelink, H. (2017). Computer games and organization studies. *Organization Studies, 38*(2), 273–284.

Warmelink, H. (2014). *Online gaming and playful organization.* Routledge.

Whitton, N. (2014). *Digital games and learning: Research and theory.* Routledge.

Wolfe, J. (1993). A history of business teaching games in English-speaking and post-socialist countries: The origination and diffusion of a management education and development technology. *Simulation & Gaming, 24*(4), 446–463.

Zynga. (2009). *Farmville* [Multi-platform]. Zynga.

4 The Limits of 'Serious' Play
Frame Disputes around Educational Games

Jonas Linderoth, Adam Chapman and Sebastian Deterding

Educational Games and 'Serious' Issues

One suggested educational use of games is promoting social change by fostering attitudes and beliefs that help solve real-world problems. As game designer and researcher Mary Flanagan put it in a recent talk at the World Economic Forum in Davos:

> There are pressing problems that all of us are here at the summit, at the forum, to deal with. Climate change, poverty, sustainability issues, gender inequity is a big topic of course this year, sexual assault. These are all massive topics and for me the first idea that comes to my mind is what could video games do in that space.
>
> (Flanagan, 2018)

This, of course, is not just a 'first idea'. Flanagan and many others have developed dozens of games that try to inform players about 'serious' sociopolitical, environmental, or historical issues, and promote certain attitudes and values towards them. Such games have been variously called serious games, persuasive games, activist games, games for social change, or games for change. Two well-known examples are *Darfur Is Dying* (Ruiz, 2006), a game about the humanitarian crisis in the Darfur province in western Sudan, and *Sweatshop* (Littleloud, 2011), an award-winning game that illustrates the work conditions under which clothes are manufactured in sweatshops. Whole organizations like *Games for Change* (G4C) have been set up to 'empower game creators and social innovators to drive real-world impact through games' (Games for Change, 2018), and games for change are receiving high-level political attention, as illustrated by Flanagan's invitation to Davos.

However, despite their good intentions, such games for change regularly become the subject of public controversies. For instance, *Sweatshop* is but one of a number of serious games that Apple deemed inappropriate for their app store (van Roessel, 2014). The game *Mission US: Flight to Freedom* (Electric Funstuff, 2012), developed to teach the history of slavery

DOI: 10.4324/9781003297406-6

in the USA, was paradoxically banned by a US school (Valley News, 2015, March 3). Notably, these controversies do not fit the usual 'harmful media' discourse that positions video games as aggression-inducing or addictive. Instead, they revolve around the notion that games as a medium are somehow *inappropriate* for the given subject matter. Leaving aside the actual impacts of playing any of these games for change, controversies strongly shape their educational uses and effects. At best, the controversies become teachable moments in themselves, and at worst, they outright prevent the usage of certain games (as in *Mission US*) or overshadow any fruitful engagement with them. This makes it worthwhile to understand how and why controversies around games for change emerge.

In this chapter, we propose Erving Goffman's theory of frame analysis (1986) and the concepts of *frame limits* and *frame disputes* as useful tools to examine such controversies with. In previous work, we have argued that establishing playful frames for sensitive topics is complicated, and that framing a game as a work of art or educational material can fail and/or have unintended adverse effects (Chapman & Linderoth, 2015; Deterding, 2016). Here we extend this line of inquiry with an analysis of the controversies surrounding two particular games for change, *1378(km)* (Stober, 2010) and *Playing History 2* (Serious Games Interactive, 2013). Particularly, we will draw on online articles and social media available in English that may have shaped people's moral evaluation of the games and the rationales behind them, as well as the views of the games' developers.

Frame Analysis

Sociologist Erving Goffman's *Frame Analysis* (1986) has proven highly productive in the academic study of play and games (see Deterding, 2015, pp. 25–30 for a review). Frame analysis is based on the core assumption that how people 'define a situation' – what type of social situation they believe 'is going on here right now' – will guide their experience and action. Borrowing the label from Gregory Bateson (2000, pp. 184 ff., pp. 192 ff.), these definitions of situations are called *frames*. To give a simple illustration: putting a hand on a shoulder will have different meanings depending on whether participants frame it as an assault, an invitation to dance, a display of affection, part of a physical examination, etc., each resulting in different likely follow-on courses of action (Linderoth, 2004). Frames are usually implicitly created, signalled, and upheld by the way participants act, although people may sometimes resort to explicit metacommunication (e.g. asking, 'Was that a joke?'). The concept of frame strongly resembles that of the 'magic circle', introduced to game studies by Salen and Zimmerman (2004) to stress that the activity of play generates its own 'sphere' of meaning and action that is somewhat 'bounded' from ordinary life. Several scholars have since argued that frames offer a more developed theoretical tool for understanding the boundaries between play and non-play (Consalvo, 2009; Stenros,

2014). This fit is not incidental, and Bateson (2000) originally developed the frame concept to explain how otters can meta-communicate to one another that although biting and other displays of aggression may be a part of the activity at hand, it is not a real fight, but is in fact play.

Keyings and Laminations

In frame analytic terms, the play-biting of otters holds a special property in that it is *re*-framed. It is already meaningful in the primary frame: biting constitutes an attack in the fight frame. A second play frame, however, transforms this meaning of the bite entirely (into a non-aggressive invitation to tumble), while its material form changes only little (the bite is softened so as not to draw blood). Play and other such secondary frames that can transform primary frames are called *keys*, in analogy to musical keys, and these transformation processes involve *keying*. Any form of *represented* experience, such as a stage play, film, or non-abstract game, constitutes a keying. Some representational keys, which Goffman calls 'make-believe', give the represented events a fictional, 'as if' status, while others do not: the TV drama is both a representation and fictional, the TV documentary is a representation but presented as non-fictional.

Keying implies the possibility of what Goffman calls *laminations*: events can be nested in multiple layers of transformations. Consider the sport of boxing, an activity we tend to treat as a keyed fight. Now imagine seeing a boxing scene in a film. Here we have a simple activity with a *rim* or 'outermost' frame that 'tells us just what sort of status in the real world the activity has' (Goffman, 1986, p. 82): 'we are at the cinema seeing a film', telling us that the witnessed events are fictional representations. The 'innermost' frame is that of two people fighting, with another frame in-between that transforms fighting into a sporting contest. Furthermore, by using this boxing film as an illustration of the lamination concept, we changed the outer rim by adding yet another layer.

Frame Limits and Frame Disputes

Notably, not all matters are easily transformed by keying. For instance, some people seek to ban boxing because they reject the idea that boxing transforms a 'real' fight into a sporting contest. Take an article in the *British Columbia Medical Journal*: 'There is no metaphor in boxing: it is the real thing. Boxing is real fighting, perfectly genuine violence, a pastime with the genuine aim of causing damage to the opponent' (Smillie, 2003). In frame analytical terms, the author here objects by pointing to the notion that in boxing, the real physical consequences (bodily harm) remain untransformed, and with it the participants' intentions. And this goes against the author's conceptions of what keying something as a 'sportive contest' *should* involve.

Put differently, frames are *normative* (Deterding, 2015). Not only do they set out expectations of how one *ought* to behave in a given situation, but different groups also hold different norms regarding what events can be 'legitimately' keyed in what way and when – a phenomenon Goffman calls *frame limits*.

Frame limits are most readily apparent in 'dramatic presentation, illustration, and documentation' (Goffman, 1986, p. 72), where they are also partly determined by the type of media involved: 'Obviously, what is offensive in a movie might not be offensive in a novel' (p. 55). Goffman stresses that these limits are culturally established and can therefore change over short time spans, as the case of depicted nudity shows (p. 73).

As seen in the case of boxing, individuals or groups can hold contesting moral views on the legitimacy of a particular framing, or even enact different framings altogether. Often, agreement is reached relatively quickly: If some people treat a fire alarm in a movie theatre as false and remain seated while others leave the building, a joint definition is likely to be established by flame and smoke or an 'official' person publicly declaring the alarm false. In some cases, however, 'parties with opposing versions of events may openly dispute with each other over how to define what has been or is happening. A frame dispute results.' (p. 322).

Two Controversies

In the following sections we analyze two controversies surrounding games in the games for change genre. These two cases lend support to a theory forwarded in previous research concerning the 'limits of play' (Chapman & Linderoth, 2015). In this, it was proposed that two fears are often at the root of controversies regarding sensitive topics in games. Firstly, the fear of trivialization through ludification, where a sensitive representational element is given a second, rules-based, meaning that may compete with its primary meaning by introducing it into a playful frame. Secondly, the fear of distasteful playable positions – positions that allow players to reenact historical episodes of cruelty, exploitation, or abuse. Negotiation of these fears seems to influence the content selected for representation in games. For example, these 'limits of play' seem to have some effect on the history selected for inclusion in historical games, where sensitive parts of some histories are more frequently left out of games in comparison to other popular media (Chapman, 2016; Chapman & Linderoth, 2015).

The game *1378(km)* (Stober, 2010) is a modification or 'mod' of the commercial game *Half Life 2*. At the time of its release in 2010, Jens Stober, its sole developer, was an art student at the Karlsruhe University of Arts and Design in Germany. The game portrays the inner German border in 1976. Players choose to play either as East German refugees trying to cross the border or as East German border guards trying to stop refugees. As a border guard, players can choose to shoot refugees. However, the game also actively devalues this: a shooting player cannot win the game, loses points and, if too many refugees are killed, will be teleported into a court in the year 2000 to face charges for crimes against humanity. The game was originally scheduled for release on the 20th anniversary of the fall of the Berlin Wall on 3 October 2010. However, led by the German tabloid newspaper *BILD*, the game was subjected to heavily negative press coverage even before its release, in response to the promotional material alone. This delayed its release to December 2010. Overall, the game spurred a massive controversy in national and international media, with coverage by more than 2,200 print and online news outlets and 400 TV stations (Stober, n.d.). Opinions were split between condemnation on the one hand and cultural appreciation on the other. In the end, the game was shown in several art game exhibitions and was elected as one of the best German video games of the past 25 years in 2013 – somewhat ironically (or in atonement) by the newspaper BILD. This emphasizes the aforementioned fluidity of frame limits/framing and the relation of this to cultural negotiations that can change rapidly.

Playing History 2: Slave Trade (Serious Games Interactive, 2013) was originally released in 2013 as an educational game targeting Danish, and subsequently UK, schools, complete with a teacher's manual with a lesson plan for grade 4–6 history classes for teaching about the transatlantic slave trade in the 18th century. The player plays as a young black slave, Tim, who works on a slave ship and tries to free all the slaves from the ship with his sister. The game comprises a range of mini-games that each depict a particular aspect of the slave trade. In 2015, the developer made the game publicly available on the digital distribution platform Steam. Almost immediately, it generated a massive uproar on social and then mass media. In social media, the controversy was focused on a particular mini-game labelled 'Slave Tetris'. The mini-game tasked the player to 'pack' slaves into the belly of a ship as efficiently as possible, emulating the mechanics of the well-known game *Tetris*. At first the developers responded by explaining the educational rationale behind the game, but then quickly resorted to removing the contentious 'Slave Tetris' mini-game from *Playing History 2*.

The Dissociation of Act and Documentation

Seemingly, the focus of the critiques against both *1378(km)* and *Playing History 2* was that the games were 'insensitive' to the victims of the represented events. In this context, it is worth stressing that a good portion of critique stemmed from communities whose identity was directly tied to the victims: family members of deceased East German border refugees in the case of *1378(km)*, and members of Black communities in the USA in the case of *Playing History 2*. If a group and its historical suffering are already culturally marginalized, its members will understandably be particularly sensitive to any further trivialization of said suffering. This is apparent in the media statements of several spokespersons of organizations that commemorate the Cold War responding to *1378(km)*, shown in the following:

> Theodor Mettrup of the Association for Victims of Communist Tyranny said the game 'makes a mockery of the victims.' (Martin, 2010)
>
> The director of the Berlin Wall Foundation, Axel Klausmeier, called the game 'tasteless' and a slap in the face of victims' families. (Price, 2010)
>
> The head of the Union of Victim Associations of Communist Tyranny (Union der Opferverbände Kommunistischer Gewaltherrschaft) said regarding the game that 'It used the trauma of the victims and turns it into a violent game', and that 'The game is simply insensitive.'
>
> (Kelsey, 2010)

What we see at work here is a particular frame limit Goffman (1986) observed for representational keyings:

> namely a limit on the dissociation between the action documented and the document itself, the concern being that if a reprehensible or horrible or improper action is represented, whether this be an unkeyed action or itself a keying, how free can the documentation be of the original sin? At first blush, of course, one might think there would be no limits, since everyone clearly appreciates that a documentation of a past event is not that past event. But, nonetheless, connection is felt, and connection is honored.
>
> (p. 70)

As a representation, a game obviously does not inflict the original physical harm, but according to Goffman (and the quoted spokespersons), it is the *symbolic* harm through acts that *show* a lack of regard that is the issue – the 'mockery', the symbolic 'slap in the face'. By representing a physically *and* symbolically denigrating act (shooting at people, stacking them into a ship), one still repeats the symbolic denigration – in the same way that re-telling an offensive joke may still cause offense despite being earmarked as 'meant in jest' or as simple reporting of a previous incident and 'not originating from me.' We find a similar logic in critiques of *Playing History 2*. Pulitzer Prize winner Dexter Thomas interviewed children's librarian Allie Jane Bruce for the *L.A. Times*:

> 'Put yourself in the shoes of a black child', Bruce said, 'watching their white classmates playing Tetris with people that look like you. Even if the classroom was all black, what kind of image is that, seeing yourself played with as a Tetris block? It's wrong on so many levels.'
>
> (Thomas, 2015)

Seeing other people treating *depictions* of your own or closely related social groups/identities as human tetrominoes is what Bruce is critiquing here, the public symbolic devaluation involved in this 'kind of image'. This raises the question (and already points to an answer): why are *video game* depictions of historical atrocities often perceived to be particularly offensive? Take the following statement on *1378(km)*:

> 'There are enough contemporary witnesses still around who suffered from the consequences of this cruel division of Germany', said Axel Klaus Meier, who heads a group devoted to the memory of successful and unsuccessful escapers. 'They don't need a computer game to remind them of these times all over again.'
>
> (Hall, 2010)

While the concern for the victims' psychological well-being is well-taken – wanting to avoid the discomfort of re-living past trauma, it is also a somewhat strange statement from an organization *devoted to remembering* said trauma. Particularly amidst a national anniversary of the Fall of the Berlin Wall that was marked with events and media commemorating the suffering of East German refugees. It is not the 'reminding' that is offensive, but rather, it seems, reminding by '*a computer game*'.

The Trivializing Cultural Meaning of Games

As Goffman (1986, p. 55) observed, the medium of representation itself plays a part in whether a keying is overstepping frame limits or not. And in fact, several voices in the controversies stated that games *in particular* are unsuitable vehicles for representing the depicted topics:

> But the Federal Foundation for the Reconciliation of the Communist Dictatorship said that while it welcomed different ways to come to terms with the 1949–1989 regime, it doubted young people would learn anything by shooting dissidents. 'Ultimately it's [*1378(km)*] just an ego-shooter game, which is unacceptable given the historical context', said Dietrich Wolf, spokesman for the foundation. (Martin, 2010)
>
> Frank Noschese, a physics teacher at John Jay High School, who tweeted about the game [*Playing History 2*], said that the biggest problem is that the game exists at all. Noschese said some topics aren't appropriate for a children's game, and the slave trade is one of them. 'I just think the whole concept of making it a game – it trivializes the atrocity of slavery. There are some topics that are just off limits'.
>
> (Quinlan, 2015)

The excerpts above illustrate how part of the controversy is made in a format where it is questioned what games, as a cultural form, can achieve. The different voices in the debates stress that in this context games are 'unacceptable', 'nonsense' and that they 'trivializes' or fail to 'address the gravity' of the topic. Both developers of the two games addressed this format of the critique in their defences. The developer of *1378(km)* wrote on the game's official webpage that:

> A large part of the criticism is a consequence of my chosen medium, the computer game. Computer games as a medium are often quick to be judged without being more closely examined, as was also the case with my art project.
>
> (Stober, n.d.)

The core of this defence is that games receive an unjust treatment as a cultural form. This position was also taken up by independent voices such as the blog *Gamescenes – Art in the Age of Videogames*:

> It's not the first time a reconstruction of a historic event in a videogame has been questioned for its credibility. It's ok to write books and make films about these stories but it's controversial to make an interactive videogame about them.
>
> (Jansson, 2010)

Here, Goffman's exact observation – something that passes in one medium becomes controversial in another – is cast as an illogical or unjust unequal treatment. In the defence against the critique the developer of *1378(km)* also compared the game with a documentary. However, he stressed the unique aspect of player agency in games.

> In this computer game – which would not be the case in, for example, a documentary film – I personally have the control over my behavior and my reactions, which take place in real time and in changing situations.
>
> (Stober, n.d.)

This argument was made to stress that the players will only be able to win *1378(km)* if they avoid shooting at refugees and that as a designer you are not fully in charge of what players do with your game. However, it can be said that part of the concerns about games not being able to portray the events in the 'preferred serious frame' has to do with this player agency. Where in historical books or movies the audience *passively observes* a depicted *Other* enacting an atrocity, in games, the audience often *directly enacts and embodies* the perpetrator. In previous research (Chapman & Linderoth, 2015) this has been described as concern over the 'playable position' offered by the game to the player. When the game allows the player to play as the perceived historical antagonist the game can generate controversy because it is perceived to implicitly endorse the perpetrator's actions or encourage the player to enjoy the reenactment of these actions. Chapman and Linderoth (2015) saw that in WWII games where the players could take on the role as Germans, political aspects and symbols of Nazism were left out of the design. While these things were still part of single player experiences where the designer was in control of the portrayal, they were not representations in games where the player could have agency over them.

As a part of the defence against the criticism, the developer of *1378(km)* stressed that player agency was used intentionally in order to enable engagement with the subject while clearly signalling its moral status:

> In a computer game – unlike for instance in a documentary film – the player has control over their behavior and their reactions . . . The game *1378(km)* doesn't force the border soldier role to shoot refugees. It leaves options. The border solider has the option to arrest refugees without the use of force, or even become a refugee themselves. You can only win *1378(km)* if you don't shoot. Who shoots, loses points and lands in a wall shooting court case in the year 2000.
>
> (Stober, n.d.)

As will be discussed in the conclusions, this form of design assumes that the player will follow a rather pre-defined trajectory of up-keyings and down-keyings (adding or removing laminated frames).

The developer of *Playing History 2* also pointed towards the unjust way of understanding games. Already before the actual controversy emerged, the game had received similar critique on Steam. The lead developer wrote in response this:

> I think it is a real shame that a lot of people are so ignorant towards the potential of games for more than entertainment. Like any medium or tool, it can be used for good or evil. It is our aim to reach people that would normally not reflect or learn about this subject. Furthermore, I have a feeling that many of the negative reactions in here are knee-jerk reactions and sheeps following what other says. Please take time to look at the game before forming your opinion.
>
> (Klepek, 2015)

One of the arguments here is made towards the fact that the game received critique from persons who obviously had not played the game. The same issue was part of the discussion surrounding *1378(km)*, where the debate emerged before the game even was released. However, given the idea that games have an internal trivializing property (see Chapman & Linderoth, 2015; Linderoth, 2013), it makes sense to criticize the actual concept of a game about a specific topic. Linderoth and Chapman (2013) stressed that even a thought experiment of some games can evoke feelings of repulsion if you have a cultural identity tied to a horrific event.

Failed Keyings – The Rise and Fall of Educational Frames

In relation to Goffman's frame theory, educational claims about games can be understood as another keying, that is, it adds another frame on how to understand the activity at hand, another layer or lamination. At its core the unkeyed events are the historical events, which are keyed into games. However, on top of this the educational layer makes it possible to frame the use of the game as education or informal learning. Defendants of both games continually stressed their framing as 'art or 'education' as justifying their form and content – a framing that was challenged by the games' critics:

> Members of the school's [Karlsruhe University of Arts and Design, where Stober made the game as an art student] faculty defended the game against moral and ethical challenges at Friday's meeting, making a case for artistic freedom.
>
> 'This work is an art project, and art has always tried to overstep boundaries', the university's head of media arts, Michael Bielicky said.
>
> But another person attending the discussion ahead of the game's launch claimed "1378 km" had nothing to do with art . . .
>
> (Price, 2010)

Similarly, the developer of *Playing History 2* stated:

> I think it is a real shame that a lot of people are so ignorant towards the potential of games for more than entertainment. Like any medium or tool it can be used for good or evil. It is our aim to reach people that would normally not reflect or learn about this subject.
>
> (Klepek, 2015)

Frame analytically, such claims constitute another keying. The unkeyed historical events are keyed into games, which are then keyed as education or informal learning. The high cultural status of the education key is thus assumed to 'override' the perceived triviality of the game key. Interestingly, this holds for *1378(km)* as well. Even though the game was mainly framed as an art project, the surrounding discourse attempted to up-key it into a didactical tool:

> Adam Rafinski, a teacher at Karlsruhe University . . . maintains that *1378(km)* is a serious game that you don't just play as a pastime, and that users can take a history lesson from the themes presented. 'I can well imagine that people who'll be playing this game will ask themselves a lot of questions', Rafinski said. 'They'll want to know more about the fortifications, the automatic firing devices and all the rest, and why they were there. And they'll realize how difficult it must have been to make it across the border.'
>
> (Graupner, 2010)

There are many competing ideas about how a game can be used for educational purposes (Linderoth, 2014). One such idea used in relation to *1378(km)* is that 'games are an appropriate medium when we have important things to tell the young' (Sharp, 2011). For example, an initial statement about the game claimed:

> Through the personal identification as a fugitive of the republic or a border guard, and the intensive experience of the border areas, the interest of the young generation in the conflict of recent German history will be awakened.
>
> (Nick, 2010)

In fact, the developer stressed this as the express purpose of the game:

> 'It's my impression that, particularly among young people, that part of history is no longer really debated and has been forgotten', he said. 'Being young, too, I myself didn't know much about the border fortifications either. Many of my peers have no idea that the inner-German border was 1378 kilometers long. They've only heard about the Berlin Wall, but that was only a small part of the border. So I wanted to bring the big picture back to young people's minds.'
>
> (Graupner, 2010)

In the case of *Playing History 2*, initial critique led its developer to explain how the mini-game dubbed 'Slave Tetris' was supposed to work in terms of education:

> Our experience is that in the game it really gets people to think about just how absurd and cruel it is – trust me nobody is laughing or finding it a joke to play that kind of Tetris. They do however get a ahaa experience that will indeed haunt them. They will also discuss afterwards, and most of them will probably remember more than [they] did from most [of] their history lessons.
>
> (Klepek, 2015)

When the full controversy emerged, the lead developer further explained:

> 'I still believe the game mechanics convey in a very powerful way one of the most important points with [the] slave trade then and now: that you dehumanize and objectify people into bricks', he said to me over email. 'It makes you think and reflect – was it really like that. Did people really do that to each other. I have been [in] a classroom using the games, and I have seen middle school students have this discussion. It is hard and sensitive – of course. Should we stop teaching kids about [it] in a

way they can understand – I don't think so. I may be wrong but that was the goal to create a strong education experience.'

(Klepek, 2015)

The educational strategy of 'Slave Tetris' is to first get players to take on the perspective of the slaver trying to pack as many people as possible on to the boat – effectively keying this cruel act as 'just a game'. Then, play would be up-keyed into a 'teachable moment' of in-class debate, making players realize in a haunting 'aha-experience' just how horribly objectifying slavery was, and how easily complicit they could become in this objectification, instilling feelings of guilt and remorse intended to become a 'strong educational experience'. Put differently, highlighting and harnessing the precise frame tension between action and document that was the main focus of the controversy was also the underlying educational strategy of the game. However, the efficacy and value of this strategy was also directly questioned by critics:

> Would a young player be able to grasp the inhumanity of the slave trade, all while being rewarded for stacking brick slaves efficiently or expertly navigating a slave ship? Allie Jane Bruce, a children's librarian at the Bank Street College of Education in New York, doesn't think so.
>
> (Thomas, 2015)

While the developers seem to ask its audience to, during their interaction with their games, go through stages of framing, the critique seems doubt that the gamers would follow these rather complicated frame shifts. A similar critique was voiced with regard to *1378(km)*:

> Physics teacher Noschese compared the game to a hypothetical one about the Holocaust, which is another example of a historical event educators shouldn't make games about. "I don't think kids have the capacity yet to do that and the topic needs to be conveyed in a different way. What about the Holocaust? Would you try to get people in railway cars or would you try to manage getting the trains from all across Germany into all of the different concentration camps?" Noschese asked.
>
> (Quinlan, 2015)

What is striking about this teacher's comparison with a hypothetical game about the Holocaust, is that a well-known art board game, *Train* (Brathwaite, 2009), indeed did just what he described, and to great acclaim: putting the player into the role of a person efficiently stacking figures into train wagons, only to learn that by 'just following rules', they made themselves complicit in transporting Jews to concentration camps.

However, unlike the wide online releases of *1378(km)* and *Playing History 2*, in the case of *Train*, the *developer* controlled how the game circulated through society: it was mainly set up in the context of art galleries and exhibitions, always exposing it to select adult audiences with the developer present to respond (Deterding, 2016). Thereby, a framing of the game as an artwork was more likely to be accepted. Hence, this game evaded the critique that particular 'vulnerable' audiences like children might not have the necessary *framing literacy* to interpret her work as intended (Deterding, 2011; see also Chapman & Linderoth, 2015; Linderoth, 2013).

Discussion and Conclusion

Games for change, designed to educate people about 'serious' issues, regularly become subject to public controversies that impede or steer their educational impact. Analyzing two such controversies through the lens of Erving Goffman's frame analysis, we find them to be frame disputes about particular frame limits concerning games documenting historical atrocities. The dissociation between historical acts of physical and symbolic harm and their documentary representation is always tenuous; to be socially legitimate, a representation needs to act in line with conventions of respectful use of themes and credibly signal moral regard for the victims and their suffering alongside moral devaluing of the perpetrators and their acts. As discussed, part of the educational or artistic idea in some of the games in the games for change genre is that the audience are to commit 'problematic' symbolic acts and then reflect upon them. This idea is utilizing the inherently trivializing nature of games in asking players to commit the symbolic actions in a 'this is just a game' frame (accepting the up-keyed frame) and then down-key their own game experience (rejecting the up-key) in order to learn and reflect. Hence, the games for change genre in itself has a complicated and not completely clear design agenda. As mentioned, this trajectory of intended frame processes that the audience are supposed to go through is highly vulnerable, since there is no guarantee that the audience will accept and follow the scripted structure of keyings built into the design.

Developers of educational games and games for change might do well in reflecting upon the social dynamics of meaning. Good intentions will not save them from creating games that potentially can be framed as being tasteless or inappropriate.

Acknowledgements

The research presented here was a part of the Linnaeus Centre for Research on Learning, Interaction and Mediated Communication in Contemporary Society (LinCS) at the University of Gothenburg and partly conducted in the Digital Creativity Labs (digitalcreativity.ac.uk), funded by EPSRC/AHRC/InnovateUK under grant no. EP/M023265/1. The authors gratefully acknowledge the financial support and productive collaboration.

References

Bateson, G. (2000). *Steps to an ecology of mind: Collected essays in anthropology, psychiatry, evolution, and epistemology.* University of Chicago Press.

Brathwaite, B. (2009). *Train* [Board game]. Self-published.

Chapman, A. (2016). It's hard to play in the trenches: WWI, collective memory and videogames. *Game Studies Journal, 16*(2).

Chapman, A., & Linderoth, J. (2015). Exploring the limits of play: A case study of representations of Nazism in games. In T. E. Mortensen, J. Linderoth, & A. M. Brown (Eds.), *The dark side of game play: Controversial issues in playful environments* (pp. 137–153). Routledge.

Consalvo, M. (2009). There is no magic circle. *Games & Culture, 4*(4), 408–417.

Deterding, S. (2011). 'Was geht hier eigentlich vor sich?' Medienrealität, mediensozialisation und medienkompetenz aus rahmenanalytischer perspektive. In J. Fromme, S. Iske, & W. Marotzki (Eds.), *Medialität und Realität* (pp. 103–126). VS Verlag für Sozialwissenschaften.

Deterding, S. (2014). *Modes of Play. A Frame Analytic Account of Video Game Play.* Doctoral dissertation, University of Hamburg, Hamburg, Germany. https://ediss.sub.uni-hamburg.de/handle/ediss/5508

Deterding, S. (2016). The mechanic is not the (whole) message: Procedural rhetoric meets framing in Train & Playing history 2. *DiGRA/FDG '16, 13*(2).

Electric Funstuff. (2012). *Flight to freedom* [Game]. Electric Funstuff.

Evening Standard. (2006, September 8). Fury over 'war on terror' board game. *Evening Standard.* www.standard.co.uk/news/fury-over-war-on-terror-board-game-7206642.html

Flanagan, M. (2018, January 25). *Game-changers: Playing games for good* [Lecture]. Presented at World Economic Forum Annual Meeting in Switzerland, Davos-Klosters. www.weforum.org/events/world-economic-forum-annual-meeting-2018/sessions/game-changers-playing-games-for-good

Games for Change. (2018). *Games for change.* www.gamesforchange.org/

Goffman, E. (1986). *Frame analysis: An essay on the organization of experience.* Northeastern University Press.

Graupner, H. (2010, September 30). Computer game recreates horrors of former East German border. *Deutsche Welle.* www.dw.com/en/computer-game-recreates-horrors-of-former-east-german-border/a-6059839

Hall, A. (2010, September 28). 'Tasteless' Iron Curtain game. *The Telegraph.* www.telegraph.co.uk/news/worldnews/europe/germany/8032121/Tasteless-Iron-Curtain-game.html

Jansson, M. (2010, October 22). Game Art: Jens Stober's "1378 km". *GameScenes.* www.gamescenes.org/2010/10/game-art-jens-stobers-1378-km-2010.html

Kelsey, E. (2010, December 14). "Insensitive" East German border video game a hit. *Reuters.* www.reuters.com/article/us-germany-video-game/insensitive-east-german-border-videogame-a-hit-idUSTRE6BD3KG20101214

Klepek, P. (2015, September 3). Backlash over supposedly educational 'Slave Tetris' video game. *Kotaku.* https://kotaku.com/this-is-a-screen-shot-from-slave-tetris-which-i-can-as-1728483373

Linderoth, J. (2004). *Datorspelandets mening: Bortom idén om den interaktiva illusionen.* [PhD Thesis, Göteborgs Universitet]. GUPEA. https://gupea.ub.gu.se/handle/2077/16217

Linderoth, J. (2014). Spel i skolan: Det regelstyrda lärandets möjligheter. In A. Lantz-Andersson & R. Säljö (Eds.), *Lärare i den uppkopplade skolan* (pp. 173–196). Gleerups.

Linderoth, J., & Chapman, A. (2013, August 28–30). *The limits of play in game narratives concerning World War II*. Paper presented at the IVth conference of the European society for the study of symbolic interaction, European studies in symbolic interaction: Traditions, contemporary perspectives, and challenges.

Littleloud. (2011). *Sweatshop* [PC]. Littleloud.

Martin, M. (2010, September 30). Berlin Wall shooting video game angers victims' relatives. *Reuters*. www.reuters.com/article/us-germany-wall-game/berlin-wall-shooting-video-game-angers-victims-relatives-idUSTRE68T1PS20100930

Nick. (2010, December 17). Controversial 1378 KM game released. *Softonic*. https://en.softonic.com/articles/controversial-1378-km-game-released

Price, A. (2010, December 14). Controversial East German-themed computer game finally goes online. *Deutsche Welle*. www.dw.com/en/controversial-east-german-themed-computer-game-finally-goes-online/a-6327242

Quinlan, C. (2015, September 1). CEO chalks up outrage over 'Slave Tetris' to cultural differences between Europe and the U.S. *ThinkProgress*. https://thinkprogress.org/ceo-chalks-up-outrage-over-slave-tetris-to-cultural-differences-between-europe-and-the-u-s-9239652ebdfb/

Ruiz, S. (2006). *Darfur is dying* [PC]. Interfuel.

Salen, K., & Zimmerman, E. (2004). *Rules of play: Game design fundamentals*. MIT Press.

Serious Games Interactive. (2013). *Playing history 2: Slave trade*. [PC] Serious Games Interactive.

Sharp, G. (2011). I love Pandemic (and I despair for serious games). In G. Costikyan & D. Davidsson (Eds.), *Tabletop: Analog game design* (pp. 129–135). ETC Press.

Smillie, M. (2003). There is no sport like boxing. *British Columbia Medical Journal*, *45*(9), 473–474.

Stenros, J. (2014). In defence of a Magic Circle: The social, mental and cultural boundaries of play. *ToDiGRA*, *1*(2).

Stober, J. (2010). *1378(km)* [PC]. Karlsruhe University of Arts and Design.

Stober, J. (n.d.). *1378(km)*. https://1378km.de/

Thomas, D. (2015, September 7). I played 'Slave Tetris' so your kids don't have to. *Los Angeles Times*. www.latimes.com/entertainment/herocomplex/la-et-hc-played-slave-tetris-kids-20150904-htmlstory.html

Valley News. (2015, March 3). Minneapolis public schools bans controversial game. *Valley News Live*. www.valleynewslive.com/home/headlines/Minneapolis-Public-Schools-Bans-Controversial-Game-294950581.html

van Roessel, L. (2014, July 22). Do Apple's policies impede the growth of serious games? *Internet Policy Review: Journal of Internet Regulation*. https://policyreview.info/articles/news/do-apples-policies-impede-growth-serious-games/305

Part II
Representing War and Armed Conflicts

5 On Wargames and War

Modeling Carl von Clausewitz's Theory of War

Ville Kankainen and Ilmari Käihkö

Introduction

The stated purpose of Carl von Clausewitz's magnum opus *On War*, in which he sought to revolutionize theory of war, was educational. For Clausewitz, theory of war investigates its nature, subjects, separate parts, and their properties and probable effects. Good theory was essentially a guide that 'facilitates . . . progress, educates . . . judgment, and shields . . . from error': theory 'should educate the mind of the future leader in War, or rather guide him in his self-instruction' (Clausewitz, 2004, p. 82).

Coherent concepts were central to Clausewitz's theory. As a result, the core of *On War* consists of 'an analysis of strategic and tactical concepts and principles' (Echevarria, 2013, p. vii). Clausewitz's theory was also intimately connected to practice. This was for instance reflected in his view of military education. Unlike his contemporary Rühle von Lilienstern who advocated officer training consisting of broader knowledge, Clausewitz emphasized narrower expertise immediately relevant for the military profession (Heuser, 2002, p. 45).

In this chapter, we follow Clausewitz's cue by investigating how some of his ideas have been implemented in non-digital *commercial-off-the-shelf* (COTS) tabletop wargames. The relationship between war and games was recognized even by Clausewitz. According to him, 'a play of possibilities, probabilities, good and bad luck . . . makes War of all branches of human activity the most like a gambling game' (Clausewitz, 2004, p. 15). Others too have described war as 'the ultimate game, which makes all the rest pale' (van Creveld, 2009, p. 67).

Like Clausewitz, we are also primarily interested in pedagogy, and the way wargames have become increasingly common pedagogic tools in both civilian and especially military education (Sabin, 2015). Our chapter aims to investigate the modeling of Clausewitz's theories of war in two popular COTS tabletop wargames through a form of ludo-textual analysis (Booth, 2021). We focus on COTS wargames because they are played much more than purely educational games, yet also attempt to model war and thus teach us about it. As a result, this chapter investigates how the different parts of Clausewitz's theory of war have been modeled in these games. It makes two contributions to the existing literature. Firstly, we summarize Clausewitz's theory of war into seven factors always present in war. Secondly, we analyze whether and how these seven factors have been modeled in two COTS wargames, and discuss how such modeling could be improved.

Simulating War to Learn War

Beginning in the 1800s, most wargames were designed by officers for educational purposes, as well as for testing military plans (Sabin, 2015, p. 331; Schuurman, 2019, p. 3). As pedagogical tools, games can be used to illustrate aspects specific to the subject matter that are hard to teach through other means. Wargames allow capturing the reality of war as a contest between two sides where the action of one has consequences for the other (Sabin, 2015, p. 332). Similarly, the use of dice and other methods of randomization brings an important element of chance and uncertainty, always present in war (Clausewitz, 2004, p. 14). Games also provide an opportunity for students to experience circumstances that have practical implications on theories, such as the stress involved with decision-making in a crisis context where full information is not available. Through the inherent requirement of participation, they encourage active learning and motivate students to discover more (Bayeck, 2020; McKeachie & Svinicki, 2013, p. 192).

Both analogue (Bayeck, 2020; Drake & Sung, 2011; Mattlin, 2018; Paino & Chin, 2011) and digital (Curry et al., 2016) COTS have been subject to a growing interest as easily available educational tools. Educational games and simulations always require abstraction. They are 'simplified representations of specific realities' in opposition to general realities (Klein, 1985, p. 676), and the extent of abstraction needs to be evaluated on a case-by-case basis. As Alonge (2019) points out: 'Wargames are all about realism. But "realism" is a cultural convention that changes through time.'

Although the designers might have taken some liberties with presentation, the activity can be more important for learning than factual accuracy (Harteveld, 2011, p. 6). In fact, Apperley (2013) argues that *counterfactual play* can be a powerful tool for learning, as it facilitates discussion on how things could have gone in other circumstances. Building on this, Antley (2016, p. 470) suggests that wargames hold tremendous potential as secondary sources on history and primary sources about modern reflections on historical experiences. Games should be considered as a method for learning, as 'by *doing*, players are *feeling*, and therefore most memorably learning' (Suckling, 2017, p. 111; emphasis in the original). What is learned from games ultimately depends on the context where they are used, and how the situation has been framed pedagogically (See Nygren et al., 2022).

Theory of War

As many of his contemporaries, even Clausewitz emphasized the interdependence between theory and reality. Proper education departed from theory and concepts, which students were encouraged to reflect over and clarify. Only after understanding theory could they successfully analyze reality (Gat, 2001, pp. 162–163). In this section, we discuss some of the main concepts in Clausewitz's theory of war presented in his *On War* and subsequent literature.

Clausewitz's *On War* has been called 'not simply the greatest book on war but the one truly great book on that subject yet written' (Brodie, 1973, p. 291). The masterpiece was nevertheless unfinished when posthumously published in 1832–1834. It was also contradictory. Clausewitz's thinking of war has been divided into two phases (Gat, 2001). Beatrice Heuser has characterized the young Clausewitz as an idealist: an ideal war, for younger Clausewitz, was the kind of absolute war he had witnessed Napoleon wage that was freed from political constraints. In 1827, Clausewitz discovered the importance of politics to war. This discovery turned Clausewitz into a realist. He saw that war is not autonomous but an instrument that would reflect the character of the politics it served as an instrument (Heuser, 2002). When Clausewitz unexpectedly died in 1831, he had begun, but not finished, revising *On War* to reflect this discovery. The manuscript thus contains both the old and the new theory of war, which are at times contradictory. This becomes clear with the seven concepts we focus on: *violence, friction, uncertainty, politics, trinity, victory* and *ethics*. All but the last have been chosen because of their centrality to Clausewitz's theory. We have included the last concept because we feel that discussing war without considering ethics would be unethical in itself. While ethics in general have been widely discussed in the context of games (e.g. Consalvo, 2009; Sicart, 2009), these discussions have rarely focused on war (Zagal, 2017).

Clausewitz's contribution to theory of war remains immense. He defined war, identified many of its constitutive parts and prescribed how it can be won. For Clausewitz, war equalled the use of force to make the enemy submit to our (political) will (Clausewitz, 2004, p. 1). In this conceptualization, the guiding principle of war is *violence*: wars are decided through fighting in battle, or through the threat of doing so. While there are less drastic solutions, political goals are best achieved in war by forcing the enemy to its knees. This requires destructing enough of their armed forces to make them defenceless. The greater the battle, the more decisive the effect (Clausewitz, 2004, p. 229). Even after losing their means of resistance, the opponents' country has to be conquered to prevent them from raising new forces and offering renewed resistance (Clausewitz, 2004, pp. 20–21). Unable to resist, the enemy must submit to the will of the victor. This violent prescription remains central in our modern, Western conceptualizations of the military, where the use of force forms the core occupation of the military profession (Huntington, 1957).

This is not to say that real war could ever be simple. In his attempt to ground his theory of war to reality, Clausewitz adopted the idea of *friction* from mechanics to describe everything that separated war on paper from war in reality – or war plans from their execution. Friction can be divided into general and incidental friction or chance. General friction first and foremost concerns danger, physical exertion and uncertainty (Echevarria, 2013, pp. 102–103). While everything in war appears simple, friction causes even the simplest thing to become difficult in practice (Clausewitz, 2004, pp. 58–60). Because fighting equals physical activity, war requires physical exertion. Fighting also invites danger, which too influences decision-making and perception. Much of general friction thus concerns psychological effects that have to do with waging war. Ultimately Clausewitz saw that war is characterized by uncertainty: 'three-fourths of those things upon which action in War must be calculated, are hidden more or less in the clouds of great uncertainty' (Clausewitz, 2004, p. 36). While never called so by Clausewitz, this is where the famous notion of 'fog of war' – poor intelligence – emerges. Because intelligence tends to be incomplete and because of the tendency to interpret it negatively, Clausewitz advised caution with it (Clausewitz, 2004, p. 80)

Incidental friction concerns the more concrete physical effects of the countless events related to possibilities, probabilities and fortune. In comparing war to a game, Clausewitz saw war as being closer to *chance* than any other human activity: 'together with chance, the accidental, and along with it good luck, occupy a great place in War' (Clausewitz, 2004, p. 14). Chance, compounded by the psychological effects described by general friction, combine to make war a gamble that can go either way.

These infinite psychological and physical effects influence attempts to establish a positive theory. Whereas some of Clausewitz's contemporaries sought to reduce war to mathematical or mechanical formulas, he remained sceptical about such endeavours: war is not a one-sided activity restricted to the material world (Clausewitz, 2004, pp. 72–81). While much of Clausewitz's theory of war described above reflects Clausewitz's earlier thinking, in 1827 he understood war to constitute a social and a *political* phenomenon (Gat, 2001, pp. 168–169, 217–219). The existence of a living opponent alone meant that war could never be one-sided. As a result of such reciprocity, no plan would suffice. What was required was a dynamic strategy continuously developed to meet the demands and opportunities offered by constantly changing circumstances. This also concerned the aims of war. War and violence constituted a means to an end that lies within the realm of politics. Changing circumstances affect political situation, and even political aims (Clark, 2015, pp. 55–56).

In the theory of Clausewitz the realist, war constitutes a political instrument, not an autonomous thing (Clausewitz, 2004, p. 18, 674ff). This realization nevertheless resulted in a contradiction in his theory: the majority of wars did not correspond with his violence-centric theory of war waged until the destruction of the enemy's means of resistance (Gat, 2001, pp. 215–216; Heuser, 2002, pp. 34–38). The recognition that every situation and war was unique made Clausewitz' simple and uniform prescription about making the enemy defenceless difficult. As Jan Willem Honig has observed, this questioning of war as a unitary phenomenon that could be regularized leads to great discomfort. If war is not about the use of force to disarm the opponent, what is it about? If war is not about violence, what should the military do? And yet, if war is about violence and the most violent party is destined to win, does this not risk total war with no limits (Honig, 2017, pp. 38–41)? Finally, if war is *not* about violence, does this not risk everything becoming war? If nothing else, this raises questions about the traditional role of the military (Käihkö, 2021).

This contradiction between different kinds of war – often called either total and limited, or regular and irregular – remains unresolved. Clausewitz's attempt to describe war as a 'thing in itself' suggests the possibility of a universal theory; his proposition that every war is unique questions it (Echevarria, 2013, p. 89). This conflict has bearing for the three remaining concepts we want to consider, *trinity*, *victory* and *ethics*. Clausewitz's recognition of the importance of the sociopolitical context for war led him to describe the existence of a 'wonderful trinity'. In fact, Clausewitz fleetingly presented two trinities. The first represents moral forces, and consists of hatred and animosity, probability and chance and reason. The second links these three moral forces to the greatest degree to three institutions: the people, the general and his army, and the government, respectively. A theory of war which does not properly consider the unique circumstances of these three – or rather, six – forces contradicts reality and is worthless (Clausewitz, 2004, p. 19). It has also been emphasized that none of the three moral forces is, *a priori*, more influential than the other. Each force is distinct, but simultaneously part of an indivisible whole (Echevarria, 2013, pp. 70, 72).

To summarize, a realist view sees war as a political instrument, never isolated from its sociopolitical context. Because of its chameleon-like character, every war is unique as it reflects the politics that guide it. Yet the trinities also suggest that politics should not be given primacy in the consideration of war, because it is affected even by other forces (Echevarria, 2013, pp. 94–97).

The conflict between merely disarming the opponent and achieving one's political goals is blaring when one considers *victory*. Clausewitz drew on several metaphors when discussing war, calling it both a game and 'nothing but a duel on an extensive scale' (Clausewitz, 2004, p. 1). While Clausewitz believed international law and custom had little limiting effect on war, he saw social conditions within and between states influence dynamics of war. The comparison of war and a duel suggested not only polarization between the belligerents (Clausewitz, 2004, p. 11), but also institutionalization of a set rules of war and warfare. When shared by all belligerents, a shared understanding of war could serve to translate violence to a decision in a way that limits bloodshed (Käihkö, 2020).

Clausewitz claimed that victories were tactical, not strategic. These tactical victories on the battlefield could, however, contribute to strategic success (Clausewitz, 2004, p. 364). While Clausewitz recognized that 'the result in war is never absolute' (Clausewitz, 2004, p. 7), he still appears to have assumed that the belligerents would largely follow the same rules or conventions when waging war. For Clausewitz, the use of force was a mere means of achieving political goals.

But what if a party to the conflict refuses to accept that a verdict of battle necessitates submitting to the political will of the victor? What if the political goals sought are conditions – such as preventing another terror attack like 9/11 or establishing democracy – that cannot be realized through military action alone (Smith, 2008)? If war is understood not primarily as mere organized violence but as a political struggle where violence is only one available instrument, it will never end like physical battles do. This is especially the case when political projects sought are mutually incompatible, and where surrender equals to destruction. Does refusing rules and not accepting defeat lead to either genocide or a war without an end (Käihkö, 2020)?

The last concept we want to discuss is *ethics*, as we feel it outright unethical to discuss war without them – and not only because we have just mentioned genocide. If war equals the use of organized violence, it will inevitably cause death and destruction. This immediately raises ethical and moral questions, which are largely missing in *On War* as Clausewitz likely understood politics to justify the use of organized violence.

While ethical considerations have always shaped war, war was considered a more mundane and almost inevitable affair during Clausewitz's lifetime (Heuser, 2002, p. 50; Paret, 1986, pp. 186–187). Recognizing violence as the essence of war, Clausewitz identified benevolence in war as erroneous, any principles of moderation absurd (Clausewitz, 2004, p. 2). We contend that ethics are inseparable from war. As sociological research has shown, we are not inherently violent, nor does organized violence come naturally to us. As a result, war must be legitimized through ideology (Malešević, 2010). Opponents must be designated as fair targets for violence as we seek to protect our own from harm.

In this section, we have discussed seven concepts intimately related to war, as well as some inherent contradictions within Clausewitz's theory. The fact that *On War* was never finished means that Clausewitz's theory can be understood in different ways. Perhaps unsurprisingly, a more superficial reading emphasizes the younger and more idealist Clausewitz. His narrow view that stressed violence, however, corresponds more closely with a modern view of the operational level of war (Howard, 2002, pp. 2–4; Strachan, 2013, pp. 14–15, 57–58). The more complex realist view that emphasizes politics is in turn more attuned to the strategic level of war. In the second part of this chapter, we investigate how these seven concepts are modeled in two COTS board wargames.

Modeling War

The Cases

We chose two COTS tabletop wargames to analyze in this study, namely *Paths of Glory* (Raicer, 1999a; PoG) and *Twilight Struggle* (Gupta & Matthews, 2005; TS). We chose them because they are popular COTS wargames and use similar type of game mechanics but model the war on different levels: TS on the (grand) strategic and PoG on the operational level. While TS does not simulate a specific war, its popularity makes it an interesting case for investigating the strategic level. The argument against TS being a (real) wargame, because it does not describe typical war (Alonge & Fassone, 2020, p. 55), further corroborates our choice. By choosing games that model war on different levels we hope to draw attention to the difference between Clausewitz the idealist and Clausewitz the realist.

PoG and TS are both amongst the most popular tabletop wargames on the market, being ranked as the first and the second[1] in the *Board Game Geek* (BGG)[2] wargame listing. Being exemplary cases of their genre, they have been compared in prior studies (Alonge & Fassone, 2020; Antley, 2016). Both games are card-driven games (CDG), where players use cards in their hand for taking actions. Typically, each card is used for a single action after which it is discarded. CDGs are considered more player-friendly, with simpler rules and shorter playing times than traditional hex-based wargames (Alonge & Fassone, 2019).

As two-player games, PoG and TS also correspond closely to Clausewitz the idealist – straightforward, without the added complexity of multiple players and a variety of goals. Further, while the historical accuracy of the games – especially for TS (e.g. Alonge & Fassone, 2020; Harrigan & Wardrip-Fruin, 2011) – can be contested, this is not the focus of our analysis. Rather, we aim to analyze how the design and gameplay of these games correspond to Clausewitz's theory of war.

Method

To analyze the two games, we operationalized each of the seven concepts of war into questions as shown in Table 5.1. The questions were formulated by studying closely how Clausewitz (2004) described and contextualized the terms. We used the physical copies and rulebooks of both games to get an overview of the central game elements that might model them (see Lankoski & Björk, 2015). Two questions were formulated for each concept. The first asked which game elements are used to represent the concept. The

Table 5.1 Summary of the concepts of war investigated and their operationalization

Clausewitz the Idealist		
Concept	**Description**	**Operationalization**
Violence	War is about fighting, and hence violence, or its threat. Ultimately fighting aims to make the enemy defenceless through the destruction of their means of resistance.	How is violence modeled with different game elements? What is the role of the violence in the game?
Friction	General friction emphasizes the psychological effects of danger, physical exertion, and uncertainty of information in war. 'Fog of war' – poor intelligence.	How is friction modeled with different game elements? How have uncertainties and the 'fog of war' been used to create it?
Chance	Chance or incidental friction refers to the infinite physical effects that arise from possibilities, probabilities, and fortune. Compounding with general friction, chance makes war an unpredictable gamble.	How is chance modeled with different game elements? What is the balance of various elements of chance in the game?
Victory	Clausewitz did not believe in international law, but in making the enemy defenceless through battle. While he did not perceive victory as absolute, he nevertheless assumed belligerents to largely follow shared rules or conventions of war and warfare.	How is victory modeled with different game elements? Can victory conditions change during the game?

Clausewitz the Realist		
Concept	**Description**	**Operationalization**
Politics	War is a political instrument, but the recognition that every war is unique questions Clausewitz' simple prescription about making the enemy defenceless.	How are politics modeled with different game elements? What is the relation of politics and war in the game?
Trinity	The trinity emphasizes the three moral forces and institutions central to war. War can never be isolated as its character reflects its socio-political context.	How is trinity modeled with different game elements? What is the balance of the six forces of the trinity in the game?
Ethics	The centrality of violence to war requires ideological legitimization, but also consideration of ethical and moral questions.	How are ethics modeled with different game elements? How do ethics affect the gameplay?

second one focused on the defining aspects of each concept to find out how well they correspond with the theory. A crucial factor in this process was that the first author had played both games several times (dozens for TS, and half a dozen for PoG), and could reflect the gameplay experience in addition to the formal game elements (see Booth, 2021).

The framework was used as an analytical lens in what Booth (2021) calls a 'ludo-textual analysis' – which, combines 'textual analysis (an examination of the actual material elements of the games) and formal analysis (an examination of structures that unite those elements)' (Booth, 2021, p. 17; see also Lankoski & Björk, 2015). The analysis paid attention to the rules, components (e.g. board, cards and tokens), visual aesthetics (e.g. card illustrations), text (card titles and descriptions), and the gameplay experience, considering how the concepts are modeled on the game as a system, but also how they can be interpreted through the gameplay dynamics (see Hunicke et al., 2004). The questions worked as a starting point for the analysis, but it was not restricted by them. The following sub-chapters will present the central findings of the analysis.

Paths of Glory – The Operational Level

Of the two games analyzed here, PoG is a more traditional two-player wargame, where one player controls the Central Powers (CP), and the other one Allies (AL) in the European and Middle East theatres of the World War One (see Figure 5.1). PoG's version of the CDG system uses two decks of cards, one for each player. These decks are further divided into three stacks describing the commitment level of the faction: Mobilization, Limited War and Total War. Some cards increase the War Status (WS) between 1 and 3 depending on the card. Players start with Mobilization cards in their deck, while the other stacks are added in that when WS reaches a certain level. This division, together with the distribution of political vs. military events between the decks, reflects the understanding of Clausewitz the idealist, that war escalates towards total war and the enemy's annihilation.

Unsurprisingly, *violence* takes a central stage in PoG. The main activity for both players is moving and fighting with their units, enacted by using cards from the players' hand. Units are represented with cardboard tokens, which are flipped over when they take damage and removed when they are destroyed, as is typical for wargames. The goal of the game is to score points by capturing strategic cities from the opponent and thus force them out of war. Violence is also present on a thematic level in some card events, like 'Lusitania', which do not directly affect player actions but do increase the WS.

Combat is resolved through dice roll, which is the principal source of *chance* and *incidental friction* in the game. The probabilities of dice rolls can be affected via playing cards or other game mechanics. Card drawing is aligned towards probabilities instead of pure chance, which allows

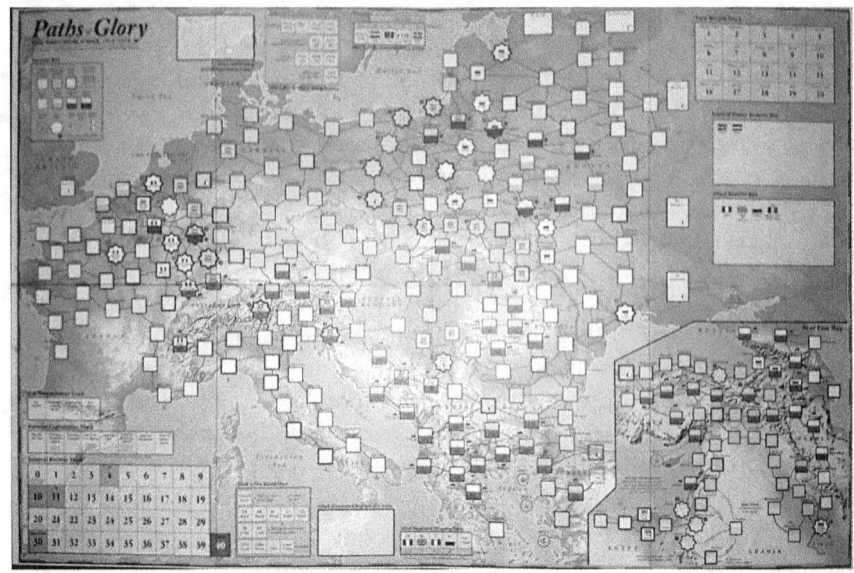

Figure 5.1 The Paths of Glory gameboard.
Source: © GMT Games Ltd, reproduced with permission. Captured by Ville Kankainen.

experienced and calculating players to take risks for greater glory. The fog of war is represented by the uncertainty of the other player's cards, and thus the choices available to them. Further, although the unit stacks are visible to both players and thus offer complete information on the current military balance, players are unaware of the reinforcement cards in the opponent's hand. This, to some extent, simulates the incomplete information common in all wars.

As noted by the game designer Ted Raicer (2016, pp. 141–142), the card play dynamic brings forth much of the *friction* in the game, even if more straightforward dynamics of PoG make this less nuanced than in TS. The design of the map (see Figure 5.1) and other game elements support the development of historical campaigns. This guides the play towards historical realism by limiting the players' options and making some actions more desirable than others (Raicer, 1999b, 2016, p. 145). Game mechanics reflect the narrative of the actual war, balancing between realism and giving a right historical 'feel' for the game. For instance, to make trench stalemate more likely in the West, German, French and British are better at entrenching than Austrians and Russians (Raicer, 2016, p. 145).

Friction is also tied into the *Politics* of PoG. Mandated Offensives (MO) present the political pressure to conduct military actions that might not be the most effective ones. They are decided by rolling a die each turn for both players. The Russian Capitulation (RC) and the US Entry (UE) tracks describe the political events leading to one nation leaving and the other entering the war by increasing the WS. Advancing the war is thus inherently connected to the larger political context, although with little possibility for players to affect it. In this sense, politics act as a tool to advance the war, thus reversing Clausewitz's hierarchy of politics and war. Most cards (see Figure 5.2) focus on the infrastructure and operational level of the war, with only a small number concerning political events, like governmental changes or war entries of neutral countries.

In addition to describing the material preparation for the war, WS also 'shows various effects of such prolonged and costly struggle on national morale, politics and diplomacy' (Raicer, 1999b). Thus, political events tied to WS offer a high-level abstraction of the war's political dimension. Still, *politics* only act as a backdrop for the war and a tool for advancing warfare. This approach suggests that politics merely add another layer of *friction* in war. As players only have minor agency in politics through choosing whether to play specific cards or not, reason becomes an attribute of generals rather than politicians.[3]

The emphasis put on the operational aspects of the war also means that civil-military relations lean towards the military as players have almost perfect control as both generals and politicians. This means that not all forces of the *trinity* are distinct. Some elements of the government are abstracted

Figure 5.2 Examples of Paths of Glory cards.

Source: © GMT Games Ltd, reproduced with permission. Captured by Ville Kankainen.

into randomization mechanics – thus aligning them more towards chance and probability than rationality. Hatred and animosity, in turn, are contained in the WS on a very abstract level as the general acceptance of the war increases among people. Scarce events like 'Russian Desertions' (see Figure 5.2) bring in human emotions as well. Hostility is generally presented at a very high level, although event names like 'Libyan Revolt' and 'Rape of Belgium' give connotations of hatred and animosity either as a motivation for military conflict or as repercussions of atrocities highlighted by wartime propaganda. For the player, however, there are no repercussions for conducting atrocities. Instead of emphasizing war *ethics*, they are diminished into side notes on the larger narrative of the war. The superficial take on the political extensions of the war and the heavy emphasis on the operational elements bring forth a representation of warfare as a clinical activity of rational decision-making void of ethical complexities. No meaningful attention is given to the suffering of civilians or to the use of questionable strategies, apart from increasing WS, as such atrocities do contribute towards war weariness.

To capture this, the game ends in *Armistice* if combined WS reaches 40. To win, players need to score *Victory Points* (VPs) by controlling specific places. If at the end of any round one side leads by 20 VP, that side gets *Automatic Victory* (AV), reflecting the opponent becoming defenseless. Otherwise, the player with more VPs in that last round is the winner. The leading player can also offer *Peace Terms* at any round, which – if accepted – ends the game in a draw and is the only way to end the game with player-to-player negotiation.

All in all, PoG is a typical wargame where the focus is on an operational level, and not much consideration is given to societal context, and thus for the *trinity*, of war. Maybe this is due to a tradition of considering wargames as apparently neutral simulations of past conflicts, that same reason might explain why the *ethics* do not have a meaningful impact on the gameplay.

Twilight Struggle – The Strategic Level

Twilight Struggle posits the players in the charge of the USA and the Soviet Union during the Cold War, covering years from the end of the Second World War in 1945 to the fall of the Soviet Union in 1989. Instead of controlling military units, players spread the influence of their respective superpower by placing 'influence markers' on countries depicted as boxes on the game board (See Figure 5.3). As noted by Alonge and Fassone (2020, pp. 69) the game does not aim to simulate the Cold War, instead being 'an attempt at recreating a specific mindset for the player, in which history is not necessarily simulated from the vantage point of reconstruction, but rather presented to the player as a set of beliefs and assumptions'.

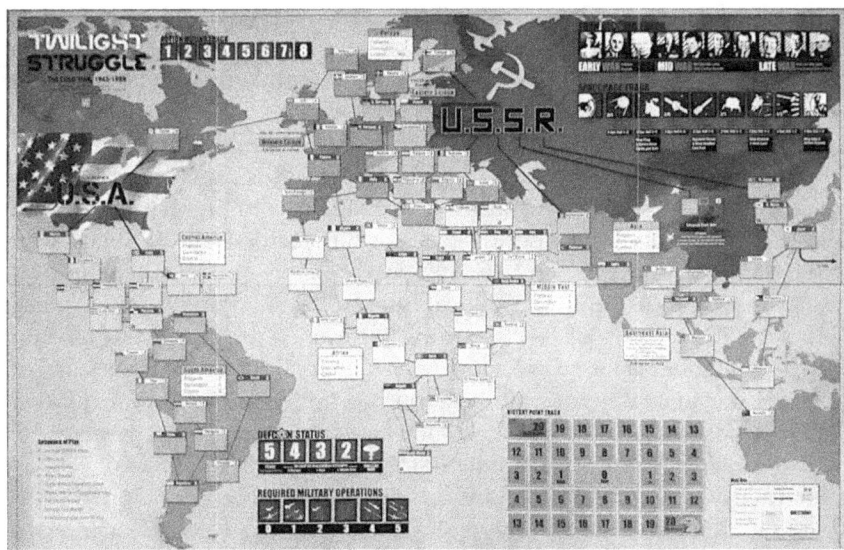

Figure 5.3 The Twilight Struggle gameboard.
Source: © GMT Games Ltd, reproduced with permission.

Antley (2016, p. 464) provides a sturdy description of the core game mechanics:

> Over the course of ten turns, . . . players are dealt hands of cards that are used either to re-create famous events of the Cold War or to place influence points among countries grouped into geopolitical regions. To win, players must capitalize on the play of region-specific scoring cards that are interspersed in Twilight Struggle's deck. These scoring cards act like a snapshot, documenting the hegemonic saturation each side possesses in that region; the higher the level of control, the more victory points are awarded to the player. Once a player reaches twenty victory points, the game ends with an ideological victory for that superpower.

If the game does not end before the last turn, the player with the most points wins. Although the *victory* conditions are yet again clear to the players from the start, gameplay dynamics do compensate this to some extent. If players are not tracking the game progression pedantically, reaching victory before turn 10 can feel surprising and thus interpreted as a sudden change of war goals. Further, as the description elucidates, TS is more of a game of *politics* than a game of war in the light of Clausewitz's theory. The game presents a prolonged political confrontation where war is – indeed – a political instrument and individual countries mere pawns in the ideological battle between the two superpowers. *Violence* is a key element in spreading political influence in this confrontation, but simultaneously only one of several means available. In the words of the game's designer Jason Matthews, the game is about 'a political struggle that held the threat of world-consuming violence in its back pocket' (Antley, 2016, p. 466). TS is thus modeled on a grand strategic rather than a narrower military strategic level. The lack of military units on the board further corroborates the statement that on a grand strategic level, the military is merely one of the many tools states possess to further their political interests, as suggested by Clausewitz.

In TS, *Violence* takes place via various war events like the 'Indo-Pakistani War' (see Figure 5.4), or *Coup* actions used to conduct 'operations short of full-scale war to change the composition of a target country's government' (Matthews & Gupta, 2009, p. 7), in a best case by replacing opponents influence by one's own. This mechanic highlights the contradictions of Clausewitz's theory of war, and the questions raised by Honig (2017, pp. 38–41) about the role of violence and the military. Violence in TS is abstracted into dice rolls or cards, and it is merely a tool to advance the overall political goal of spreading the superpower's influence over the world. This design choice emphasizes the interpretation where other reasons for war become

Figure 5.4 Examples of Twilight Struggle cards.

Source: © GMT Games Ltd, reproduced with permission.

irrelevant compared to the struggle for global political hegemony. It also reduces other countries to mere superpower proxies.

Conflict within countries progresses players in the 'Military Operations' (MilOps) track and raises the overall tension of the world by degrading the status of the 'DEFCON track' (see Figure 5.3). Each step down closes one of the three key geopolitical areas (Europe, Asia, and the Middle East), for Coups and Realignment rolls (which reflect less drastic measures for shifting the influence in the country), echoing the heating politics and the passions of the people. If the DEFCON status degrades to one, the game ends in a thermonuclear war and in the loss of the player who caused it. Using one's military deprives the opponent of a chance to advance their goals by preventing the play of certain cards or making a comeback coup. In this light, wars in TS are therefore not about disarming the opponent, but about countering and restricting opponents' political options, or leveling the playing field in the political struggle. Just like in the Cold War, conflict management is necessary to avoid the nuclear holocaust.

The representation of violence in TS seems – if possible – even more cynical than in PoG. Still, it is encouraged, as the opponent scores 'free' VPs if the player does not have enough 'MilOps' by the end of the turn. Thus *violence* is a necessary part of the grand (political) strategy, as this can make or break the game. Aesthetically, *violence* is present only in the titles and imagery of several cards, such as 'Marine Barracks Bombing' or 'East European Unrest.', and for game dynamics, aesthetics has scant meaning – not least due to the miniscule size of the images on the cards.

The looming threat of nuclear war and restrictions posed by the DEFCON status are also sources of *friction*, by posing the psychological effects of danger. However, the main source for the *friction* is in the play of the cards. The events in them are either neutral or related to one of the superpowers. When playing their own or a neutral event, the player gets to decide whether to use the card for the event or to use its value for manipulating the 'influence markers' on the board. Players are often forced to play opponent's events, meaning they can use it for influence, but the event benefiting the opponent still triggers. Minimizing harm to oneself is one of the key tactical elements in the game. This dynamic introduces a new layer to the feeling of danger, as some events allow the opposing player to degrade the DEFCON status during the acting player's turn. Because this can cause the acting player to lose the game, it is imperative to get rid of such events without allowing the opponent to act. In general, the CDG system is an elegant way of introducing the fog of war into the game, and much of the uncertainty and danger defining the *general friction* is hidden in the dynamics of the card play.

Dice become a very simple, yet effective way of emphasizing the idea put forth by Clausewitz as war being in closer connection to *chance* than any other human activity (2004, 14). The use of force is ultimately a gamble that can go either way, which is concretely represented by using dice. In TS dice rolls are used to resolve 'Coups' and 'Realignment rolls', and card events like wars. The rolls are affected by the 'Stability Number' of the country, depicting 'the country's overall stability, independence and power' (Matthews & Gupta, 2009, p. 2), and the amount of influence in the target country. The more enemy influence present, the harder the dice roll. From the perspective of Clausewitz's theory, influence markers, 'Stability Number', and the dice rolls can represent the three tips of the *trinity* – *the people, the government*, and *the general and his army*, respectively. Influence affects the attitudes and emotions of the people – that is their hatred and animosity towards the opponent. Governments in countries with higher 'Stability Numbers' are more difficult to reason with, while staging coups or using less violent means to make countries realign with you brings in the element of *chance*. Thus, the success of these depends on the balance of the three forces.

The *trinity* is also present on a higher level, in the core dynamics of the game. Here, the player represents the *reason* as the government of the superpower, elements of *chance and uncertainty* manifest in card drawing and dice rolling mechanics, while the *hatred and animosity* in any given moment of the game are represented by the DEFCON track and the players' cards. While DEFCON reflects the overall tension of the world, each hand of cards can be seen as a 'montage' portraying the stage of world *politics*, and the options this affords for the player-government. The quality of each hand is relative, as by not knowing what the opponent has in theirs, it is obfuscated by the fog of war. Planning how to play thus becomes war on paper compared to war in reality as strategies must be adjusted to the opponents' response to each card you play. To triumph, players need to balance between the trinity's three elements.

The paradigm of understanding warfare mostly as a rational pursuit that leaves little room for ethical or moral considerations is prevalent in TS as much as in any wargame. Most of the time the game mechanics do not force the players into ethical decisions, apart from starting a nuclear war. Although the players can choose to avoid actions they feel are morally questionable (e.g. playing the 'Captured Nazi Scientist' event or starting a proxy war), the design supports and rewards an opportunistic approach. Yet again, the people and their passions and ethics are merely side notes on the narrative of the superpowers' Cold War grand strategies. Nevertheless, due to the completely different perspective and level of abstraction, TS captures the influence of *politics* better than PoG (or most other wargames, in that regard). Just like Clausewitz theorized, in TS war serves politics and not the other way around.

Conclusions

In this chapter we have investigated pedagogy of war, and how Clausewitz's influential theory of war has been modeled in tabletop wargames. We have focused on seven factors always present at war – *violence, friction, chance, politics, trinity, victory,* and *ethics* – in two popular tabletop wargames, *Twilight Struggle* and *Paths of Glory*. As our analysis suggests, while many of the factors, central to Clausewitz's theory of war, are present in wargames, some have been difficult to model, or have been overlooked for better playability and other reasons. As a result, many COTS wargames offer a rather conventional understanding of war, which steers players towards a specific 'regular' type of war.

In the analyzed games, modeling of chance, uncertainty, and friction come in the form of rolling dice or drawing cards from a shuffled deck. They, in addition to polarization, are also affected by the presence of a living opponent. Latter however offers the first complication to modeling war. Like in many wargames used in military education, the typical scenario envisages two somewhat equally strong adversaries who 'fight it out'. This kind of polarization does not exist in many real wars, which encompass multiple sides with a plethora of varying interests and goals, not always compatible. In the so-called *Counterinsurgency* (COIN) line of tabletop wargames, this kind of complexity is accounted for by letting players control different factions with individual victory conditions and differing game mechanics in an unbalanced situation. For instance, in *Fire in the Lake – Insurgency in Vietnam* (Herman & Ruhnke, 2014), the USA wins by exiting the conflict without giving any of the competing factions enough control over Vietnam to reach their victory goals.

In real life, organized violence is also used in a context, and rarely as the only means for achieving political goals. While this context could be implemented through the trinity, aspects of it appear difficult or unimportant to reproduce in wargames. We do wonder whether this is because of the burden of wargaming tradition, the influence of the hegemonic understanding of the nature of war, or something else entirely?

As discussed in the analysis, the absence of context is particularly noticeable in games that focus on the operational level, and which thus closely corresponds with the early idealist thinking of Clausewitz. The narrowness of this view of war becomes obvious as games that focus on battling armies tend to neglect the equally important people and governments, as well as the often-difficult relationship between the three. This, we argue, narrows understandings of not only civil-military relations but of war as a phenomenon, and partly explains why ethics are rarely considered in wargames (see Alonge, 2019). Still, their importance cannot be emphasized enough. Some designers do understand the ethical problem of wargames, as several games depict a critical stance towards war in the game title and the imagery (Alonge & Fassone, 2019). Games like *This War of Mine* (Włosek, 2014) go even a step further, by presenting the war from the civilian point of view.[4]

In both of the analyzed games, ethics are displayed as a thin aesthetic layer. While imagery and descriptions on game boxes and cards bring flavour to the game experience, their exact contents have minimal influence on the overall gameplay experience. Thus, we can agree with Alonge and Fassone (2019) that these games do not reflect the ethical and moral elements of war. From the perspective of pedagogy, we disagree with their notion that 'a wargame is a wargame. Its main goal is simulating fighting not mourning'; we believe the main goal of wargames to be not simulating war but learning about war.

Games that are more educational are not necessarily the most entertaining ones. For instance, consider a game whose mechanics allow insurgents to hide among unarmed civilians. While it can make a lot of sense to shoot at them from a tactical point of view, this might not be the case on the strategic level. Implementing such murkier issues into the core experience of wargames – that is on the game mechanical level – can be necessary for retaining the ethical dimension in games; blurring the horrors of war may make war more acceptable.

If we accept Clausewitz's maxim of war as a continuation of politics by other means, it is necessary to consider what victory consists of. The example of shooting civilians illustrates how victory on a tactical level may contribute to strategic failure. Unlike limited war where military goals can be specified and wargames where victory conditions are known from the start, politics do not have an end state. Like limited war, even wargames offer set rules that must be followed in a way that considerably reduces the uncertainty and fog of war. This is not the case in real war, where it is predominantly ethics, moral forces and material considerations that set the limits of what is possible. Adversaries and others can choose to act by other, often for us unconventional ways.

To summarize, we find that modeling war in wargames that focus on the operational, or even strategic level remains a challenge. As TS illustrates, the strategic level may in some ways be the easier of the two. After all, TS arguably succeeds in emphasizing the primacy of politics and treats military force as only one of the many instruments a state can employ to further its political goals. This is in contract with PoG, where the *Mandated Offensive* mechanic frames *politics* as a necessary evil causing friction to well-laid plans. This said, TS similarly illustrates how several of the more sociological factors, that Clausewitz the realist believes affect war, are difficult to model or are overlooked for other reasons. Due to the importance of wargames as pedagogical instruments, these difficulties risk reproducing a narrow understanding of war that guides thinking toward limited conventional war. Considering that few contemporary wars offer a good fit with this type of conflict, we find this troubling. In conclusion, we offer some suggestions on how the often-missing factors of war can be modeled to advance pedagogy of war.

While we consider especially ethics to be lacking in these games, addressing this factor is tricky. Both wargames investigated here take several ethically problematic events for granted as inevitable historical facts. Neither of the games allows players to act for ethical reasons if they still wish to win. This type of paradigm supports the view that to win a war, one should not bother too much with ethics. This approach, which diminishes the role of ethics in war, is the approach more generally taken in wargaming. As many games aim to simulate past conflicts, understandably, certain disturbing elements must be present for the sake of historical accuracy. However, all wargames are to some extent alternative histories – otherwise, there would not be any room for player agency. Some elements of reality have been given factual leeway to allow players to influence the outcome of the conflicts. Why should we then take the ethically questionable elements for granted, and not allow players to try finding more ethically sustainable solutions through counterfactual play? This approach might offer fruitful venues for educational purposes.

The pedagogic use of wargames can be traced to the professionalization of the military, which by and large has built on the notion that waging war is a practical skill and activity where politics are best held at arm's length (Huntington, 1957). This notion has no doubt contributed to also making wargames a rather technical affair. To offer only one example, we rarely consider what happens to civilians and governance structures when territory is captured. This is especially the case in contexts where political authority is asserted by force. This often happens in civil wars but was equally the case in the Second World War where advancing German and Soviet forces murdered undesirable groups like Jews and rooted out (suspected) political enemies. Recent Russian wars in Syria and Ukraine illustrate that such practices are not bygone. In wargames the presence of civilians is often disregarded with only military units present on the board, contrasting with ideas of modern wars as being fought amongst the people in a manner that demands taking them into account (Smith, 2008). These examples illustrate how war and warfare should never be considered as a merely apolitical, technical activity.

What we find problematic is that wargames tend to model more comfortable limited regular war, and thus a less complicated view of war that does not match reality. Similarly, the focus tends to be on the operational, not the strategic level of war. From the perspective of the pedagogy of war, Clausewitz's theory still offers useful concepts for understanding the phenomenon in its complexity. We hope that this chapter can assist in future attempts to model this theory in wargames.

Notes

1 This was the situation on 23 March 2020.
2 Board Game Geek is the most popular online community and database for tabletop games listing over 101 000 tabletop games. It has been online since 2000 and passed two million registered users in February 2019: https://boardgamegeek.com/thread/2147066/2000000-users/page/1.
3 In comparison, there is a full political phase during each turn in *Triumph of Chaos* (Dockter, 2005), a CDG about the Russian civil war, giving players more agency in politics, thus emphasizing its importance for war.

4 After the Russian invasion of Ukraine in February 2022, the sales of the game, surged thousands of percent (Zeitchik, 2022), as a result of publisher's charity campaign for Ukraine.

References

Alonge, G. (2019). Playing the Nazis: Political implications in analog wargames. *Analog Game Studies, 6*(3). http://analoggamestudies.org/2019/09/playing-the-nazis-political-implications-in-analog-wargames/

Alonge, G., & Fassone, R. (2019). Playing the Great War. In R. Fernández Sirvent & R. A. G. Lloret (Eds.), *Del siglo XIX al XXI: Tendencias y debates (Alicante, 20–22 de septiembre de 2018): Actas del XIV congreso [de la] Asociación de Historia Contemporánea*. Biblioteca Virtual Miguel de Cervantes.

Alonge, G., & Fassone, R. (2020). Twilight struggle, or: How we stopped worrying about the hexagons. In D. Brown & E. MacCallum-Stewart (Eds.), *Rerolling boardgames: Essays on themes, systems, experiences and ideologies* (1st ed., pp. 48–68). McFarland.

Antley, J. (2016). Struggling with deep play: Utilizing twilight struggle for historical inquiry. In *Zones of control: Perspectives on wargaming* (pp. 463–470). MIT Press.

Apperley, T. (2013). Modding the historians' code: Historical verisimilitude and the counterfactual imagination. In M. W. Kapell & A. B. R. Elliott (Eds.), *Playing with the past: Digital games and the simulation of history*. Bloomsbury Academic. https://doi.org/10.5040/9781628928259

Bayeck, R. Y. (2020). Examining board gameplay and learning: A multidisciplinary review of recent research. *Simulation & Gaming, 51*(4), 411–431. https://doi.org/10.1177/1046878119901286

Booth, P. (2021). Meeples, miniatures, and cubes – Ludo-textual analyses of board games. In *Board games as media* (pp. 17–29). Bloomsbury Academic.

Brodie, B. (1973). On Clausewitz: A passion for war. *World Politics, 25*(2), 288–308.

Clark, I. (2015). *Waging war: A new philosophical introduction*. Oxford University Press.

Clausewitz, C. von. (2004). *On war*. Barnes & Nobles.

Consalvo, M. (2009). *Cheating: Gaining advantage in videogames*. MIT Press.

Curry, J., Price, T., & Sabin, P. (2016). Commercial-off-the-shelf-technology in UK military training. *Simulation & Gaming, 47*(1), 7–30.

Dockter, D. (2005). *Triumph of chaos* [Tabletop Wargame]. Clash of Arms Games. https://boardgamegeek.com/boardgame/15826/triumph-chaos

Drake, P., & Sung, K. (2011). Teaching introductory programming with popular board games. In *Proceedings of the 42nd ACM technical symposium on computer science education* (pp. 619–624). https://doi.org/10.1145/1953163.1953338

Echevarria, A. (2013). *Clausewitz & contemporary war*. Oxford University Press.

Gat, A. (2001). *A history of military thought: From the enlightenment to the Cold War*. Oxford University Press.

Gupta, A., & Matthews, J. (2005). *Twilight struggle* [Board game]. GMT Games.

Harrigan, P., & Wardrip-Fruin, N. (2011). Twilight struggle and card-driven historicity. In G. Costikyan & D. Davidson (Eds.), *Tabletop: Analog game design* (pp. 156–166). ETC Press.

Harteveld, C. (2011). *Triadic game design: Balancing reality, meaning and play*. Springer. https://doi.org/10.1007/978-1-84996-157-8

Herman, M., & Ruhnke, V. (2014). *Fire in the lake* [Board game]. GMT Games.

Heuser, B. (2002). *Reading Clausewitz*. Pimlico.
Honig, J. W. (2017). Uncomfortable visions: The rise and decline of the idea of limited war. In B. Wilkinson & J. Gow (Eds.), *The art of creating power: Freedman on strategy* (pp. 29–48). Hurst.
Howard, M. (2002). *Clausewitz: A very short introduction*. Oxford University Press.
Hunicke, R., LeBlanc, M., & Zubek, R. (2004). MDA: A formal approach to game design and game research. In *Proceedings of the AAAI workshop on challenges in game AI, 4*(1), 1722. https://www.aaai.org/Papers/Workshops/2004/WS-04-04/WS04-04-001.pdf
Huntington, S. (1957). *The soldier and the state: The theory and politics of civil-military relations*. Belknap Press of Harvard University Press.
Käihkö, I. (2020). War as nothing but a duel: War as an institution and the construction of the Western military profession. *Journal of Military Studies, 9*(1), 11–23. https://doi.org/10.2478/jms-2018-0003
Käihkö, I. (2021). The evolution of hybrid war: Implications for strategy and the military profession. *Parameters, 51*(3), 115–127.
Klein, J. H. (1985). The abstraction of reality for games and simulations. *The Journal of the Operational Research Society, 36*(8), 671–678. https://doi.org/10.2307/2582262
Lankoski, P., & Björk, S. (2015). Formal analysis of gameplay. In P. Lankoski & J. Holopainen (Eds.), *Game design research: An introduction to theory & practice* (pp. 23–35). ETC Press.
Malešević, S. (2010). *The sociology of war and violence*. Cambridge University Press.
Matthews, J., & Gupta, A. (2009). *Twilight struggle deluxe edition rulebook*. GMT Games.
Mattlin, M. (2018). Adapting the DIPLOMACY board game concept for 21st century international relations teaching. *Simulation & Gaming, 49*(6), 735–750. https://doi.org/10.1177/1046878118788905
McKeachie, W., & Svinicki, M. (2013). *McKeachie's teaching tips: Strategies, research, and theory for college and university teachers*. Wadsworth.
Nygren, N. V., Kankainen, V., & Brunet, L. (2022). Offsetting Game – Framing Environmental Issues in the Design of a Serious Game. *Simulation & Gaming, Advance online publication*. https://doi.org/10.1177/10468781221126786
Paino, M., & Chin, J. (2011). MONOPOLY and critical theory: Gaming in a class on the sociology of deviance. *Simulation & Gaming, 42*(5), 571–588. https://doi.org/10.1177/1046878110391022
Paret, P. (1986). Clausewitz. In P. Paret (Ed.), *Makers of modern strategy: From Machiavelli to the nuclear age* (pp. 186–216). Princeton University Press.
Raicer, T. (1999a). *Paths of glory* [Board game]. GMT Games.
Raicer, T. (1999b). Design notes. In *Rules booklet – Paths of Glory the First World War, 1914 1918*. GMT Games.
Raicer, T. S. (2016). The paths of glory lead but to the gaming tablet. In P. Harrigan & M. G. Kirschenbaum (Eds.), *Zones of control: Perspectives on wargaming* (pp. 141–147). MIT Press.
Sabin, P. (2015). Wargaming in higher education: Contributions and challenges. *Arts & Humanities in Higher Education, 14*(4), 329–348.
Schuurman, P. (2019). A game of contexts: Prussian-German professional wargames and the leadership concept of mission tactics 1870–1880. *War in History, 28*(3), 504–524. https://doi.org/10.1177/0968344519855104
Sicart, M. (2009). *The ethics of computer games*. MIT Press.
Smith, R. (2008). *The utility of force: The art of war in the modern world*. Vintage.

Strachan, H. (2013). *The direction of war: Contemporary strategy in historical perspective.* Cambridge University Press.

Suckling, M. (2017). Board with meaning: Reflections on game design and historiography. *CEA Critic, 79*(1), 110–119. https://doi.org/10.1353/cea.2017.0007

van Creveld, M. (2009). *The culture of war.* Spellmount.

Włosek, R. (2014). *This war of mine* [PC, Mobile]. 11 Bit Studios.

Zagal, J. P. (2017). War ethics: A framework for analyzing videogames. In *DiGRA '17 – Proceedings of the 2017 DiGRA International Conference, 14*(1). http://www.digra.org/digital-library/publications/war-ethics-a-framework-for-analyzing-videogames/

Zeitchik, S. (2022, March 2). Here's how new technology is bringing home Ukraine's tragedy. *Washington Post.* www.washingtonpost.com/business/2022/03/02/virtual-reality-ar-ukraine-russia/

6 Wargames as Reenactment
An Ecological Framework for the Development of Military Games for Education

Adam Chapman and Jonas Linderoth

Introduction – Explanatory Models vs. Systems for Reenactment

The potential of wargames as *explanatory models* of conflict is frequently highlighted. As Sabin puts it, 'Where wargames differ from books and films on war is that they focus on systematic interactive modelling of the hypothetical possibilities inherent in a limited set of conflict dynamics' (2015, p. 333). Definitions of wargames also generally emphasise (implicitly or explicitly) the importance of agent-focused elements such as decision-making. An example of this is Perla's definition where a wargame is 'a warfare model or simulation whose operation does not involve the activities of actual military forces, and whose sequence of events affects and is, in turn, affected by the *decisions* made by players representing the opposing sides' (1990, p. 164, our emphasis). Sabin makes a similar argument saying: 'Traditional didactic means such as books, films and lectures focus on the one-way transmission of information [. . .]. Wargames, by contrast, require players to engage with and master the simulation system sufficiently to make sensible command *decisions*' (2015, p. 334, our emphasis). Research exploring the educational use of historically themed games has also marked decision making as valuable (e.g. McCall, 2011). Decision-making in wargames is hence highlighted as a unique educational quality. For example, Sabin later adds: 'Actually grappling with such dilemmas at first hand rather than simply reading or hearing about them has enormous educational potential' (2015, p. 333).

As such, a core aspect of wargaming seems to be the attempt to construct a system in which the player assuming a role will face similar *decisions* to those faced by an agent – a situation, which to some degree must be modelled from past experiences. Hence there is a connection to conventional historical reenactment, communities who seek to learn about everyday *decisions* made in the past by experiencing the *challenges* presented by utilising historical material culture to perform past activities in particular environments.[1] This similar concern with learning about past decisions through facing challenges seems to imply that at some level wargames are inherently concerned with reenactment of historical events. Even when hoping to prepare students for, or test, future scenarios such games are constructed according to insights into processes and dynamics gleaned from previous conflict situations. As Rubel writes, the famous military theorist Clausewitz 'regarded history as a real-life laboratory of war, one that can be mined for information useful for preparing the minds of future commanders' (2006, pp. 116–117).

Teaching students tactics or strategy without at least some basis in previous conflict situations would seem to be unsound pedagogy. Similarly, if a wargame's represented scenarios held no relation to past events (even in the loosest sense of the 'historically typical'), there would be no referents to establish criteria for critical judgements as to educational quality, rendering the whole exercise useless for anything other than entertainment. Furthermore, any training manual, accepted technique, or approach is generally codified due to its proven utility in past actions, even if these actions in themselves might not be sharp conflicts – that is one might have to model something based on data from an exercise, real life simulation, or make an estimation based on how similar phenomena have behaved in the past.

It therefore seems appropriate to accept that history, at least in the broader sense of past events, is important to educational wargames – that part of the idea of such games is to learn from the past to prepare for the future. Indeed, history is a social practice that is generally seen to only have value in terms of its capacity to inform us about the present or future. As Pihlainen puts it, 'As far as I can see, claims for the *intrinsic* value of studying the past make no sense' (2017, p. xv).

This emphasis on learning from the past through facing *decisions* and *challenges* seems to imply the possibility of understanding wargames as a form of historical reenactment – the reenactment of past experiences in order to gain insight. This is not to argue that information about military skills (or indeed history) cannot be learned in other ways. Some games offer explanations of theories or systems through abstraction, metaphor, and metonym (Chapman, 2016) rather than by offering reenactment. In such cases, just as with conventional historical writing, insights are gained by moving beyond the possible experiences of individual historical agents to a larger, macro scale in which multiple sources of information can be considered and synthesised in ways unavailable to historical contemporaries.

However, games offering reenactment differ, at least from the perspective of this chapter, by offering *a more direct form of learning*. We argue from the basis of ecological psychology that this form of learning can be understood as: *confronting players with information fields and challenges that are related to earlier situations so that they can adapt their perception-action system to specific sets of affordances that are predicted to be relevant to future situations.*

This explanation of the educational possibilities of wargames therefore differs from the view that they are mainly models in which abstracted theory is explained, grounded in the idea that cognitive models are then created that can be applied in future, completely different situations. By comparison, in a reenactment wargame, action and perception are trained directly in an environment that intends to echo past environmental challenges experienced by historical agents and foreshadow future conflict environments that might be experienced by players. Put simply, whilst we often think of wargames as offering a simulative explanatory model *of battle*, a reenactment wargame differs by offering a *perceptual experience similar to* experiences of past agents *in battle*. As the earlier cited literature indicates these two capabilities of wargames are frequently tangled. Our separation of them has mainly an analytical purpose.

If we accept these arguments – that educational wargames in general are based to some degree in history (however recent or unspecific); that this history is potentially pedagogically valuable; and that reenactment of past decisions and challenges is one potential path to realise these lessons – then considering how to best implement the reenactment aspect of wargames seems a viable line of inquiry.

Ecological Psychology and Its Application to Games

Ecological psychology, or the ecological approach, was founded by James and Eleanor Gibson. Though starting as a theory of visual perception, James Gibson's ideas were so fundamentally different from other ideas of perception that it eventually entailed a full ontology, as well as groundbreaking ideas about information and knowing (Gibson, 1986). With the contribution of Eleanor Gibson, the approach also developed a theory of learning (Gibson & Pick, 2000). The core of the ecological approach is to understand humans (as well as other animals) as having intertwined perception and action systems that they modulate in relation to their environments. An environment has a potential for action that is dependent on the perception-action systems of the human or animal. Gibson labelled these potentials as affordances, a concept that has gained recognition and use far beyond the ecological approach, sometimes without an understanding of the original theory's idea of the reciprocal relation between animal and environment.

Learning, according to this perspective, is to develop one's action system in order to be able to realise new affordances. However, learning is also about becoming more perceptually attuned to the environment. To use opportunities for action one must be able to *perceive* these opportunities. This *perceptual learning* is, according to the ecological view that Gibson and Pick endorse, a process of *differentiation* (Gibson & Pick, 2000). The available information the perceiver has about the environment is rich and complex. Hence, living beings must manage the task of separating between information that is relevant or irrelevant to their actions, goals, and tasks at hand. In other words, perception is about picking up the information that specifies the affordances of the environment. Information flows in the perceptual field surrounding the observer. The perceptual field is structured in variants and invariants, features that change and features that remain during different transformations (movement, events, change of illumination etc.). It is in this flow that the observer discovers the affordances of their immediate surroundings. The invariants will specify the available affordances since affordances themselves are invariant, in that they do not change with the mental state of the observer (Gibson, 1986, pp. 140–141).

Hence, pictures are samples of perceptual fields and when we see them we pick up some invariants of the portrayed features. Still, there will be information in the perceptual field where the picture is seen that reveals the fact that it is a picture and not the portrayed object or event (unless the painting is made to be deliberately misperceived like in the case of trompe-l'œil paintings, however, these misperceptions are most often temporary and remain until the observer has picked up more information). In general, we have no problems understanding that a picture does not have a majority of the affordances of the portrayed thing.

Linderoth (2012, see also Linderoth, 2013; Linderoth & Bennerstedt, 2007) has used this framework to theorise how gamers learn and how the concept of gameplay can be understood. According to Linderoth, gameplay is '*to perceive, act on and transform the affordances that are related to a game system or other players in a game*' (2012, p. 52). Linderoth makes an analytical separation between the part of a game that is a control function, where the player's agency is extended into the game realm (player-controller-avatar unit, cf. Wilhelmsson's, 2008 concept *game ego*), and the other parts of the game (that the player manipulates through the control function). Hence, Linderoth treats avatars, the extended agency in the game, as a tool. The affordances of a game are then located between this tool and the rest of the game environment. To perceive affordances in games is therefore always a matter of relating the game environment to the properties of the tool.

Reenactment, from an Ecological Perspective

For anyone studying James Gibson, using the concept of reenactment might initially seem counter-intuitive. The related concept of representation was, according to Gibson, misleading since there could never be a re-presentation of an earlier perceptual field (1986, p. 279). However, just as a picture can display some of the information it shares with the phenomenon it displays (the information that is invariant between display and displayed), a reenactment can be seen as an activity that has some invariant features (both in terms of information and affordances) with the activity it attempts to model.

The possibilities of the ecological approach to wargaming have previously been recognised by Granberg and Hulterström (2015), who use ecological psychology to offer an approach to wargame design that is practically focused on affordances and tools as an alternative to costly high-fidelity approaches.

Chapman (2016) previously argued that video games could function as a form of reenactment when their screens produce information that is invariant with the information experienced by historical agents. This resonates with how Gibson saw the possibility of learning from film, where he saw the camera as being analogous to the perceptual field of an observer (Gibson, 1986, p. 297). However, he also stressed the limitation of film:

> The beholder is helpless to intervene. He can find out nothing for himself. He feels himself moving and looking around in a certain fashion, attending now to this and now to that, but at the will of the filmmaker. He has visual kinesthesis and visual self-awareness, but it is passive, not active.
>
> (1986, p. 295)

Games of course differ by offering players precisely the kind of agency that is missing in film. By allowing players to experience similar information fields and, importantly, related challenges to historical agents, games offer players the possibility of learning to differentiate information and develop skills in similar ways to these agents.

Learning through Reenactment

Conventional reenactment is about 'skill acquisition – particularly through group learning and sharing of techniques' (Johnson, 2015, p. 197). As this implies, the social aspect of reenactment is an important issue. Similarly, Agnew (2004) argues that the central narrative of reenactment is:

> one of conversion from ignorance to knowledge, individualism to sociability, resistance to compliance, and present to past . . . [reenactors] . . . begin as novices . . . undergo trials, acquire skills and experience, and are finally inducted into a community of dedicated reenactors.
>
> (2004, pp. 330–331)

From the perspective of the ecological approach, learning transfer (Greeno et al., 1996) from reenactment becomes a twofold issue. Firstly, there is the question of if the information that the game provides allows the player to perform differentiations that have some similarity with the reenacted situation, some invariant aspects. Secondly, there is the question of whether the affordances that the reenactor is supposed to realise force them to adapt to the reenactment in such a way that they develop behaviours and predispositions that are useful in the reenacted situations (cf. Linderoth, 2012). The pedagogical argument for the reenactment game, at least from an ecological point of view, is then the notion that facing similar information fields and challenges to those that agents have faced in past situations might train players in skills of perception and action that are useful to future situations.

However, as Gibson stressed, there really is no full *re-*presentation and hence, no matter the visual or audio fidelity, we must expect large deviations between reenactment and reenacted. This is even more so in the case of affordances. While it is possible to create illusions of the available information in the reenacted setting, particularly technical interfaces, it is harder to represent affordances, especially in the case of wargames where the affordances of real war would be dangerous, unethical, or impossible to mimic. As such, it is important to note that reenactment wargames differ from the original situation(s) upon which they are based. Unlike the original historical agents (who presumably should have been already attuned to the environment), the player of the reenactment games is in a context of learning and should at some point in the process be offered feedback. Hence, in the ecological framework the deviations between reenactment and reenacted is an important realm for the instructor (Sellberg, 2017). However, following Linderoth (2012), too much assistance may eradicate the challenge of the wargame environment, too little and the environment may be overwhelming to the relatively unskilled student.

Reenactment Wargames – Challenges Instead of Explanation

The core idea of the reenactment game is that learning should occur through facing challenges from the past that have predicted relevance to future scenarios within the context of carefully chosen resources for perception and action (i.e. an information field). These games are not focused on *explanation* of the underlying dynamics of combat situations (theoretical knowledge) as much as offering opportunities to directly train *skills of differentiating information* relevant to these challenging environments. As such, the focus in reenactment games is primarily on presenting an information field for the player that has overlapping invariants with the reenacted situation, with the simulation of the battle itself merely underpinning this aspect. Such games are about providing opportunities for environmental attunement through direct experience of the challenges and information of a similar environment, rather than abstracted explanations about that environment through another mode. Wargames that function as explanatory models often offer theoretical abstracted knowledge that it is unlikely that historical agents had access to. For example, a wargame can offer complete or near-complete, real-time information on a large scale. By comparison, reenactment games focus on the 'black boxing' of information to reproduce the kinds of challenges that faced individual agents in these scenarios (and may in future). As this implies, the *presentation* of a reenactment game is just as important as its *content.*

From the ecological perspective this means that a 'presumption is that a sensitive exploring agent can pick up the affordance of an environment directly through exploration, discovery, and differentiation' (Young, 2004a). It is this focus on direct experience that the reenactment game seeks to harness. If we accept this idea, and students are sufficiently motivated, the problem then does not become *if* students will learn in the game environment but *what* they will learn.

Reenactement Games Are Not about Fidelity

Approaching the design and evaluation of wargames from a perspective of ecological psychology means attempting to ensure that this knowledge is valid and useful by adding elements to the environment of the student that offer possibilities to become attuned to invariant information in ways that will be useful to them in future situations. As this implies, one of the easiest ways to do so is to ensure similarities in these two environments and (as we cannot see the future) naturally this involves drawing from previous environments that we predict will have similarities to future ones (hence the intrinsically historical nature of such games and their status as a form of reenactment).

This should not be mistaken for a simple concentration on nebulous concepts such as 'realism'. All thematic games are representations and are therefore intrinsically different from the phenomena they seek to represent (otherwise they would simply *be* that phenomena). There will always be information in the environment of the student that specifies different affordances to that of the soldier. The student, for example, will not experience the threat of violence as part of the environment. Similarly, even the very knowledge that the environment is intended to be educational is significant and introduces its own pressures (e.g. the social affordances of instructor surveillance often means students performing good intent and commitment to an activity). These environmental factors may be helpful to learning outcomes, but they also emphasise that the reenactment wargame has limitations, like all forms of representation. Sabin (2012) notes the complexities of representing conflict in wargames to an accurate degree, arguing that, alongside military factors, complex social, political, and cultural factors would also have to be included. He adds: 'Even if such daunting levels of knowledge and understanding could be gained in the first place, incorporating all this detail into the game would make it unplayable complex and time-consuming' (Sabin, 2015, p. 344).

The focus on 'black boxing' information in reenactment games offers a way out of this bind to some degree. Reenactment games are about reflecting the information challenges of battlefield environments in relation to human perception (and information technologies), thus offering a potentially transferable experience. This often means deliberately restricting information about the game-state from the player and presenting information in purposely less efficient 'second-hand' ways (e.g. relying on messages from other players rather than 'real-time' maps). This black boxing means the problem of representing every factor in a conflict scenario becomes far less important. Rather than attempting to model an entire conflict situation for explanation, reenactment games only simulate the part of the system that an individual agent typically experiences. As long as it generates the appropriate reactive changes and maintains the challenges in the information field that the player is confronted with, the rest of the system that lies beyond the player's direct perception (i.e. that is 'black boxed') can be constructed in any way we consider appropriate.[2]

The reenactment wargame should therefore not be mistaken for a simplistic, expensive high-fidelity approach (see also Granberg & Hulterström, 2015). Instead, this is about focusing in on important invariant aspects of an environment that offers particular challenges we wish to prepare students for. Naturally this involves a subjective design process that chooses to emphasise some environmental elements while minimizing others. However, using a theoretically informed approach and a historically grounded mind-set we can try to isolate those aspects that might be most pertinent to particular tasks (enabling further research). Doing so may offer an alternative perspective on educational wargames beyond high fidelity or explanatory model approaches.

An Ecological Framework for Using Wargames as Reenactment

What elements should then be taken into consideration in the design, evaluation, or implementation of reenactment wargames? The central idea of a reenactment game is to present players with an information field that specifies similar affordances and contains similar challenges to previous agents' experiences of conflict environments. They aim to give players the opportunity to learn to differentiate information in ways that are useful to environmental pressures we expect they might face in the future and provide opportunities for assessing student learning.

From this perspective it is the structuring of the interactive information processes of play and the relation of this to previous/future environments that is most important. Despite the historical aspect, these games are not intended to *describe* past events. Instead of learning what *did* happen, a reenactment game allows players opportunities to explore what actions *could* be performed given the context of the environment and the ability to negotiate the information within it.

Since affordances are not simply stable properties of the environment but are codetermined by the agent's skills and abilities (Young, 2004a) they will differ between individuals. Hence students may realise different affordances despite encountering the same wargame environment. This makes reenactment an unpredictable activity and students are unlikely to have exactly the same experience or results as the original agent. It should be noted that the point of a reenactment game is not to learn from the actions taken by historical agent(s) so much as the situation in which they found themselves. Even if player's solutions may vary, there are still aspects of the environment important to constructing particular challenges and encouraging students to discover particular affordances. Some of these aspects, which we term *agent to player relation; goals; challenge; information type; information quantity;* and *information mode*, will be considered in greater detail in the following text.

Historical Agent to Player Relation

As reenactment is about trying to learn through exposure to the perceptual information and challenges of the past, the activity should structure and maintain information that has some invariant properties of the past environment, that is the visual fields of agent and player should have commonalities. The relationship between player and past agents is therefore important. Perspective is of particular significance. Wargames that utilise visual perspectives impossible for human agents to commonly experience cannot constitute reenactment. In reenactment games one must not only play *with* a system but actually take on the feasible role of a particular *agent* within the system that the game seeks to represent. The player should occupy only *one* agent position within a given play through and the affordances (both possibilities and limitations) of this player position should echo those of the real agent(s) upon which this is based. This is about embodied action in past, present and potential futures.

Sabin argues that 'Wargames model a conflict as an endlessly replayable game of "glorified chess" . . . whereas books and films zoom in to highlight sporadic experiences of selected "pieces"' (2015, p. 333). The reenactment game rejects both the eclectic movement between positions of books and film and simultaneously rejects the zero focalisation perspective of the chess player common in wargames. In the reenactment game we play as a single 'piece' (agent) on the 'board' (conflict situation) and learn precisely from the challenges of restriction this information field implies. The various military tools (technologies of surveillance, communication etc.) that extend the perception of soldiers should still be a part of the game. However, information offered by these tools should be presented to the player only in the manner it can be experienced by a single agent (see the following sections on information).

Previous work (Chapman, 2016) has concentrated on reenactment in first-person shooter games, that is at the level of individual soldiers. However, games on higher tactical and strategic levels can also offer reenactment as long as they isolate the experience (information field and challenges) of a particular commanding agent in this strategic system. As the original agent's experience in such roles will typically involve understanding the battlefield through perceptual tools (e.g. maps, reports, surveillance footage/information) rather than direct perception of the space, this often means inhibiting the player perspective in comparison to conventional strategy games.

Goals

Goals are integral to the relationship between player and agent to ensure the reenactment experience encourages the player to learn what we wish them to. Goals influence the player's *intention* and thus *attention*. Hence, if students are to *attend* to particular affordances of the wargame environment, then goals are a central design feature. As such, if students are to learn through reenactment, game developers should ensure that the goals resonate with the practice the students train for. This encourages them towards the affordances of the environment that we deem potentially useful in future situations (based on our understanding of, or guidelines formed from, previous situations).

Learning, from the perspective of ecological psychology, is about educating *intention* and *attention*, with goals being a facilitator (Young, 2004a). In training the aim is that students treat the game seriously and pursue the educational outcomes. The agency offered by games means that some goals would only emerge during play. As Young (2004b) points out: 'The education of intention describes how new intentions emerge as compactified fields during the pursuit of existing goals. Consider that as a video game unfolds, new sub goals and problems emerge that allow for new intentions to be adopted' (p. 4).

This has implications for reenactment wargames. The context of play should encourage players to adopt broad goals, which are meaningful in relation to the training goals. A degree of alignment between the goals of the player and the agent makes it possible for players to discover affordances that may be useful to future scenarios. As noted earlier, reenactment experiences are inherently unpredictable because perception and action are based on activity *in situ*. However, clear goals can be used as to narrow this gap between player and agent. For developers it becomes important to ensure that players can adopt useful intentions (and thus attend to useful affordances) and prevent them entering the 'gamer mode', that is the risk that players just focus on the goals of the game and not learning objectives (Frank, 2012). In the framework we put forth here, that would be a player behaviour that utilise gameplay affordances unavailable in real situations (c.f. Linderoth, 2004, 2012). Hence students should be provided with goals (implicitly or explicitly) that exert pressure similar to those experienced by agents in the previous environments from which we wish students to learn. This should also drive students to attend to the information in, and contexts of, the environment in ways that test or develop their skills of perception.

However, some degree of discrepancy is necessary and/or unavoidable. It is inevitable that students will have other goals than the agents (e.g. students may wish to demonstrate understanding to instructors, but do not have to worry about surviving the exercise). Furthermore, sometimes we may want players to discover new goals (intentions).

Whilst goals are important, they are rarely solely internal to the wargame. The system design may exert pressures pointing to particular goals as necessities, but often much of this work is done externally to the game in the framing and contextualisation offered by instruction. Often secondary goals implicit in real battlefield situations, such as preserving one's life and the lives of one's soldiers, must be made explicit in the wargame to prevent players utilising affordances they cannot rely on in real situations. Even if this can be remedied somewhat by intrinsic goals (e.g. scoring partly based on number of friendly units left), the wider ethical and humanitarian aspects of such a goal are difficult to include as part of the game system and must be reinforced by surrounding social and educational structures.

Challenge

Considering goals and environmental pressures necessitates considering *challenge*, a core aspect of games. Educational wargames should confront students with challenges expected of future conflict environments, aiding in the development of transferable skills. These challenges should be constructed partly in line with past events likely to hold relevance to future ones. Within ecological psychology, actions are divided into two categories: exploratory (what possibilities for action you can perceive) and performatory (what actions you can do) (Reed, 1996, pp. 80–82). 'The exploratory aspect of actions is to yield knowledge about the affordances of the specific situation. The performatory aspect of action is about realizing [utilising] affordances that are already discovered' (Gibson & Pick, 2000, p. 21). Linderoth (2013) argues that challenges in games can be similarly divided. Some challenges in games primarily test the exploratory aspect of action and some game challenges primarily test the performatory aspect. Games with a high degree of exploratory challenges are those where performing actions are relatively easy but *knowing which actions to take* is challenging. Chess is one example. For most humans moving chess pieces is easy, but knowing which pieces to move and where to move it is challenging when facing a competent opponent. Comparatively, in games of performatory challenge the actions the player should take are apparent, but performing these actions is difficult. For example, in a running race the action to be taken is clear (run faster than the opponent) but the performing of this action is challenging. As Linderoth stresses (2013), games often contain both forms of challenge but generally have an emphasis on one or the other.

It is important to think about what kinds of past challenges can be reenacted with ecological validity in different kinds of games. Digital games have been argued to be capable of offering reenactment of historical exploratory challenges (Chapman, 2016, pp. 180–230). This includes command during conflict because the performatory abstraction of using a controller does not really matter when reenacting this challenge of the past that was also primarily exploratory (giving orders is easy, knowing which orders to give is challenging). This is possible because the digital game can produce and maintain (despite player agency) visual information that is structurally similar to that experienced by historical agents, meaning that player and agent have part of their information field in common. 'This commonality allows for the possibility of the player to reenact exploratory historical challenges that were part of some of the practices of the original historical agent, because these challenges rely only on differentiating visual information' (Chapman, 2016, p. 184). This means that games can allow players to reenact exploratory challenges *related* to performatory challenges (e.g. skills of perception related to the use of weaponry or tactical movement). However, digital games are generally not well suited to the reenactment of performatory challenges themselves – the abstraction between facing physical challenges (such as carrying or using heavy gear) and sitting down with a game controller is too great. These games can make us *aware* of the performatory challenges of the past (and even make arguments about difficulty) but this is through the use of metaphor rather than reenactment.

These limitations, however, become less problematic the further we move up the echelons of command (hence the concentration on strategy games below). Such roles are naturally more focused on exploratory challenges and thus work well within reenactment games. All this means that care should be taken as to exactly what past challenges we seek to represent in the reenactment wargame and player roles should be those focused on exploratory challenges, with performatory challenges left to other kinds of exercises. It is important to attend to the limitations of reenactment games alongside their possibilities.

This said, whereas the challenges of command (e.g. negotiating and collating limited information to inform tactical/operational actions) are generally exploratory, the ability to give clear, coordinated orders to multiple actors through necessarily limited means of communication has a performatory aspect. Single player games struggle to represent this. In *Brothers in Arms* (a WW2 FPS), for example, there is no chance for failure in giving an order. Orders are always received and understood by the fire teams under the player's command when the player presses the relevant button. In reality, of course, miscommunication is always possible. Some wargames attempt to model this possibility through randomness (e.g. dice rolls), once again an abstraction that significantly differs from the actual challenges of interpersonal, multi-personnel communication. However, multiplayer wargames can offer reenactment of the challenges of communication, as long as information *mode*, *type* and *quantity* resonate with the experience of past agents.

Information

Thinking about different types of challenges helps focus us on what skills it is possible to develop through game-based reenactment. Considering the exploratory challenges of visual and auditory perception involved in command leads us to consider the information fields that should confront players of reenactment games. As information in the environment is what specifies affordances to an actor, if we wish players to become attuned to the affordances of particular situations then they must experience the important invariant information in training. As noted, in the reenactment wargame this often means deliberately restricting information from players or delivering it in purposely less efficient ways in comparison to conventional wargames. These black boxing techniques reflect the inherent limitations of both human perception and technologies used to extend perception/action. The movements of the battlefield are therefore not the only challenge in a reenactment game; negotiating the available information itself is a challenge. Design in such games should therefore focus on the information flow from the environment, particularly towards the player and the exploratory challenges this entails. Attending to these flows requires examining three particular information categories: *type, quantity*, and *mode*.

Information Type

Three types of information must be considered in the player/agent relationship: Firstly, there is information experienced by both player and agent. As this allows reenactment to occur at all, this type of information should ideally outweigh the others in the game environment. However, whilst as far as possible information available to agents should be available to players, inevitably there will be other types of information. Secondly, there is environmental information experienced by agents that cannot feasibly be experienced by the player (e.g. information specifying the affordances of real violence). Thirdly, there is also information available to the player that was not experienced by the agent. For example, the game room may contain extra visual information and the wider educational environment will contain information that specifies, for example, that the exercise can be stopped if the player needs/wishes it to, something unavailable in real conflict situations without severe penalties. Some of these discrepancies are inevitable, but some can be remedied. For example, extra-mimetic information in the player environment can be partly removed by having the game take place in a darkened room or curtained area (a technique used in cinemas to encourage audiences to attend primarily to the affordances of the screen). This is particularly important when using digital games because the information beyond the screen often specifies affordances unavailable to the original agent. Sometimes we may wish to train players to attend to relevant information despite surrounding distraction. However, even in such cases the distracting information should relate to likely future scenarios that we wish skills of differentiation to transfer to.

From the ecological perspective, invariance in the environment is key to learning, in this case invariance in the information shared between past, likely future and game environments. Because affordances are complicated relations between environments and the perception and action cycles of organisms, removing or adding particular pieces of information can result in unpredictable results. This is indicated by the complexity of experiments of ecological psychology attempting to isolate invariants in even relatively simple activities such as catching a ball or walking upstairs (for an overview see Gibson, 1991). This means that similarities *and* differences between the situated domains of practice, and hence the information fields of agent and player, should be constantly attended to because we do not always know precisely what aspects of the environment might contain important information about the affordances to be perceived/utilised.

Information Quantity

It is impossible to have perfect information about an environment available to us, particularly when dealing with something as complex, rapidly changing, and large-scale as armed conflict and war. Despite this, many wargames offer players comprehensive information about and/or vast perspectives on the state of the represented conflict. This is appropriate when using wargames as models for explanation and tools of representation that extend human perception, thus offering students as much information as possible about the scenario. Such games will not, however, prepare students for the challenges of information limitation within individual roles in conflict, as reenactment games attempt. In reenactment games the idea is to directly train skills rather than offer only theoretical knowledge. Giving the players' perception support that is not part of the setting they train for will interrupt this learning process by eradicating challenge.

As Linderoth (2012) argues, progression in games is not necessarily an indication of learning. Instead, the nature of the challenge offered in relation to the tools provided to the player must be considered. Tools to aid differentiation common to mainstream games (e.g. those that visually highlight important aspects of the game environment) are therefore frequently unsuitable for reenactment games. Such wargames should therefore not offer, for example, maps with real-time updated information about unit movements (i.e. requiring no coordination with other kinds of information/actors in order to update) and without the possibility for this information to be wrong, ambiguous, or limited, despite the fact that this is often part of the design of conventional wargames. Instead, a map in a reenactment wargame should function only as a tool to aid visualisation of information acquired by other means rather than a direct source of information about the environment. This maintains the challenges of gathering multiple and often incomplete sources of information to understand a current conflict environment.

This is not to say that this issue is entirely ignored in conventional wargame design. For example, 'fog of war' mechanics attempt to simulate some of the challenges of limited information. 'Players may, for instance, make unwarranted assumptions about the location of enemy forces due to a lack of information; they might equally do so in the real world, and such imperfection of information does no violence to the intellectual validity of cause and effect or critical analysis' (Rubel, 2006, p. 115). The reenactment game takes this even further and restricts the information available to players to only that which could feasibly be available to individual agents in the situations upon which the game is based.

The quantity of information available from other players should be carefully monitored. For example, if agents did not have access to body language (another form of information) when communicating with other actors (e.g. through radio or written communication) then neither should players, as this may interrupt the challenges of these kinds of communication. This also means that outgoing information from the player to other actors should be similarly restricted in terms of quantity to maintain challenge. For example, the delivery of detail is frequently impacted by the performative pressures introduced by time-sensitive situations in relation to the means of communication available and should therefore be represented through the challenges of the reenactment game.

Information Mode

The final information category *mode* focuses on the *means* by which information is presented to the player. In a reenactment wargame the information the player receives should, where possible, be presented through the modes in which this would be experienced in actual conflict environments. If information about unit movements was/is likely to be received through radio or text-based messages, then the game should similarly present players with information in this way.[3] This gives players opportunities to develop skills of information differentiation, that are key to performance in future environments (based on our understanding of previous ones). Such skills would not be possible to develop in relation to alternate abstract information sources (such as dice rolls and real-time updated maps). If the modality of the presented (and outgoing) information is not attended to then a game is probably not training the same skill. Consider an oil painter suddenly being asked to swap to watercolour painting. Some aspects of their training might be transferable, but it is clear that the affordances of the situation have somewhat changed. Different modes of information also have different affordances in terms of specificity/ambiguity, with different modes entailing different kinds of *epistemological commitment* (Kress, 2010). For instance, whilst drawings must make commitments as to spatial, shape and size relations, language must make a commitment to naming and the relations between names, that is X *has* Y (Machin, 2013). Mode therefore plays an important part in the black boxing that is intrinsic to the reenactment wargame's representation of the information challenges of conflict command.

Mode must therefore be a focus during the development of educational wargames intended for reenactment. The precise affordances information specifies necessarily has at least some relation to mode (i.e. content is partly determined by form) and different skills may therefore be needed to differentiate different modes of information, even if the information sought for perception indicates the same thing about the environment. This is particularly important in reenactment games because they are not only about teaching the underlying mechanics of warfare but also aim to train players in the skills necessary to negotiate the exploratory challenges of obtaining sufficient information to negotiate these mechanics given limited means.

Despite the obvious logistical advantages of conventional approaches to designing wargames with limited numbers of information modes, commanders and their immediate subordinates must become skilled at synthesizing many different modes of information in order to understand a conflict environment (e.g. audio communications, text communications, images on maps, video feeds and intelligence information such as radar or sonar etc.). Reenactment wargames, through concentrating on information mode, ensure the best opportunities to directly train skills related to the negotiation of these kinds of information fields.

Conclusion

In this chapter we have sketched a framework for the development of wargames with an educational purpose. The framework rests on two interlocked ideas: (1) Wargames can, in a productive way, be seen as historical reenactment. (2) Ecological psychology is a theory that provides new and interesting heuristics for the development, use and analysis of wargames in military education.

Taken together, these ideas lead to a discussion about the relation between the affordances and information in the game and the affordances and information in the historical context. One of our main conclusions is that a wargame has somewhat limited possibilities when it comes to teach performatory aspects of action but rather high potentials to teach how to overcome exploratory challenges i.e. allowing players to learn how to discern important information in the situation. A necessary condition for this is that the game builds on the principles of reenactment, that is it places the player within the system as an actor, rather than putting the player in control of the full system. The ecological perspective, being a strict non-dualistic theory of mind, rejects an understanding of perception and cognition as a processes of enrichment, that is the idea that the mind adds something to imperfect, sparse information. This perspective instead holds that information is rich and overwhelming. Learning is about differentiation rather than enrichment (Gibson & Pick, 2000).

The principles of reenactment are discussed in relation to six different aspects of game development. Using them means to be aware of the *agent to player relation* in terms of similarity and differences in regard to affordances. The framework stresses that *goals* should be designed to create incentive structures that point the player to the learning objectives. When designing *challenges*, the developers should regard the differences between exploratory and performatory modes of action. Finally, *information type*, *information quantity*, and *information mode* should be designed in such a way that the player is forced to make distinctions that in some respects overlap the situation they train for. Ideally the players' and the agents' information type, quantity and mode should overlap to some degree (have invariant features).

By offering this type of reenactment, grounded in tangible affordances of skill, action and challenge, games also sidestep the potential epistemological problems introduced when reenactment is focused on more ephemeral notions such as 'empathy' or 'thought' (as it tends to be when discussed in relation to historical writing). Indeed, the medium offers support for Reed's claim that the ecological approach 'offers the possibility of genuine cross-cultural and cross-temporal comparisons' (1996, p. 188). As such, the ecological approach allows the evaluation of reenactment experiences in a new way, one 'rooted more in ideas about the reenactment of challenge, skill, action and perception than in the reenactment of consciousness' (Chapman, 2016, p. 181).

Reenactment games aim to prepare students for future conflict environments as much as possible by allowing them to experience the challenges of the information fields that such environments are likely to involve (by drawing on previous situations predicted to be relevant). However, of course real environments are unpredictable, chaotic, and based on many variables (not the least of which is the actions of many actors). As such, whilst it seems possible that reenactment wargames might teach students how to negotiate particular kinds of information fields and the challenges of doing so, the underlying events that these information fields describe may differ in future situations – in essence meaning that reenactment activities reach the limitations of all pedagogical exercises.

Acknowledgements

The research presented here was funded by the Swedish Defence University, the University of Skövde and the University of Gothenburg. The authors gratefully acknowledge the financial support and the productive collaboration.

Notes

1 This is also connected to the idea of learning by reenacting past thought processes, often argued to be a key part of the historian's method (e.g. see Collingwood, 2000).
2 This raises the question of whether this system beyond the player's perception need even be a game at all.
3 This can be logistically trying, but supplementary options are available that maintain some modality. For example, pre-recorded sound files can be used instead of live radio transmissions. This, however, depends on the emergence of the game structure (more emergence meaning greater difficulty implementing this). But in games where some of the event structure is decided *a priori* in the construction of the challenge environment, this is a feasible option for part of the information experienced by players.

References

Agnew, V. (2004). An introduction: What is reenactment? *Criticism*, *46*(3), 327–339.
Chapman, A. (2016). *Digital games as history*. Routledge.
Collingwood, R. G. (2000). *Idea of history*. Oxford University Press.
Frank, A. (2012). Gaming the game: A study of the gamer mode in educational wargaming. *Simulation & Gaming*, *43*(1), 118–132. https://doi.org/10.1177/1046878111408796
Gibson, E. J. (1991). *An odyssey in learning and perception*. MIT Press.
Gibson, E. J., & Pick, A. D. (2000). *An ecological approach to perceptual learning and development*. Oxford University Press.
Gibson, J. J. (1986). *The ecological approach to visual perception*. Lawrence Erlbaum Associates.
Granberg, S., & Hulterström, P. (2015, July 17–21). Ecological psychology: A framework for wargame design. In *ISAGA/JASAG 2015, 46th ISAGA conference*, Kyoto, Japan.
Greeno, J. G., Collins, A. M., & Resnick, L. B. (1996). Cognition and learning. In D. C. Berliner & R. C. Calfee (Eds.), *Handbook of educational psychology* (pp. 15–46). Macmillan Library Reference.
Johnson, K. M. (2015). Rethinking (re)doing: Historical re-enactment and/as historiography. *Rethinking History*, *19*(2), 193–206.
Kress, G. (2010). *Multimodality*. Routledge.
Linderoth, J. (2004). *Datorspelandets mening: Bortom idén om den interaktiva illusionen*. [PhD Thesis, Göteborgs Universitet]. GUPEA. https://gupea.ub.gu.se/handle/2077/16217
Linderoth, J. (2012). Why gamers don't learn more: An ecological approach to games as learning environments. *Journal of Gaming and Virtual Worlds*, *4*(1), 45–62.
Linderoth, J. (2013). Beyond the digital divide: An ecological approach to gameplay. *ToDIGRA: Transactions of the Digital Games Research Association*, *1*(1), 85–113.
Linderoth, J., & Bennerstedt, U. (2007, September). This is not a door: An ecological approach to computer games. In *Situated play: Proceedings of DiGRA (Digital Games Research Association) Conference*, *4*, 600–609. http://www.digra.org/digital-library/publications/this-is-not-a-door-an-ecological-approach-to-computer-games/
Machin, D. (2013). What is multimodal critical discourse studies? *Critical Discourse Studies*, *10*(4), 347–55.

McCall, J. (2011). *Gaming the past.* Routledge.
Perla, P. (1990). *The art of wargaming.* U.S. Naval Institute Press.
Pihlainen, K. (2017). *The work of history: Constructivism and a politics of the past.* Routledge.
Reed, E. S. (1996). *Encountering the world: Toward an ecological psychology.* Oxford University Press.
Rubel, R. (2006). The epistemology of wargaming. *Naval War College Review, 59*(2), 107–128.
Sabin, P. (2012). *Simulating war.* Continuum.
Sabin, P. (2015). Wargaming in higher education: Contributions and challenges. *Arts and Humanities in Higher Education, 14*(4), 329–348.
Sellberg, C. (2017). *Training to become a master mariner in a simulator-based environment: The instructors' contributions to professional learning.* [PhD Thesis, Göteborgs Universitet]. GUPEA. https://gupea.ub.gu.se/handle/2077/54327
Wilhelmsson, U. (2008). Game ego presence in video and computer games. In A. Fernandez, O. Leino, & H. Wirman (Eds.), *Extending experiences: Structure, analysis and design of computer game player experience* (pp. 56–72). Lapland University Press.
Young, M. (2004a). An ecological psychology of instructional design: Learning and thinking by perceiving-acting systems. In D. H. Jonassen (Ed.), *Handbook of research for educational communications and technology* (pp. 80–108). Erlbaum.
Young, M. (2004b, July 23). An ecological description of video games in education. In *Proceedings of the international conference on education and information systems technologies and applications* (EISTA), Orlando, FL. http://web.uconn.edu/myyoung/EISTA04Proceed.pdf.

7 The Grasping Eye
Wargames and the Ideal-Typical Field Commander's Inner Vision

Tomas Karlsson

Introduction

In a study of renaissance warfare biographies, historian Noa Yuval Harari points out that battle narratives as told by eyewitnesses often utilized 'the birds eye point of view', as if told from an 'all knowing' and 'objective' historian, even though the stories were of events experienced by the writers (Harari, 2004, p. 85), and much like wargaming rules, often 'as dry and colorless as a CV' (p. 79). But besides this dry recounting of 'facts', there is an element in the cultural understanding of war that has a dramatic streak. We might think of tales of warrior heroes and heroic deeds, great characters like Alexander the Great or Napoleon Bonaparte that leap on to the stage of history and through success on the battlefield change the course of history. We know that war means suffering and pain, yet many of us are drawn to those kinds of tales. Some of us like to play wargames, and playact with the fantasy as one of those great figures of the past. We wage wars of fantasy in an orderly and safe space of a gaming table, in an act of simulation that strikes the right balance of feeling realistic, whilst leaving out the horror, pain and suffering that we know is part and parcel of real armed conflicts. It is a guilty pleasure imagining oneself stepping into the shoes of a great commander of the past. But what kind of ideal type do we imagine that we are in those moments? How do we remember wars of the past when we play a wargame?

This chapter combines military history, masculinity studies and game studies, with the aim to use those different perspectives to provide a reflection on how the imagined internal cognitive qualities of an ideal-typical field commander echoes throughout the ages as an assemblage in wargames, and how wargames may be used as tools of playful identification with ideal-typical field commanders. I explore how aspects of the alluring quality of ideal-typical field commanders' *coup d'euil* is codified in wargames. I argue that both rules and aesthetics in wargames are used as attempts to codify those inherent qualities. Furthermore, the reader is introduced to the ideal typical field commander as a masculine stereotype, as portrayed in some works of military theory from the Enlightenment era. This gives a backdrop to a discussion on how wargamers may playact as field commanders in an act of playful identification, and I explore the idea that the field commanders also playact as gamers. I argue that descriptions of the field commander's inner cognitive abilities and descriptions of war in 18th- and 19th-century military theory point toward making the ideal-typical field commander into a gamer on the field of battle.

In this chapter I also discuss masculine warrior virtues, and those imagined feats of warrior commanders as expressions of some of those virtues on yesteryears' battlefield. These are things that are remembered in awe, and are prevalent in the way contemporary wargames contextualize historical warrior-commanders. In this text I will discuss how some of their qualities have been codified in wargames.

This chapter draws on sources stretching from works of military theory to contemporary boardgames. Besides references to wargames, I also use instructional notes from two 18th-century field commanders, Frederick the Great and Maurice de Saxe. Carl von Clausewitz's idea of war as a gambling game is also briefly discussed. I also use archival material in the form of commercials from print media, and essays on wargaming as a hobby from the periodical *Vecko-Journalen* from 1915, as well as Swedish 19th-century wargames. Miniature wargame rules and board wargames are used as examples of how one might approach wargames as expressions of what military thinkers from the Enlightenment period and onwards called the *coup d'euil*.

Wargames as Expressions of an Ideal-Typical Field Commander Mind's Eye

In 18th-century military theory, it was commonplace to think that certain field commanders had the ability that enabled him to play out the probable outcomes of various maneuvers in each tactical situation before their inner gaze. This internal cognitive quality was referred to as *coup d'euil*. Translated *coup d'euil* means roughly a glance that takes in a whole view. But in the military sciences of the Enlightenment, the term had a more specific meaning, defined as a skill deemed essential to a military commander. According to Frederick the Great, *coup d'euil* was twofold. First, it was the ability to judge how many troops could be deployed at a given geographical space, which included the ability to calculate space and distance. This was an ability that had to be learned by practice. The other was the ability to 'distinguish at first sight all the advantages of which any given space of ground is capable', and also this skill could be honed 'to perfection though a man be not born with absolute military genius' (Frederick II, 2005, article IV, p. 24).

A successful field commander must have the ability to 'read the battlefield' and intuitively recognize what features are of military importance as well as what possibilities for action are available to him with regards to the landscape and resources available in terms of soldiers and materiel. He must also be able to recognize the potential abilities for action available to his opponents.

To be able to 'read' means to able to translate signs in a system of symbolic representation into meaning, and a wargame is a symbolic representation of certain aspects of warfare. If *coup d'euil* could be taught, as Frederick suggested, and if a wargame is a symbolic representation of those features in war that are considered tactically important, then it could be argued that the line between 'recreational' wargaming and wargames as professional training tools is thin. Though wargames can be 'either a hobby or deadly serious' (Sutton-Smith, 1997, p. 7), one should not overemphasize the differences between the civilian and military sphere. In the digital age there are many examples where wargames, such as tactical training tools or flight simulators, are similar in many respects and use the same kind of symbolic representation and physical modeling (Lenoir & Lowood, 2005; Lowood, 2016, pp. 83–106).

This, however, is not a new phenomenon. Consider the wargame constructed by Johann Ludwig Christian Hellwig (1743–1831). He was a multidisciplinary academic, a professor of philosophy in Braunschweig, teaching mathematics and natural history. He also taught military science to young officers, and his wargame was designed to be a pedagogical tool for educating officers in the art of war. Originally published in 1780 in Braunschweig, his wargame predates and probably inspired the more famous Prussian wargame designers such as father and son von Reisswitz. The Reisswitz's wargame has been described by many authors and scholars (Hilgers, 2012; Perla & Curry, 2011, pp. 31–32; Peterson, 2012, pp. 214–216; Vego, 2012). Hellwig perfected his wargame over the years. In 1803 a version called *Das Kriegspiel* was published, and a version of that game can be found in the Swedish book *Hand-bibliothek för sällskapsnöjen, eller systematiskt ordnande spel, lekar och konster* (*A collection of games to be played in pursuit of leisure and pleasure* (1838–39)). Hellwig's *Kriegspiel* is presented as an effort to 'in an almost chess-like way, closely examine how war is conducted' (Hand-bibliothek, 1838–1839, p. 586). It is a contest of skill in coordinating troop movements in time and space. The game was brought to conclusion 'not as in chess with the capture by a certain figure, but by conquering the land of the opponent . . . above all by capturing his fortresses' (Hand-bibliothek, 1838–1839, p. 610). Players were awarded points in the form of 'victory signs' by destroying enemy troops and capturing strategic points.

> The more victory signs a gamer possesses at the end of the game . . . the greater his glory and profit, provided the game is played with money at stake.
>
> (Hand-bibliothek, 1838–1839, p. 612)

In Hellwig's Kriegspiel, geography impacts troop movement and decides what is possible to achieve for the player. Various troops have various abilities.

For instance, if a player wants troops to cross the river running across the game-board, then markers representing engineering troops can deploy pontoon bridges at selected points to facilitate crossing. Engineers can also perform other tasks that change the function of the terrain on the game-board, such as build or destroy fieldworks. A player can also choose to raze his own cities, since a ravaged city is worth less to the opponent if captured, which was also a recommended tactic (Hand-bibliothek, 1838–1839, p. 588).

In Hellwig's wargame a player can perfect his *coup d'euil* during game set up by combining the interrelated functions of the gaming pieces to the best of his abilities.

> In times of war the commander will place his troops in accordance with his wishes and his knowledge. . . . The greatest feat in the art of war is to position one's army in such a way that it can be used effectively on the attack as well as the defense.
> (Hand-bibliothek, 1838–1839, pp. 608–609)

In this game the *coup d'euil* is translated into the representation of the battlefield and the rule mechanics for moving troops in different types of terrain, as well as the military value of this terrain. The player sees the battlefield though the *coup d'euil*, and the codified landscape help her do the planning.

Great Battles of Alexander (Herman & Berg, 1991) is an example of a game that codifies different historical commanders' *coup d'euil* by rating their skill as field commanders. As the name suggests, it features historical battles of Alexander the Great, a tabletop hex and counter wargame to be played solitaire or against a human opponent. This game features representations of a variety of historical battles, with the geography of the battlefield codified as hexagons. The troops, represented by cardboard counters, have different strength and weakness, partly depending on what type of ground they use for military operations. However, the only counters with real agency are the commanders and subcommanders. Each player controls several of these, who are activated in turn to move troops. To reflect the skills of the different commanders, they have been given ratings showing how well they rally their troops and how many moves their troops are allowed to make. Every commander has a set of ratings that, among other things, decide how many troops they may move and the likelihood that they will 'activate' to move troops. To decide who gets to move when, the commanders have an 'initiative rating' which 'denotes his basic ability to control forces and make rapid decisions' (Herman & Berg, 2014, p. 8). These commanders include various historical persons such as Darius III the King of Persia, and various Macedonian commanders including Philip II of Macedon, Parmenion and Ptolemy. And then we have Alexander, with the highest ratings of them all. This means that in the game, the player who commands an army that is commanded by Alexander can do more with less.

If you play a scenario featuring Alexander the Great the game the rules in a sense force you to view Alexander as a great field commander, since his abilities usually allow his troops to move and fight more efficiently than the opponent. Commanders can also influence the outcome of the battle through bonuses in fights and in attempts to rally fleeing troops. Alexander has the highest rating possible of any character in the game. This makes it possible for the player using his as the commander, not only to 'to do more things' in every turn, but also to use the game-environment more efficiently. I would suggest, such a player has more affordances to play with. This design feature, with ratings of historical commanders, is integrated in many wargaming rule systems. They are an attempt to present the knowledge a commander had about troops, other commanders and terrain, and how those things interrelate. According to the designers of *Great Battles of Alexander*: 'It was Alexander's genius that he could combine all of these aspects: it is the player's challenge to see if he can equal – or even-best him' (Herman & Berg, 2014, p. 2). In this example, one could argue that the designers of the game have codified their interpretation of each commander's *coup d'euil*, and consequently their ability to operationalize available resources according to changing circumstances in the game.

To some degree, wargames codify cultural norms about warfare and some aspects of the 'art' or 'science' of war in a cultural context. As visual aids they streamline the wargamer's perception by enhancing certain aspects of war while downplaying others, both by rules and by aesthetics. A hexagon map, for instance, portrays a landscape in a simplified way, as an estimation of direction and position, and the rules tell you what you can and cannot do in each hex. Thus, it shows the relative potential military usability of various places for different troops. In that way the wargame makes it easier to show the potential usability of the combined troops, material and landscape by means of codification into rules. In ecological psychology the concept 'affordance' is used to describe how the environment one interacts with is perceived as a set of possibilities to utilize (Gibson, 1979). Granberg and Hulterström define affordance as 'a resource that the environment offers to a specific agent, who in turn has both the capability to see and use it (2016, p. 6). What affordance an actor perceives and/or has the necessary capabilities to utilize varies. Affordances are always dependent on any agent's given ability of perceiving the resource and translate it into something that is useful for the agent's purposes. Granberg and Hulterström (2016) suggest that such an approach is well suited to be codified into the design of wargames. The usefulness of tools at the commander's disposal in a tactical setting, such as battalions of troops and tanks, depends on how well they interact with a variety of factors in the environment. This is something different than the 'simulation-approach' used in professional wargames, such as command bunker and cockpit simulations, wherein procedurals of decision making in a complex man-machine-environments interaction is portrayed.

The focus on portraying the combat environment in total as an affordance to be used by the commander, with a varying degree of skill, is in many respects similar to what 18th-century military theorists called *coup d'euil*. According to 18th-century military sciences, a commander with a good *coup d'euil* is someone who is able to perceive the environment, potential obstacles, and the resources available in such a way as to facilitate planning and execution of battlefield maneuvers. It means thinking in terms of moves and potential countermoves in order to be prepared for contingencies. *Coup d'euil* is the cognitive ability to recognize and utilize the affordances of a tactical situation.

Coup d'euil means the cognitive skill required to plan an action, it is not the same as taking action. *Coup d'euil* is a cognitive portrayal of warfare and the commander from the vantage point of potential agency, having a superior ability to recognize what can be done in any given tactical situation, whilst simultaneously calculating the risk and potential rewards resulting from those actions before taking action.

War as a Game of Playful Identification of What Might Have Happened

Since warfare and the experience of battle traditionally has been an arena reserved for 'men', or even an activity that defines 'manhood' (Ehrenreich, 2011, p. 127), it is not a great stretch of the imagination to regard the commander of an army as a masculine stereotype. 'Masculinity' is a changing set of qualities that may refer to male bodies or certain activities that in certain contexts are associated with being 'masculine'. It describes how someone at a certain time and place ought to behave to be masculine (Connell, 1996). Since notions of history and notions of culture are interrelated, using what is perceived as a common history can operationalize notions war in the past as justification and inspiration. In this respect, the game is an example of how notions of military history and masculinity is used to justify warfare. The commander's role was to represent this collective entity on the stage of history to settle old scores by playing the game of war. One might even think of a militarized male gaze, which codifies the observed world and categorizes it into its military usefulness utilizing *coup d'euil* symbolically translated into a wargame.

Masculine stereotypes can be used as objects of playful identification in a game of mimicry on the individual level as well. In one of the first commercial wargame rules for toy soldiers, *Little Wars*, written by science fiction author H. G. Wells, there is a description of a playful act of transformation. It reminds us of those kinds of playful activities game theorist Roger Caillois (2001) and others call mimicry, a playful act that involves imitation and roleplaying. Upon starting a game, Wells says that as a part of getting in the mood for the wargame, he constructs a fictional stereotypical ideal commander. Indeed, he says that he likes to think of himself being transformed into a character called 'colonel Wells', and the transformation is profound as H. G. Wells undergoes an act of playful identification with a stereotypical masculine warrior hero:

> His inky fingers become large, manly hands, his drooping scholastic back stiffens, his elbows go out, his etiolated complexion corrugates and darkens, his moustaches increase and grow and spread, and curl up horribly; a large, red scar, a saber cut, grows lurid over one eye. He expands – all over he expands. He clears his throat startlingly, lugs at the still growing ends of his moustache, and says, with just a faint and fading doubt in his voice as to whether he can do it, 'Yas, Sir!'.
> (Wells, 1913, pp. 63–64)

In other acts of playful identification players may make themselves into kings. During the first winter of World War One, readers of a Swedish newspaper could find an advertisement for a wargame in which people could relive the 'excitement' of the first autumn of the conflict in Europe (Dagens Nyheter, 1914). The game was called *Floods krigsspel* (1914, [transl. *Flood's wargame*]). The advertisement read that the game was an accurate representation of the now ongoing war. 'You will be astonished as to what lengths the actual war can be replicated on the game-map'. Each player plays the role of a supreme commander of the warring nations as, according to the advertisement for the game 'Each is his own Hindenburg!'. Flood's wargame was not a propagandistic tool, but more of an educational one. The players represented all warring parties, and each warring party had a roughly equal chance to win. War, the advertisement informs us, was exciting and the outcome uncertain, and 'excitement brought to you by this game is stupendous!'.

Reading the rule's pamphlet, one sees that the games designer chose to portray the causes war as a combination of realpolitik and notions of masculine virtues, such as honor, duty, and an obligation to live up to the standards of a perceived heritage. The German player was, for instance, told that (translated from Swedish by the author):

> As the brave German army goes into combat you feel the power it wields. Everyone recognizes your courage, the strength of your arms and your exceptional army and its leaders. They hold their breath and expect to see the arms of Germany covered with glory once more.
> (Floods krigsspel, 1914, pp. 7–8)

For the French player it was the proud heritage of Napoleon and the history of war against Germany became something to measure one's efforts against since:

> . . . there is a huge task before you, taking on Germany, but history shows what your armies are capable of. Perhaps now is the time for Your

revenge and maybe once again You will appear covered with that glory that always surrounded the great Napoleon.

(Floods krigsspel, 1914, p. 8)

Accordingly, both Russia and Great Britain was forced into this war since it was expected of them to keep promises made (Floods krigsspel, 1914, p. 8). We might assume that a true gentleman is expected to be someone who always keep his promises. Consequently, the decision to go to war stems in part from a desire to live up to ideal typical masculine notions of honor. This wargame can be viewed as an attempt to use the symbolic representation of *coup d'euil* on a macro scale to show what might happen if the different warring nations acted in particular ways. It was not a 'serious' military simulation of such potential events, but since it was marketed as a parlor game to be played amongst friends, perhaps it can be described as an attempt to facilitate a discussion amongst those friends about potential outcomes.

What is striking in *Floods krigsspel* is the way masculine stereotypical qualities tied to a historical heritage of military culture and nations are used to explain why the various nations contemplate going to war. Across the board, going to war had all the connotations of living up to the perceived proud heritage of warriors, including to be a trustworthy and forthright person to prove one's worth. It signals the idea of absolute necessity for a collective, such as a nation or army, to live up to ideals of culturally specific notions of masculinity.

Similar descriptions are found in one of Wells' contemporaries, Ossian Elgström. He was a Swedish author of adventure books for boys who also liked to play wargames with his toy soldiers. Elgström published his own set of wargame rules for toy soldiers in 1914. In a Swedish magazine article, he described his hobby and mused over the 'joy of being king in a land of one's own making and to kill and fight to one's hearts content' (Elgström, 1915, p. 372). Elgström's rules provide tips on how a wargamer should draw maps that mimic those found in works of military history and how to document the battles, so that one could go back and 'remember one's feats on the field of battle'.

A modern example of playful identification with the ideal typical field commander as a masculine stereotype is *Black Powder*, a set of miniature wargaming rules published by Warlord Games. With a description echoing Wells' and Elgström's jargon, *Black Powder* is intended for 'military inclined gentlemen with straight backs, bristling beards and rheumy eyes that have seen a thing or two' (Priestley, 2009). The text goes on to warn those who find no excitement in tales of historical combat to 'be glad that you have saved yourselves the discomforting spectacle of grown men attempting to relive great conflicts of history with armies of toy soldiers' (Priestley, 2009).

Hail Caesar, another of Warlord Games' miniature wargaming rules, presents similar sentiments of nostalgia:

> Our ambition is to breathe life into the warriors and tales of former days; to paint a picture that lacks nothing of the colour and splendour of an era long past; even if imagination alone must paint the hue and cry of battle, the whistling flight of arrows and the flash of plunging spears ... And though our efforts may never topple tyrants nor change the history's long course, let us summon the ghosts of Hannibal, Xerxes, Alexander and even Caesar himself, to stand at our shoulders, watch and hopefully approve.
>
> (Priestley, 2011)

Miniature wargaming rules are often written in a self-deprecating manner. When a game is contextualized as just a game it signals that it is not to be taken seriously, which in turn facilitates usage of nostalgic notions of 'great commanders of the past' without making it unpalatable. Statements such as 'let us summon the ghosts of Hannibal, Xerxes, Alexander and even Caesar himself, to stand at our shoulders, watch and hopefully approve' even make playful use of the idea that these historical figures might serve as judges of the players' ability to play the game of war. Nevertheless, herein lies an echo from more 'jingoistic', older works of military history. Consider for instance how the military exploits of one of Napoleon's marshals, Michel Ney, is described in a 19th century biography. They are said to be great works of art, that should be preserved and revered to posterity:

> Like the cartoons of Raphael, they constitute a monument ... Soldiers of genious, finished tacticians, like the poets and painters, are seldom seen: and if in an age a Dundas appear in Britain or a Prince de la Moskowa on the Continent, their labours become the property of the world, and, like the sacred fire of the temple, should be religiously preserved.
>
> (Chauncer, 1833, p. 16)

One way of celebrating such perceived feats of military history, is to emulate historical examples by enacting them in games. Nowadays warfare is rarely described as a glorious affair, but descriptions of 'brilliant' tactical maneuvers of 'great' commanders are commonplace throughout popular history and in wargames.

This way of thinking about wars and battles is not something of the past; indeed the 'ghosts of the past' can be represented by symbols on a screen, or as counters or miniatures in a tabletop wargame. As symbolic representations, their *coup d'euil* abilities are codified. They become, to use the language of ecological psychology, 'affordances' for the player to utilize. The choice of commander makes it possible to do certain things, that other commanders do not. In these games, players may be playacting as generals, by moving representations of commanders they playact as across the board. In the *Black Powder* and *Hail Caesar* rules, players are encouraged to expressively use their voice or writing notes as a historical commander would do, ordering symbolic troops of toy soldiers across a model landscape.

Playful identification becomes an attempt at acting out cognitive processes by externalizing them on a wargaming table. In theory, such cognitive processes only occur in the mind of an ideal – typical field commander. In a wargame, the *coup d'euil* is translated into symbolic representations in a wargaming-setting filled with affordances. The wargame thus becomes an attempt to interpret aspects of *coup d'euil* and bestow counters or miniatures with those perceived qualities. In theory *coup d'euil* is an ungraspable internal cognitive process, but in a wargame with representation of commanders with different abilities to move and rally troops, *coup d'euil* is primarily translated into an affordance amongst others in the game. Only in part does it become part of players' playful identification, using symbolic representations and rules as guidelines for how the *coup d'euil* is believed to function. Examples of such guidelines can be found in *Great battles of Alexander*, which feature a probability table for calculating results in combat. Such a table can be viewed as a heuristic map of intuitive calculation, as part and parcel of a commander's *coup d'euil*.

In *Black Powder* and *Hail Caesar* die rolls are modified due to different circumstances, such as terrain, troop quality or abilities of certain commanders. These modified rolls are used to determine things like damages and troops reactions. Here modified die rolls function as guidelines for players to determine the probability of a certain outcome.

In *Great Battles of Alexander* or *Black Powder*, troops have different ratings of probable efficiency in combat against other troops, codifications of information about troops and terrain along the lines of a commander with a good *coup d'euil*. I suggest these examples are instructional for how one might think that an ideal commander ought to calculate probabilities for success and risk. Even in games that do not feature commanders with different abilities, the playful identification becomes more a matter of a players using the wargame's symbols and rule-system as guidelines for *coup d'euil*.

There and Back Again: *Coup d'euil* from Intuition to Calculation (and Back Again) in Wargames from 18th to 20th Century

In Early Modernity, aspiring field commanders had to negotiate a growing body of literature in the quest for a universal science of war. When the size of armies grew and the procedures of warfare gradually changed, there was a discussion of what qualities the field commander ought to have, including signs of shifting stereotypical masculine qualities associated with field commanders. Though robust mental qualities were always seen as important, they became even more so in an era where war was viewed as both a science and an art. This meant a combination of things that could be quantified and calculated, and those things that could not, and consequently were described as 'sublime' or elements of 'chance'.

In Marshal de Saxe's *Reveries*, an 18th-century treatise on warfare, the commander of armies is for example instructed to not show emotions to his subordinates, as well as 'possess a talent for sudden and appropriate improvisation. He should be able to penetrate the minds of other men, while remaining impenetrable himself' (Saxe, 1776, p. xxxi). If a field commander felt insecure, he should outwardly play-act the role of an ideal typical field commander and perhaps take solace in a science of war turning warfare into a rule governed game. According to Frederick the Great's *Instructions for his generals* (a handbook on military matters written to educate the kings' generals on Frederick's art of war), deception is not only used to fool the opponent, but also to instill confidence in the troops and provide them with a fighting spirit, regardless of what the real feelings of the commander might be. Saxe claimed that the commander was required to be well versed in the military sciences (to know the rules, so to speak), but he also stressed the role of being prepared for the unforeseen, for contingencies, the unpredictable and the role of chance. He referred to this uncodifiable aspect of war as the 'sublime' element of warfare. Nothing was as unpredictable and unquantifiable as the mind of a great commander, who possessed the quality referred to as 'genius'. A successful military commander needed to be gifted with 'those peculiar strokes of genius, adapted to occasion, which characterize the great captains' (Saxe, 1776, preface ix). For military thinkers of de Saxe's and Frederick's sort, warfare was wedged between both the natural, quantifiable sciences and the arts. de Saxe stated that the commander should make himself busy with preparations before battle, but that he on the day of battle should do as little as possible, let the events unfold and be guided by senses and intuition. It was important to have an inner stillness amidst the chaos of battle. The commander should have sufficient room for calmly sensing unfolding events intuitively and be prepared to immediately exploit any possibilities that might occur (Saxe, 1776, p. xxxi).

To assert some degree of control over probable events, one could rehearse them before one's inner gaze. A commander with a good *coup d'euil* would be able to see what effect different terrain was likely to have on the troops moving through it, and what the probability of success or failure of attacks was during various conditions. Once this was premediated upon, a decision could be made.

There was one school of thought in which warfare was discussed in mathematical and geometrical terms, and that precision in military drill, linear tactics, and to some degree, the emergent standardization of mapmaking was part and parcel of that discourse. One example was the theories of Dietrich Heinrich Freiherr von Bülow (1757–1807), who argued in his

Geist des Neueren Kriegssystems (1799), that natural sciences should be used to bring the chaos of war under control and thereby limit the suffering brought on by war. According to von Bülow, war should be a precise science based on the concept of lines, lines of communication and deployment. A science of war formulated in geometrical terms would have as its aim to outmaneuver the opponent, and thereby making battles unnecessary (Gat, 2001, pp. 83–85). Von Bülow used a triangle as a universal allegory to understand the relationship between logistics and troops in the field. His theory was an inspiration for wargame designer, polymath and military scholar Johann Georg Julius Venturini (1772–1802) who used Bülow's military theory as inspiration for a remake of his earlier, chess-based wargame of logistics. Venturini's wargame was published in Sweden in 1826. His gamification of von Bülow's military theory consisted of a map upon which a grid of triangles was superimposed to signify lines of communication and deployment (Krigs-Spelet, 1826). Bülow's military theory emphasized the triangular relationship between the tip of the triangle – representing the troops at the front, and the base, representing logistics and lines of communication. In Venturini's wargame both the strategic and tactical aspects and Bülow's theoretical model is visualized by this triangular relation, and consequently von Bülow's theory is expressed in how pieces of the wargame interact. I suggest that this wargame is an expression of how a commander's *coup d'euil* could be trained based on von Bülow's geometrical theory of war. A commander in the military cultural context that emphasized mathematics and linear warfare, would probably have to view the environment in those terms. Codifying a landscape into what parts are beneficial or harmful for military maneuvers means translating hills, fields, forests, troops and cannons into instruments of potential military agency, each with a certain degree of usefulness. That degree of usefulness would have to be 'recalculated' with changing circumstances, such as a change in the weather or a lack of ammunition due to logistical problems.

However, it is an oversimplification to say that all 18th- and 19th-century military thinking revolved around geometry and mathematical codifications of warfare (Gat, 2001, p. 96). Amongst 19th century Prussian military wargames, increasing complexity in rules and mathematical models led to a shift that gradually gave way to a more intuitive kind of wargame (Perla & Curry, 2011, pp. 42–45). Military theorist and staff officer Carl von Clausewitz was skeptical of military thinkers who discussed theories of war through the lens of mathematical, quantifiable determinism and science of war. He described battle as a sort of staged drama, and in his writing he evoked the image of increasing friction the closer one gets to the battlefield. Friction is the gap between intention and execution, it is the consequence of inaccurate information and human error. As an allegorical description of the unpredictabe results of warfare, von Clausewitz describes the outcome of battle as being about as predictable as a lottery, or dice-throwing. In a game of chance, or *alea*, the player is inactive and just awaits the outcome of a die roll. According to Roger Caillois, *alea* typically signifies an equality of risk and benefits to participating players, which means that skill is not a factor (Caillois, 2001, p. 17). Therein Caillois' interpretation of *alea* is only in part applicable to ideal typical commanders' struggles for success on battlefield. However, the role of chance is a central part of 18th and 19th century military theories. Clausewitz writes:

> We see, therefore, how from the commencement, the absolute, the mathematical as it is called, nowhere finds any sure basis in the calculations in the art of war, and from the outset there is a play of possibilities, probabilities, good and bad luck, which spreads about with all the coarse and fine threads of its web, and makes war of all branches of human activity the most like a gambling game'.
>
> (Clausewitz, 1997, pp. 19–20)

Commanders are themselves occasionally portrayed as, if not wargamers, then at least gamblers in works of military history and military theory. One of the most well-known utterances from antiquity refers to this: 'The die is cast', is according to Suetonius, what Julius Caesar uttered as he inaugurated a civil war (Suetonius, 2001, p. 37). They signify that the outcome of war is always uncertain and consequently that commanders are allegorically linked to players partaking in a game of hazard. When the die is cast there is no return.

Any player worth their salt must master the rules. In most games there is a fixed set of rules to follow combined with an interaction with the opponent. When playing an agonistic game, the goal is to outwit each other whilst playing according to the rules. That means you cannot do whatever you please, but that it is alright to deceive the opponent to some degree. One also must understand the opponent's intentions and take these into consideration in one's own planning. To be good at deception, you must be good at pretending, put up an act towards the opponent and in general have a vivid imagination to concoct make-belief. Additionally, one must be lucky to win. As Clausewitz described war as a 'gambling game', he perhaps inadvertently by means of allegory turned commanders into gamblers, agents that operated by means of probability and chance.

According to Clausewitz, the result of a battle can never be calculated beforehand due to the complex nature of opposing human wills acting in a theater of war. Thus, if you cannot know the outcome of your decisions, or even the likely outcome, then what is the point of making decisions? If you are not in a position of making decisions, how can you then influence events? Wargame rules do not represent truths, they are interpretations of theories that try to balance a deterministic set of mathematical rules, with the agency of free will. Whilst Clausewitz describes the friction of the battlefield and 'fog of war', the field commander appears as immersed in uncertainty and with a limited possibility to affect the outcome. To fight a battle is to play a game of chance. Frederick and Maurice de Saxe, on the other hand, both stressed the need for commanders to plan their battles, and then distance themselves during the battle. After rigorous planning they must relax and trust their intuition, the sensibilities given by an internal wargame, courtesy of *coup d'euil*. When we imagine the field commander watching events unfold beforehand, we might even think that he knows how everything will turn out? After all he might have already 'played the game' of a particular battle, and perhaps even many versions of it beforehand, before his mind's eye, so to speak. This could be likened to the commander playing an internal wargame, moving bits and pieces on a gaming board only visible before his inner gaze. That would be the function of the *coup d'euil*, to function as such an internal wargame.

Imagined Memories Shaped by Coup d'euil

In a Belgian documentary on the battle of Waterloo 1815 (Lanneau, 2015), Wellington and Napoleon are positioned on opposite sides of a wargaming table. They push toy soldiers representing brigades to new positions on the table to illustrate their tactical decisions. This illustrates how the ideal-typical field commander is portrayed as a wargamer, also how the *coup d'euil* itself can be represented as a wargame. Wargames provide an imagery of war from a detached perspective as does the *coup d'euil*.

However, emotions do have a part to play in this process, and the *coup d'euil* can be utilized to provide emotional content to a battle narrative. Consider for instance that in the later parts of the 19th century, wargaming umpires well versed in military history or with actual combat experience was highly sought after in the Prussian military (Perla & Curry, 2011, pp. 42–45). An ability to translate the wargame into an exciting narrative was deemed important for pedagogical reasons. In a Swedish version of Reisswitz's kriegspiel, revised by Julius von Verdy du Vernois dating from 1878, says that the umpire should be able to see the events unfolding on the gaming table with his inner gaze and be able to vividly relate to the participants the drama unfolding (Kleen, 1878). A subsequent version of Swedish military wargame rules from 1904, states that complex rules and calculations are to be avoided, lest the participants might fall asleep (Immanuel, 1904). The umpire has become a storyteller, using a keen *coup d'euil* to keep his audience engaged in exciting tales of battles played out on the war gaming table. It was believed that a skilled umpire's intuitive understanding of warfare made it possible to discard much of the wargaming rules. The umpire would make a swift decision to facilitate gameplay making use of his *coup d'euil*. As he vividly described what he intuitively saw happen in the game, the wargaming session came alive with exciting tales of dramatic scenes.

Summary

The perspective of the field commander is a privileged one. It represents war from an instrumental point of view, highlights possibilities and risks in the manner an ideal typical commander ought to perceive a battlefield. It is a perspective from the vantage point of agency, not the perspective of victims or masses obeying orders. In this chapter I have briefly discussed how an ideal typical field commander gaze, his *coup d'euil* is described in older and contemporary wargames, as well as in a few sources of 18th- and 19th-centuries military theory.

The coup *d'euil* is an instrumental of reduction of information that is divided into those parts that were beneficial, those parts that were threatening or those parts that were of no consequence with regards to how to go about in each tactical situation to subjugate an opponent to one's own will. Wargames may be a subjective way of making visible what goes on inside the mind of ideal typical masculine military geniuses. Above all, these wargames were used to show historical or hypothetical events from the perspective an ideal-typical commander.

A wargame becomes an attempt to portray certain aspects of *coup d'euil*, and the rule system can in part be viewed as a way of enhancing certain aspects of the qualities inherent in a *coup d'euil*, such as the ability to codify troops and landscapes according to their potential military usability. As a concept *coup d'euil* appear to have some similarities to the concept affordances, as it is used in ecological psychology. Furthermore, I argue that there is a cultural understanding surrounding the history of war and warfare that makes it possible for both wargamers and commanders to approach war and warfare as a sort of game. Wargamers may play-act as stereotypical masculine warrior heroes in the guise of historical or make-belief commanders, whilst commanders (perhaps in an attempt to cope with the horrific realities of real war), may play-act as, if not wargamers, then perhaps gamblers partaking in warfare from the perspective of viewing war as a game.

The wargaming rule-systems and wargaming aesthetics are all attempts by game designers to codify their own interpretation of how the world might appear when viewed from the perspective of an ideal-typical field commanders' *coup d'euil*. Indeed, it may be argued that one the reasons wargames were devised was to facilitate players honing those qualities. I also suggest that we need to recognize the many similarities between older wargames and more contemporary ones, as examples of how we think about and imagine war. Those imaginations may emanate from culturally embedded ideal-typical notions of masculine warrior heroes in the shape of 'brilliant commanders' waging war. Consequently, notions of how warfare 'functions' as well as notions of the 'function' of warfare in history, can be intertwined in culturally saturated representation of war embedded in a discourse regarding war as a sort of contest, and 'brilliant commanders' viewed as gifted athletes or artists. That way of representing war appear to remain the same in many respects, regardless of obvious changes in both mediation and media culture of war.

References

Caillois, R. (2001). *Man, play and games.* University of Illinois Press.
Chauncer, G. H. (1833). *Military studies of Marshal Ney: Written for his officers, translated from the Marshal's original manuscripts by G. H. Chauncer Esq. with introduction and diagrams by Major A. James.* Bull and Churton.
Clausewitz, C. V. (1997). *On war.* Wordsworth.
Connell, R. (1996). *Maskuliniteter.* Daidalos.
Dagens Nyheter. (1914, December 18). Floods krigsspel [Advertisement]. *Dagens Nyheter.* https://arkivet.dn.se/
Ehrenreich, B. (2011). *Blood rites: Origins and history of the passions of war.* Granta Books.
Elgström, O. (1914). *Hur man för krig med tennsoldater.* Bonnier.
Elgström, O. (1915). Min'hobby' – leka med tennsoldater – uppseendeväckande avslöjande om Ossian Elgströms psyke. *Vecko-Journalen, 372.*
Floods krigsspel. (1914). *Victor Pettersons bokindustriaktiebolag.* https://digitaltmuseum.se/011025168588/sallskapsspel
Frederick II. (2005). *Instructions for his generals.* (Original work from 1797). Dover Publications.
Gat, A. (2001). *A history of military thought: From the Enlightenment to the Cold War.* Oxford University Press.
Gibson, J. J. (1979). *The ecological approach to visual perception.* Lawrence Erlbaum Associates. (Original work from 1986).
Granberg, S., & Hulterström, P. (2016). Ecological psychology: A framework for wargame design. In T. Kaneda, H. Kanegae, Y. Toyoda, & P. Rizzi (Eds.), *Simulation and gaming in the network societchauncery.* Springer. https://doi.org/10.1007/978-981-10-05
Hand-bibliothek för sällskapsnöjen, eller, systematiskt ordnande spel, lekar och konster. (1838–1839). Utg. af G. J. Billberg.
Harari, N. Y. (2004). *Renaissance military memoirs: War, history, and identity, 1450–1600.* Boydell and Brewer Limited.
Herman, M., & Berg, R. (1991). *Great battles of Alexander: The Macedonian art of war* [Tabletop]. GMT Games.
Herman, M., & Berg, R. (2014). *Great battles of Alexander: The Macedonian art of war* (Deluxe 5th ed.) [Rules]. GMT Games. https://s3-us-west-2.amazonaws.com/gmtwebsiteassets/gbad/DelAlex5_Rules_FINAL.pdf
Hilgers, P. V. (2012). *War games: A history of war on paper.* MIT Press.
Immanuel, F. (1904). *Handledning och exempel till regements-krigsspelet: med kartbladet Château-Salins af tyska rikets karta 1: 100,000 samt 6 skisser i texten* [Tabletop]. Stockholm.
Kleen, G. (1878). *Försök till handbok i krigsspel.* Norstedts.
Krigs-Spelet, grundadt på Bulows nyare krigs-systems esprit [Tabletop] (1826). Carl Deleen. Tryckt hos Carl Deleen. https://weburn.kb.se/metadata/051/EOD_2409051.htm
Lanneau, H. (Director) (2015). *Waterloo l'ultime bataille* [Motion picture]. Arte.
Lenoir, T., & Lowood. H. (2005). Theaters of war: The military-entertainment complex. In H. Schramm, L. Schwarte, & J. Lazardzig (Eds.), *Collection, laboratory, theater: Scenes of knowledge in the 17th century* (pp. 427–457). Walter De Gruyter.

Lowood, H. (2016). War engines: Wargames as systems from the tabletop to the computer. In P. Harrigan & M. G. Kirschenbaum (Eds.), *Zones of control: Perspectives on wargaming* (pp. 83–105). MIT Press.

Perla, P. P., & Curry, J. (2011). *Peter Perla's the art of wargaming: A guide for professionals and hobbyist.* Lulu.com.

Peterson, J. (2012). *Playing at the world: A history of simulating wars, people and fantastic adventure, from chess to role-playing games.* Unreason Press.

Priestley, R. (2009). *Black powder* [Rule book]. Warlord Games.

Priestley, R. (2011). *Hail Caesar: Battles with model soldiers in the ancient era* [Tabletop]. Warlord Games.

Saxe, M. Count de. (1776). *Reveries, or, memoirs concerning the art of war* [Electronic resource]. Alexander Donaldson. https://babel.hathitrust.org/cgi/pt?id=pst.000010595725&view=1up&seq=9

Suetonius. (2001). *Kejsarbiografier.* Wahlström & Widstrand.

Sutton-Smith, B. (1997). *The ambiguity of play.* Harvard University Press.

Vego, M. (2012). German wargaming. *Naval War College Review, 65*(4), 106–147.

Wells, H. G. (1913). *Little wars* [Tabletop]. Project Gutenberg Literary Archive Foundation.

Part III
Critical Perspectives on Conflicts in Games

8 War Never Changes? Creating an American Victimology in *Fallout 4*

Ryan Scheiding

Introduction

In August of 1945 the United States dropped atomic bombs on Hiroshima (6 August 1945) and Nagasaki (9 August 1945). These remain the only atomic or nuclear weapons to be dropped on a civilian population during wartime. In the decades that have followed, American collective/cultural memory has developed based on arguments that the bombings were either necessary or justified. This has led to the erasure and subsequent invisibility of Japanese victims within collective/cultural memory as these victims contradict or complicate the popularized ideas of the bombs being moral, saving lives, or shortening the war. As a result, when atomic or nuclear weapons are mediated (either historically, allegorically, or fictionally) the tendency in American media is to mourn potential American victims rather than historical Japanese victims. This is the case in Bethesda Game Studios' action role-playing game, *Fallout 4*, from 2015. A close examination of American historiography and *Fallout 4* through the lens of historioludicity, premediation/remediation, and collective/cultural memory theory provides a relevant example of how American atomic fears focus on the potential of Americans becoming victims of atomic or nuclear attacks rather than on the historical experience of the largely Japanese victims. This type of video game representation effectively obscures the real conflict from the past and transposes that conflict to be American-centric. It can be said then that *Fallout 4* represents conflict in a unique and important way as it represents the past for use in the present.

This chapter begins with a historiographical examination of the atomic bombs in an American context to establish how the bombs have been formally 'remembered' and to illustrate which arguments have been institutionalized and legitimized by formal power structures.[1] The second section introduces general collective/cultural memory and key game studies theory to help establish a framework for examining the influence of formalized memory structures and their influence over the content within a video game. The final section briefly examines the setting, lore, and selected characters of *Fallout 4* as a case study. Ultimately, the chapter argues that established collective/cultural memory of the atomic bombs is remediated through a process of historioludicity within *Fallout 4*. This provides a unique representation of conflict in video games that alters the past and introduces an American victimology.

Historiography

To determine how established collective/cultural memory is reflected within video games and provide a unique example of how video games represent conflict it is necessary to establish the predominant way the atomic bombs have been remembered. One way to accomplish this is to examine available historical texts and create a historiography of the event(s). While perhaps not always widely read by the public, the works of professional and amateur historians help to establish collective/cultural memory because they help to formulate the major arguments that become institutionalized (typically through educational systems) and legitimized (by established systems of power such as governments). In regard to the atomic bombings of Hiroshima and Nagasaki, there is a strongly established collective/cultural memory that has proven to be influential beyond academia.

In general, American historiography of the atomic bombings can be categorized as being in favour of or supportive of the use of the bombs. This is typically argued through numerous means such as ideas of the bomb's 'necessity', wartime justifications, or a form of grim moral calculus arguing that they 'saved lives'. As a consequence of these arguments, it has also been necessary to erase Japanese victims because of the difficulty of explaining away the value of individual lives within the larger calculus of war. This section draws on a sample of selected texts that can be considered to be emblematic of the larger historical discourse.

Alperovitz (1995) and Lifton and Mitchell (1995) are two works that summarize the early years of American atomic bomb memory, and thus explain how their use have become largely accepted within American historiography and popular perception. Both works focus on the early conceptions/reportage of the atomic bombs and how they were presented to the American public. As outlined by Lifton and Mitchell (1995), early atomic bomb discourse was highly structured and limited by censorship orchestrated by the American government and occupation forces. Indeed, early reporting on the bombs had to rely solely upon government-sanctioned information (p. 11). Alperovitz (1995) points specifically to three prominent American politicians, Henry Stimson, Harry Truman, and James F. Byrnes, as central forces behind early attempts at engineering American public opinion about the bombs (pp. 448–588). In addition to these measures, General Douglas MacArthur denied journalists access to both Hiroshima and Nagasaki, even going as far as to deny gasoline to planes after two reporters broke the ban (Lifton & Mitchell, 1995, pp. 47–49).

These tactics allowed the government to control all outgoing information about the bombs and the victims. This control allowed for an official discourse of the atomic bombings to be established and become the only substantial discourse in the direct aftermath of the bombings. An essential element of this effort, that remains important to this day, was the establishment of a theory that the atomic bombs saved millions of lives that would have been lost in a potential invasion of the Japanese home islands. Alperovitz traces this argument to a 1947 article in *Harper's Magazine* written by former Secretary of War (1911–1913 and 1940–1945) and Secretary of State (1929–1933) Henry Stimson. Alperovitz debunks the article point by point within his larger analysis (1995, pp. 448–497). Regardless of Alperovitz's historiographical effort, which displays that the 'million lives saved' argument is untruthful, the theory has remained popular and led to two major trends within American historiography and popular perceptions: The justification of the use of the bombs and the subsequent erasure and discounting of Japanese victims within the larger discourse.[2]

Brewer (2009) summarizes the popular American perception of the war as follows:

> Americans preferred to remember the propaganda version of a noble war fought for democracy and freedom by innocent people forced to defend themselves against a vicious enemy, a war fought overseas by decent men while on the home front everyone contributed, a war in which the Americans played the starring role and the Allies had big parts, a war that delivered a better life.
>
> (p. 140)

This perception extends to the use of the atomic bombs which Minear (1995) describes as, for most Americans, having become a part of a matched pair of bookends with Pearl Harbor, where the Japanese started the war via a sneak attack, and Hiroshima and Nagasaki, where America ended it with atomic bombs (p. 363). Furthermore, Minear (1995) argues that this has resulted in a system where Americans do not consider the Japanese victims of the bombs, for a variety of reasons, and instead create memorials to Hiroshima and Nagasaki that, '. . . are to the victimizers, not the victims, and there is no debate' (p. 365). The works of Brewer (2009) and Minear (1995) show the continued influence of the early American governmental efforts to control public opinion about the bombs.

In the larger historiography of the atomic bombings, this is replicated quite frequently. Texts examining the atomic bombs, such as Bernstein (1996), Bix (1996), Frank (2005), and Lewis (2020), argue that the bombs were justified or necessary in some way. Bernstein (1996) provides an emblematic example of how American historians have written about atomic bombs as he grounds his argument in the idea that they helped to bring a quick end to the war, arguing that it was far from definite that a combination of non-nuclear options could have ended it. For Bernstein (1996), the result of the gap between 'likely and 'definite' opens the possibility of a brutal alternate history where the war was extended and resulted in many more battles and many more deaths.

However, he notes that this possibility of an extended war does not provide an ethical justification for the bombs (p. 39). He argues that the use of the bombs should be considered using moral standards of the time in which the 'older morality' of sparing civilians was disregarded in the total war of the Second World War (p. 76). The logical conclusion from his line of argumentation is that atomic bombs were justified by moral standards of the time. While he does admit that it is appropriate to question the bombings, he ultimately supports their use based on the idea that different systems of thought existed at the time and that it was possible that not using the bombs would have lengthened the war and resulted in more deaths (i.e. an example of the 'saving lives' argument).

Further examples of support for the atomic bombs can be found in generalized textbooks on the Second World War and American history. This can be seen in the works of Spector (1985), Diggins (1989), Murray and Millet (2001), Costello (2009), and Burleigh (2010) where limited space and a generalized scope lead to reliance on the accepted ideas that the bombs were justified or necessary. Indeed, these ideas have become accepted to the point that they are frequently defended as 'correct' and, as a result, works that argue against these interpretations of the past are derisively labelled as 'revisionist' or 'counterfactual'. A vehement defence of the status quo interpretations of the use of the atomic bombs can be found in O'Reilly and Rooney (2005). In their work about the Enola Gay controversy,[3] they create a strict dichotomy between 'true' history based upon 'facts', and 'revisionist' history based upon 'distortions', in which the true history justifies the atomic bombs being dropped and false history reinterprets this traditional view (pp. 1–16).

This brief historiography is emblematic of the larger historical discourse surrounding the atomic bombs in the United States. This discourse largely defends the use of the atomic bombs while downplaying or erasing the suffering of Japanese victims. This is used, in part, as a way of justifying past actions and formulating an understanding of the past that can be used to serve power in the present. For example, a defence of the atomic bombs can be used as justification for the use of military force in the present (i.e. if military force was justified against past enemies, it can be justified against current enemies). Additionally, an erasure of historical civilian victims at the hands of American military power allows for the continued argumentation of the nobility of American military action.

This defence or justification of the use of the atomic bombs will be presented as the primary way of depicting the atomic bombings in American historical discourse and collective/cultural memory throughout the rest of this chapter. However, there are two important caveats. Firstly, it should be made entirely clear that the chapter argues that this is the *predominant* way of representing and remembering the bombs, not the *only* way. For example, the works of Walzer (1977) and Zinn (2010), among others, are American texts that specifically argue against the decision to use the atomic bombs. Yet, it should be noted that even those that do argue against pro-atomic bomb discourse recognize and lament its hegemonic position. For example, Jacobs and Zwigenberg (2020) liken American atomic bomb memory to a statue that must be torn down, thus showcasing both their opposition to the use of the atomic bombs in the past *and* the hegemonic memory discourse that continues to defend or support their use in the present.

Secondly, it should be noted that this chapter focuses exclusively on the atomic bombings of Hiroshima and Nagasaki. Of course, numerous historical events have affected representation of the atomic bombs and, later, nuclear fears. These include events that occurred in or close to the United States such as the Cuban Missile Crisis (16 October 1962–28 October 1962) and the Three Mile Island accident (28 March 1979) and those that occurred far outside the United States but still affected global nuclear fears such as the Chernobyl nuclear disaster (26 April 1986) and the Fukushima nuclear disaster (11 March 2011). Additionally, one of the core issues of the Cold War was, of course, nuclear weapons and their potential use against civilian populations which also stoked nuclear fears.

This chapter focuses solely on Hiroshima and Nagasaki not to discount other atomic or nuclear conflicts and events from the past but instead to focus attention on the genesis of atomic fears and thought. Hiroshima and Nagasaki remain the only instances of atomic or nuclear weapons being used against civilians during a war. The purpose of this chapter is to examine how and why the victims of these events are absent from American collective/cultural memory and the implications of that erasure.

Collective/Cultural Memory and Game Studies

Having established the specifics of the predominant historiographical discourse of the atomic bombs in the United States, it is necessary to describe the systems that allow for that discourse to appear within other media. To accomplish this task, this section will provide a brief framework based upon collective/cultural memory theory, game studies, and remediation/premediation theory. Through the use of these theoretical systems, it is possible to describe how official discourses influence and become part of video games, even those that are not 'historical' but rather rely on fictionalized depictions. Collective/cultural memory theory is an interdisciplinary field with roots in the early 20th century French sociological and German critical theory traditions. To cover the breadth and depth of this field is beyond this chapter's scope. Instead, key early works and those that describe how the field has been adapted for contemporary media will be the focus.

In *The Collective Memory*, Halbwachs (1980) outlines the basics of this theoretical concept. He argues that, as people living in organized societies, we are never alone and, as a result, we formulate our memories collectively based upon shared data or conceptions (pp. 23–31). This means that memory is not a process that is located in the individual, but rather, *always* occurs through group processes. In Halbwachs' words, 'a person remembers only by situating [themselves] within the viewpoint of one or several groups and one or several currents of collective thought' (p. 33). Crucially, Halbwachs (1980) argues that individuals believe themselves to be free when they actually yield to external suggestion and obey unperceived social influences (p. 45). Thus, each individual remembers within a collective memory framework, but those memories can change based upon place, space, and temporality.

Halbwachs (1980) argues that pasts are remembered only through reconstructions of the past with data borrowed from the present (p. 64). Collective memory is not necessarily 'accurate' but, instead, represents the wants, needs, and understandings of contemporary society. Society uses the past to explain and order the present. Contemporary society has, of course, changed drastically in the decades since Halbwachs formulated his theories in the 1920s and 1930s, but the creation and maintenance of memory through groups and the idea that collective memory is created for use in the present are tenants of collective/cultural memory theory that remains unchanged since the original publication of the work.

Assmann (1995) and Erll (2007), expanded upon Halbwachs' original theorizations as a way of making the theory better reflect contemporary society. Assmann (1995), who prefers the term cultural memory, updated the field through his ideas on 'objectivized culture' (i.e. cultural artifacts) which he argues have the structure of memory (p. 128). In other words, these artifacts function beyond their physical form and help to structure and formulate cultural memory. These artifacts of objectivized culture then become the building blocks of cultural memory, which Assmann (1995) defines as:

> that body of knowledge of reusable texts, images, and rituals specific to each society in each epoch, whose 'cultivation' serves to stabilize and convey that society's self-image. Upon such collective knowledge, for the most part (but not exclusively) of the past, each group bases its awareness of unity and particularity.
>
> (p. 132)

Erll (2007) re-examined cultural memory and further updated the field with focus on technology and media. For Erll (2007), 'Cultural memory would be inconceivable without the role that media play on both levels – the individual and the collective' (p. 113). She argues that media are directly connected to memory and are instrumental to the creation of cultural memory because they work as an interface between individual memory and collective memory. Within Erll's theorization cultural memory in contemporary society cannot be created or exist without media.

It must then be asked: How are video games theorized to interact with the past/history/historiography? Squire (2004) studied how players could learn world history through playing *Civilization III*, arguing that students are able to examine relationships among geography, politics, economics, and history over thousands of years from multiple perspectives by playing the game (p. 9). This allows students to understand social phenomena from deep systemic perspectives and helps them see beyond stereotypes, scripts, or simplifications of complex historical phenomena (Squire, 2004, p. 56). Thus, video games can become valuable teaching tools that help to reinforce students' historical knowledge through gameplay. Squire (2004) labels the game and gameplay that *Civilization III* produces as a 'historical possibility space' (p. 120). For Squire, historical video games can be seen as teaching tools that help to reinforce previous knowledge of the past through gameplay. In addition to this, video games and gameplay produce their own historical discourses through coded rulesets.

For Kapell and Elliot (2013) video games act as a form of myth rather than history, but also as a democratization of the past where narrative of the past is no longer the purview of professional historians. Instead, it is available to anyone who plays historical games (pp. 363–367). This has potentially both positive and negative connotations, as each player, game, and experience will be unique. Regardless, Kapell and Elliot (2013) outline how games interact with and depict the past in a unique fashion that has larger implications for how games can be viewed as historical practices.

Chapman (2016) theorized how video games can be understood as part of traditional historical methods. He frames his arguments through the idea that history is a construction that is neither factual nor entirely fictional and, as such, there needs to be a definition of history that extends beyond ideas of accuracy (pp. 8–10). Continuing this line of reasoning, Chapman (2016) states that history, as most people know it, is constructed by historians and multiple cultural products, but the past is only relevant to many people when it can be contextualized in the present (pp. 12–13). This importance in the present can be derived from video games.

However, despite similar outputs, Chapman does not believe that history and historical games generate historical representations in the same way. He offers the idea of historioludicity to describe how video games engage in historical practice. Historioludicity is the representation of history, as well as thought about history, through visual images and ludic discourse. This can also be understood as the rules and opportunities for action within games (p. 22). The result of playing a historical video game is the creation of a historical ludonarrative (Chapman, 2016, p. 125). Ultimately, historioludicity and historical ludonarrative argue that digital historical games create new opportunities for making arguments about the past through present actions (Chapman, 2016, p. 271).

Game studies provides multiple perspectives for assessing how video games interact with the past on a theoretical level whether that be the 'historical possibility space', as myth, or through historioludicity. These interpretations also fit well within established collective/cultural memory theory as they stress the importance of interacting with the past for the benefit of the present. It can be said that video games, especially historical video games, function as an extension of collective/cultural memory. However, it must be theorized specifically how established collective/cultural memory become the content of video games. This can be described through processes of remediation and premediation.

Remediation is, '... the representation of one medium in another ... [wherein] the content has been borrowed, but the medium has not been appropriated or quoted' (Bolter & Grusin, 1999, pp. 44–45). This process can be used to describe how historiography can be incorporated into a video game. Erll (2009) expands upon remediation, coining the term 'premediation', which she defines as, 'a cultural practice of experiencing and remembering: The use of existent patterns and paradigms to transform contingent events into meaningful images and narratives (p. 114). When an event is premediated, historical events are used as narrative schemata to create successful stories where an event or person will be compared to some historical referent in order to shape a narrative. This means that historical events or people work as pseudo-blueprints that will make new stories about the past more palatable and easily understandable in the present. The new narrative thus grounds itself in the collective/cultural memory and formulates how the new events or person will be understood. Ultimately, Erll (2009) uses the theory of premediation to describe how existing collective/cultural memory influences the content of media and how these media then effect and interact with collective/cultural memory.

A combination of these theories can be used to analyze the content of a video game and help to determine how its content is influenced by the past. Taking *Fallout 4* as a case study, which is not a 'historical' game but has obvious connections to historical discourse surrounding atomic and nuclear weapons, it is possible to examine how this works. This process can be described as follows: There is an established historiographical discourse surrounding the atomic bombings of Hiroshima and Nagasaki that has influenced or become part of group processes of collective/cultural memory formation. As such, depictions of atomic or nuclear annihilation have been heavily premediated. Thus, when remediation occurs, as it does in the creation of a video game, the 'correct' or 'desirable' way of depicting that narrative and world has, in large part, been predetermined. The process of developing a game based on this can be described through the theory of historioludicity. In the case of *Fallout 4* the result is the historioludic replication of historical discourses that lament fictional potential American victims while erasing real historical Japanese victims.

Fallout 4 – A Collective/Cultural Memory Case Study

Through processes of premediation, remediation, and historioludicity, *Fallout 4* engages with American collective/cultural memory as established by historiographical representations of the atomic bombs. This section will examine the series background, setting, lore, and key characters in the game to showcase how *Fallout 4* utilizes pre-established ways of representing the past in the creation and representation of its fictionalized post-nuclear universe within the medium of a video game. Comparison of the game to historiography of the bombs reveals several overlapping representations that help to elucidate how video games interact with the past and help to foster historical knowledge even when the video games in question are not based on factual events from the past.

Fallout 4, released on 10 November 2015, was developed by Bethesda Game Studios, and published by Bethesda Softworks.[4] The game is massive in scope and content which makes a full analysis difficult to undertake and well beyond the scope of this chapter. For current purposes, the setting, the roles of the United States and China within the game's lore, and the ghoul characters found in the game will be focused upon. It is also important to note that, for the purposes of this analysis *Fallout 4*, will be understood as a text and visual representation rather than as a set of rules and gameplay.

The main story of *Fallout 4* is set in the Commonwealth, the remains of the pre-war city of Boston. In *Fallout 4* the nuclear post-apocalypse is depicted in a way that blends the true-to-life experiences of Hiroshima and Nagasaki with more fanciful aspects. For example, the Commonwealth is filled with scorched landscapes and many gutted buildings which resembles Hiroshima and Nagasaki in the aftermath of the bombs. In Hiroshima and Nagasaki, buildings that were not made of concrete were mostly destroyed by the tremendous heat and blast generated by the atomic bombs. Concrete or other reinforced structures, such as the Atomic Bomb Dome that has become a well-known UNESCO heritage site in Hiroshima, remained standing but were mostly gutted or became unstable. The Commonwealth mimics this as mostly large brick or concrete buildings remain. These buildings populate the map of *Fallout 4* and provide the player spaces to fight enemies and scavenge for materials that can be used to build settlements, customize weapons, or reinforce armor and equipment.

In addition, there is limited flora in the Commonwealth, none of which would be classified as 'normal' or 'healthy'. This feature of the landscape also causes the Commonwealth to resemble Hiroshima and Nagasaki in August of 1945. For example, the trees of the Commonwealth are twisted, burned, and lack foliage which is similar to trees in both Hiroshima and Nagasaki in the direct aftermath of the atomic bombings. Thus, the

Commonwealth remediates and mimics the past through its depiction of the destruction of a city by an atomic or nuclear weapon. The result is a scarred landscape, scantly populated by survivors who struggle to survive in the shadows of collapsing infrastructure.

Yet, at the same time, *Fallout 4* differs from the historical record in the permanence of the destruction. Whereas Hiroshima and Nagasaki recovered both naturally (through the dissipation of radiation and the recovery of plants) and through human intervention (through economic recovery and rebuilding efforts) the Commonwealth is destroyed and, as revealed in the narrative of *Fallout 4*, has remained a radiation-riddled nuclear wasteland for over a century. For example, the majority of the fauna has been mutated and become monstrous. In addition, radiation is a continuing problem in the Commonwealth, as it is ever-present even centuries after the use of nuclear weapons. The end result is a wasteland full of debris, partially destroyed buildings, permanently scorched landscapes, and numerous enemies which presents a blend of historically accurate aspects with ahistorical touches that make *Fallout 4*'s world interesting to explore and fun to play in for the player. The Commonwealth can be said to be a premediation or remediation of what is known about cities destroyed by atomic or nuclear weapons as informed by historiography that is accomplished through a video game-centric representation. Since this representation is connected to historical events, it can be said that the Commonwealth's design is an exercise in historioludicity.

The setting of *Fallout 4* is relevant because of this unique blend of the historical and fictional. Setting a game in a post-nuclear wasteland easily lends itself to comparisons to Hiroshima and Nagasaki yet the fictional elements of the setting, which we can categorize as allegorical, can be equally thought-provoking. What is unique, and important to consider, is the fact that the Commonwealth is a distinctly *American* city, based upon a real-world counterpart. The use of real-world landmarks places the player in a (potentially) familiar position and results in the creation of an American victimology where *Americans* are the victims of nuclear attack. The result is a commentary and condemnation of the use of nuclear weapons that originates not from a historical perspective (i.e. Hiroshima and Nagasaki) but from a theoretical lens where Americans *could* become victims. *Fallout 4*'s setting encourages the player to mourn *fictional American* victims rather than *historical Japanese* victims.

This is not to argue that all games (or media in general) that make references to atomic or nuclear bombings *must* depict Japanese victims in some form. A science-fiction based game is under no obligation to be historically accurate and can certainly create its own story, lore, characters, and settings. However, it is notable that, in *Fallout 4*'s depiction of nuclear aftermath, historical victims are erased just as historical Japanese victims have been erased from larger American historiography. The developers of the game have not created a discourse that prioritizes potential American victimization over the actual historical victims of American military power, but they have capitalized on the existing collective/cultural memory discourse and (knowingly or unknowingly) remediated it into their game. The erasure of historical victims occurs which, simultaneously, allows for the depiction of distinctly American victims. This perpetuates established atomic bomb discourse found in American historiography that erases Japanese victims. In *Fallout 4* the player is introduced to issues of nuclear annihilation and presented with thousands of distinctly American victims. This American setting is essential when understanding other aspects of the game.

Of particular interest are the 'ghoul' characters of the world. In the *Fallout* universe a ghoul is a person that encountered massive amounts of radiation and was subsequently mutated. A ghoul retains their mental capacities, but their bodies and faces are horribly disfigured, and their voices become much hoarser. In addition, a person who has become a ghoul will no longer age and, seemingly, cannot die of natural causes. Eventually, a ghoul may become 'feral' which entails losing all reasoning and turning into a viscous, unthinking monster that attacks other non-feral ghouls and humans on sight.

Narratively, feral ghouls serve as an allegorical reminder of the constant suffering that radiation victims experience after surviving an atomic or nuclear blast. In terms of gameplay, they become a memorable group of enemies that are similar in nature to fast-moving zombies found in wider popular culture. As such, they can be seen as a blend of historical victims and popular culture references that are expressed, once again, through historioludicity. Ghouls, given this interpretation, are particularly important to exploring the connections between the game and collective/cultural memory stemming from historiography of the atomic bombs. To further illustrate this, it is insightful to examine ghouls from *Fallout 4* that are emblematic of their general representation within the game. In particular, the companion character Hancock, the NPC Zao, and the feral ghoul enemy type are worthy of further analysis as they provide insights into how radiation victims are depicted in *Fallout 4*.

John McDonough, pseudonym John Hancock, is the de facto mayor of the city of Goodneighbor. If the player so chooses, Hancock can be recruited as a companion character (i.e. he will fight alongside and travel with the player) and can become a love interest. He becomes a fascinating character when analyzing him within the established discourse of the atomic bombings of Hiroshima and Nagasaki. Visually, Hancock resembles an atomic bomb victim, albeit in an exaggerated form, because of his disfigurement. His hardened discoloured skin resembles the keloid scars which were common among survivors of the atomic bombings. His rasping voice also echoes the experiences of some Japanese survivors. Indeed, the permanence of his suffering has some symmetry with real-life survivors (as many Japanese atomic bomb survivors continue to suffer to this day). However, these exaggerated physical symptoms are the only overlap with Japanese atomic bomb survivors.

It is important to recognize that, not only is Hancock an American, but he has also adopted the clothing, name, and righteous patriotic attitude of an American Revolutionary figure, John Hancock (1737–1793). In other words, he is not only an American, but also a representation of a specific type of American (i.e. white, Anglo-Saxon, male, patriotic, nationalist, etc.). Hancock is exactly the type of person that was not targeted with atomic weapons in 1945, yet he is one of the most prominent representations of victimhood and triumph of an indomitable spirit within *Fallout 4*. The permanence of his victimhood is tragic, but Hancock represents an overtly ahistorical representation of atomic victimhood where potential American victims are created to be mourned rather than historical victims. This, in itself, is not an issue as *Fallout 4* is a work of fiction that is under no obligation to (and does not purport to) maintain historical accuracy. However, the ahistorical nature of this depiction is significant because it is indicative of adherence to larger established ways of remembering the past in the United States and a specific American-centric version of historioludicity.

Much of American discourse of the atomic bombs have, as a matter of convenience or shame, discounted and excluded discussion of atomic bomb victims in their arguments. This leaves a gap for fictional, historioludic representations of that past because there is no established way of including victims. *Fallout 4*, as evidenced by characters such as Hancock, fills this gap with distinctly American victims. In a system where, to borrow a term from Chomsky and Herman (2002), historical Japanese victims are 'unworthy victims', it becomes necessary to create examples of 'worthy victims'. John Hancock, a white American, is a worthy victim.

Fallout 4 furthers its historioludic narrative of potential American victimhood in the form of the NPC character Captain Zao. When exploring the Commonwealth, the player can come across rumors of a sea monster just off the coast, triggering a mission called *Here There be Monsters*. When the player decides to explore these rumors, they discover that the 'sea monster' is actually the Chinese submarine that launched the nuclear attack on Boston at the beginning of the game. As the crew attempted to escape, the submarine struck a mine and became stuck in the harbor. Upon exploring the submarine, the player meets Captain Zao whom was 'ghoulified' along with his crew after damage from the mine caused a radiation leak in their nuclear reactor. He has since remained on the submarine and is the last of the crew to avoid becoming feral. At this point the player can either pick a fight with Zao and kill him or help him repair the submarine and return to China. If the player decides to help Zao he will reward the player with his personal sword along with some beacons that can be used to call down tactical nuclear strikes anywhere on the map at a later time (based on player action and player choice).

Zao is the antithesis of Hancock. Whereas Hancock was an American victim, Zao is a Chinese perpetrator. This is ahistorical as it creates an Asian instigator of nuclear war against (predominantly white) American victims. The ahistorical nature of this depiction is, once again, unimportant on its own. Its significance is found in the further insight it provides into the influence of established memory discourse on the way that *Fallout 4* represents nuclear war. Given that American discourses of the atomic bombings have (1) argued for the necessity and legal right of dropping the bombs and (2) generally discounted and erased the victims of Hiroshima and Nagasaki within these arguments, there has been little discussion of the place of victims. When a video game engages in historioludicity and remediates these discourses there is no framework for the inclusion of victims and that information must be filled in by the developers. So, the question for these developers becomes: How do we represent victims? Or, how do we make our audience empathize and care about victims? While it is impossible to speak to the intentions of creators, we can examine their output and see that these questions are answered through the creation of *American* victims and non-American (notably Asian) perpetrators.

In addition to this, it is particularly interesting that, though he shows contrition for his past actions, Zao unlocks the power to rain down further nuclear attacks on the United States. Zao becomes a physical manifestation of a category of American nuclear fears, where Americans are victims or potential victims, that are better understood as ahistorical outputs of the remediation of established collective/cultural memory. The fact that the fictional aggressors are Asian is further important because it follows historical fears of 'the yellow peril' and interacts with and supports the idea, often acted upon in American history,[5] that the use of force in the region is justified. *Fallout 4* makes Zao, the only overtly Chinese character (and one of the few Asian characters) in the game, an aggressor that is responsible for the bombing of Boston and allows the player to order future strikes through interactions with Zao. This interacts with the two essential elements of the established collective/cultural memory of the atomic bombings of Hiroshima and Nagasaki (i.e. justification of the use of the bombs and erasure of Japanese victims) while also drawing upon other historical fears (i.e. the yellow peril).

An examination of the feral ghouls of the game helps to further elucidate the connection between *Fallout 4* and established American discourses on the atomic bombs. As mentioned above, feral ghouls are former humans that were ghoulified by radiation and later became feral, dangerous monsters. A feral ghoul resembles a ghoulified human with some notable differences, such as rarely wearing clothing and being different in color, often emitting a 'nuclear' glow.

The resemblance between ghouls and feral ghouls is telling as the ghouls are the *Fallout* universe's stand-ins for radiation victims. Once again, the feral ghouls, as with the example of Hancock previously outlined, are

American victims. But their feralization holds increased significance. The monstrous fate of the radiation victims, wherein the ghouls become aggressive, vicious, unthinking, and unfeeling, is important within the context of American culture. Americans were, largely, not the victims of atomic attacks and, as a result, there is not a large population of American radiation victims. This may be why the historioludic depiction of radiation poisoning in *Fallout 4* is unsophisticated and depicts radiation victims as monstrous.

Within Japan there is still a sizable, though dwindling, population of *hibakusha* (literally translated 'bomb affected persons'). In a 6 August 2020 article *The Japan Times* reported that there is an estimated 136,700 living hibakusha with an average age of just over 83 (Agence France-Presse & Jiji Press, 2020). Through the 'peace movement' *hibakusha* have put forth ideas of nuclear disarmament through political action, numerous public demonstrations, and the authoring of media (especially literature). *Hibakusha*, and their continued suffering caused by radiation, are publicly well-known in Japan and occupy an essential place within war memory. However, as outlined in the historiography section, *hibakusha* have been largely erased from American collective/cultural memory. As a consequence, when American collective/cultural memory is remediated into *Fallout 4* ghouls (i.e. victims of the nuclear attacks) can be entirely fictional rather than based on historical victims. Through a process of historioludicity, the real, lived experience of being an atomic bomb victim can thus be entirely fictionalized.

This fictionalization, born out of the remediation of American collective/cultural memory, has potentially problematic results. When there is no risk of offending a real-world group of human beings (such as *hibakusha* in Japan) it becomes easier to take artistic license when practicing historioludicity and creating allegorical depictions of a group. Once again, the developers of *Fallout 4* are under no obligation to depict radiation sicknesses accurately. Yet, the depiction of survivors as monstrous represents a distinctive interaction with historiographical discourse of the atomic bombs. In a system that has generally disregarded and erased historical victims, such as the *hibakusha*, there are no premediated examples to be remediated. When allegorical representations are created, they have no starting point to be based on. The result with feral ghouls is a depiction that is potentially disrespectful towards the trauma of Japanese victims of the atomic bombs as the results of 'ghoulification' manifest and turn tragic victims into vicious monsters.

Hancock, Zao, and the feral ghouls represent each type of character in *Fallout 4*: A companion, a NPC, and an enemy type. They also, through their appearances, functions within the game, and personalities, reveal the more complex ways that *Fallout 4* remediates historiography through a process of historioludicity. A general acceptance or excusal of the atomic bombs by Americans, and subsequent dismissal of Japanese victims, means that potential American victims (like Hancock) are the focus of fictional concerns about bombing. This leads to a situation where a fictional enemy (like

Zao) is created that does not match the experiences of the past. Finally, real-world victims of tragedy that have been excluded from historiographical discourse become lost as their experiences are fictionalized as an enemy type (like the feral ghouls as enemies).

Conclusion

This chapter has engaged in an analysis of aspects of *Fallout 4*, namely its setting, lore, and characters, to examine historioludic creation and the linkages between historiographical representations of the atomic bombings of Hiroshima and Nagasaki, collective/cultural memory, and video games. The connections between *Fallout 4* and these larger social systems can be understood through the concepts of historioludicity, premediation, and remediation. The predominant historiographical representations of the bombings have justified or excused their use, often to the detriment of discussing Japanese victims. This, in part, has helped in the establishment of a collective/cultural memory in the United States that remembers the bombs as justified or necessary. As a result, when this established discourse is remediated into another medium (i.e. historiography or collective/cultural memory becomes the basis for a fictional video game) there is already significant premediation that will partially determine how a game represents atomic or nuclear war through a historioludic creation process. In the case of *Fallout 4* the game follows the established ways of remembering the past and, when confronted with the gaps that are found in that collective/cultural memory, fills them in with fictionalized representations. The end result is a fictionalized, historioludic universe that remediates significant imagery and historical facts into its game world while also creating new victims. It is significant that these fictional victims are *American* victims.

However, it is necessary to acknowledge that this analysis finds only correlation with collective/cultural memory and does not argue causation. A variety of resources could have influenced the creation of *Fallout 4*. Indeed, collective/cultural memory can be such a hegemonic way of thinking about the past that major events, and how they are represented, can become considered a part of common knowledge (and therefore may be discounted as sources by the creators). Yet, connecting a game like *Fallout 4* to larger collective/cultural memory is important because it reveals linkages between the medium of video games and historical pasts, how these connections are rendered, and, importantly, what these connections can tell us about how the past is used to structure the present. *Fallout 4*'s American victimology lays bare American atomic and nuclear fears (i.e. the possibility that nuclear weapons could be used against Americans) while displaying a continuing dedication to defending the use of the atomic bombs and conveniently forgetting historical victims. The *Fallout* series famously opines that 'War never changes'. Yet, through *Fallout 4*'s American victimology we can see that, while war may not change, the past certainly does; usually as a way of servicing entrenched thought/power systems for the purposes of structuring the present through distorted views of the past.

Notes

1. For the purposes of this chapter, the term 'American' is used when describing the chosen historiography and collective/cultural memory. 'American' is used due to the hegemony of American viewpoints, historiography, discourse, and collective/cultural memory. Consideration was given to using the term 'American/Western', but this terminology was found to be imprecise, especially given the focus on sources that are 'American' in a traditional sense (i.e. written by Americans, originating in the United States, or heavily influenced by American hegemony).
2. It is important to note that, even within the 'million lives saved' argument, the lives being 'saved' are those of American soldiers and not Japanese victims. Therefore, Japanese victims are always being discounted and devalued even within arguments that claim to advocate for saving lives. Additionally, the argument works under the assumption that the only option to end the war was unconditional surrender and, as a result, diplomacy was not an option. Under this assumption the options were: (1) the invasion of the Japanese home islands or (2) the use of the atomic bombs. Thus, 'saving lives' has little if anything to do with valuing Japanese civilian lives. Indeed, to view the bombs as saving lives (and thus being 'just' or 'good') necessitates the erasure of Japanese victims from the moral calculus of using the atomic bombs.
3. The Enola Gay, piloted by Paul Tibbets, is the Boeing B-29 Superfortress bomber that was used to drop the atomic bomb on Hiroshima. For the 50th anniversary of the bombings an exhibition was planned in Washington at the Smithsonian with the plane as the central piece. The organizers planned to have a section of the exhibit that would display what happened on the ground to Japanese victims. This decision incited outrage among many Americans and, eventually, the exhibit was changed to not include this section. This is, quite literally, an example of the erasure of atomic bomb victims within American historical discourse.
4. This case study is based on the PlayStation 4 version of the game including the base game and all major pieces of DLC content.
5. American military involvement in Asia, of course, extends well past the Pacific War and the atomic bombings of Japan. This includes, but is not limited to, colonialism within former Spanish-held territories post-1898 (especially in the Philippines), involvement in the Korean War (1950–1953), the invasion of Vietnam (1955–1975), and the illegal bombing of Laos and Cambodia that became part of that conflict.

References

Agence France-Presse & Jiji Press. (2020, August 6). 75 years on, abolition pleas from the last generation of hibakusha. *The Japan Times*. www.japantimes.co.jp/news/2020/08/06/national/abolition-pleas-japans-last-hibakusha/

Alperovitz, G. (1995). *The decision to use the atomic bomb*. Vintage Books.

Assmann, J. (1995). Collective memory and cultural identity. *New German Critique, 65*, 125–133.

Bernstein, B. J. (1996). Understanding the atomic bomb and the Japanese surrender: Missed opportunities, little-known near disasters, and modern memory. In M. J. Hogan (Ed.), *Hiroshima in history and memory* (pp. 38–79). Cambridge University Press.

Bethesda Game Studios. (2015). *Fallout 4* [PlayStation 4]. Bethesda Softworks.

Bix, H. (1996). Japan's delayed surrender: A reinterpretation. In M. J. Hogan (Ed.), *Hiroshima in history and memory* (pp. 80–115). Cambridge University Press.

Bolter, J. D., & Grusin, R. (1999). *Remediation: Understanding new media*. MIT Press.

Brewer, S. (2009). *Why America fights: Patriotism and war propaganda from the Philippines to Iraq*. Oxford University Press.

Burleigh, M. (2010). *Moral combat: A history of World War II*. Harper Press.

Chapman, A. (2016). *Digital games as history: How videogames represent the past and offer access to historical practice*. Routledge.

Chomsky, N., & Herman, E. S. (2002). *Manufacturing consent: The political economy of mass media*. Pantheon.

Costello, J. (2009). *The Pacific War 1941–1945*. Harper Perennial.

Diggins, J. P. (1989). *The proud decades: America in war and peace, 1941–1960*. W. W. Norton & Company.

Erll, A. (2007). *Memory in culture* (S. B. Young, Trans.). Palgrave Macmillan.

Erll, A. (2009). Remembering across time, space, and cultures: Premediation, remediation and the 'Indian Mutiny'. In A. Erll & A. Rigney (Eds.), *Media, remediation and the dynamics of cultural memory* (pp. 109–138). Walter de Gruyter GmbH & Co.

Frank, R. B. (2005). Ending the Pacific War: No alternative to annihilation. In D. Marston (Ed.) *The Pacific War: From Pearl Harbor to Hiroshima* (pp. 227–245). Osprey Publishing.

Halbwachs, M. (1980). *The collective memory* (F. J. Ditter and V. Y. Ditter, Trans.). Harper & Row, Publishers, Inc.

Jacobs, R., & Zwigenberg, R. (2020, August 6). The American narrative of Hiroshima is a statue that must be toppled. *CounterPunch*. www.counterpunch.org/2020/08/06/the-american-narrative-of-hiroshima-is-a-statue-that-must-be-toppled/

Kapell, M. W., & Elliot, A. B. R. (2013). Conclusion(s): Playing at true myths, engaging with authentic histories. In M. W. Kapell & A. B. R. Elliot (Eds.), *Playing with the past: Digital games and the simulation of history* (pp. 357–367). Bloomsbury Publishing Inc.

Lewis, T. (2020). *Atomic salvation: How the a-bomb attacks saved the lives of 32 million people*. Casemate Publishers.

Lifton, R. J., & Mitchell G. (1995). *Hiroshima in America: Fifty years of denial*. G. P. Putnam's Sons New York.

Minear, R. H. (1995). Atomic holocaust, Nazi holocaust: Some reflections. *Diplomatic History*, *19*(2), 347–365.

Murray, W., & Millett, A. R. (2001). *A war to be won: Fighting the Second World War*. The Belknap Press of Harvard University Press.

O'Reilly, C. T., & Rooney, W. A. (2005). *The Enola Gay and the Smithsonian Institution*. McFarland & Company, Inc., Publishers.

Spector, R. H. (1985). *Eagle against the sun: The American war with Japan*. Vintage Books.

Squire, K. D. (2004). *Replaying history: Learning world history through playing Civilization III*. [Dissertation, Indiana University]. ProQuest Dissertations and Theses. www.proquest.com/docview/305195950?pq-origsite=gscholar&fromopenview=true

Walzer, M. (1977). *Just and unjust wars: A moral argument with historical illustrations*. Basic Books.

Zinn, H. (2010). *The bomb*. City Lights Books.

9 Are the Bullets Going over Our Head? Designed Ambivalence in the Representation of Armed Conflict in Games

Patrick Prax

Introduction

The ways in which armed conflict is represented in games are a contested field both in games research and journalism and in the games industry and community. Games research is struggling with how perspectives that take a critical look at political economy of game production, specifically the connections between military forces and the games industry, can be squared with the various ways in which player interact with and interpret these games. There is a body of established work that convincingly argues that the games industry is intimately connected to warfare. Examples ranging from the use of gaming controllers to steer military drones (Lindley & Coulton, 2015) over digital games being developed and used as training and recruitment tools (Dyer-Witheford & De Peuter, 2019) make a strong argument that there is a connection between digital games and modern warfare. This critical research has argued convincingly that games and warfare are so tightly connected on a number of levels that it makes sense to see them as part of a *military-entertainment complex* (Andersen & Kurti, 2011; Dyer-Witheford & De Peuter, 2009; Lenoir, 2000; Robinson, 2012).[1]

These authors show that the notion of the military-entertainment complex not only refers to games portraying the army favourably, games featuring armed conflict as a preferred and legitimate way of solving problems and doing politics, or even the use of games as recruitment tools. It also means that on a more material level the technologies of war and digital entertainment converge. Gaming creates a market for tech and ICTs that, by offering an added use, make the development of military hardware more financially viable (Lenoir & Lowood, 2005). The flip-side is the colonial exploitation of for example the Republic of Congo, and thus the supply of rare earth minerals that are needed for the continued development of digital technology and thus games that are trade for military hardware (Ayres, 2012; Mantz, 2008).[2] Other intersections of the way armed conflict is represented in games are frequently connected to questions of humanism vs. nationalism (Dyer-Witheford & De Peuter, 2009; Mukherjee, 2018;

Robinson, 2012; Seiwald, 2020) or systemic racism and colonialism (Šisler, 2008). Capitalist market logics as well as the colonialist and fascist history of games and the games industry (Lundedal Hammar, 2020) give a clear reasoning for how the economic system that requires the exploitation of colonial areas to function is upheld via the use of the military. Games help to sell weapons and weapons are traded for resources that build gaming hardware. This kind of permanent war economy requires media to normalize it, and games are a part of this effort. For a recent overview over these perspectives and a contextualization of contemporary research, see Hammond & Pötzsch (2019) in the introduction of *War Games: Memory, Militarism and the Subject of Play* Even parts of analogue gaming, specifically strategy games and role-playing games, have their roots in and aesthetics borrowed from training tools for warfare (Trammell, 2015).

However, these arguments and modes of analysis run into a problem: in order to be able to claim that this origin and production of games impact players and culture they should be able to show these consequences in some way. Somehow, it should be possible to detect this influence either on games or on players. After all, what is the point of rigorously tracing and criticizing the influence of the military and the interconnectedness of games and the military industry from a political economy perspective if this influence is invisible in games and their players?

Attempting to answer this question leads to a body of equally as established and well-argued research in media- and game studies that makes a strong argument for the importance of the player as an active creator of the message of a game. This argument could be seen as a development of the understanding of how active audiences make meaning in general, coming out of communication research and being most succinctly embodied by 'the death of the author' (Barthes, 2001). In games, a medium that stresses interactivity, the impact of the player on the message of the game can be argued to be considerably greater than in other kinds of more linear or one-directional media. Players might subvert the games they are playing (Tanenbaum, 2013), might play them critically (Flanagan, 2009), engage in transgressive play and dark play (Jørgensen & Karlsen, 2019; Mortensen et al., 2015), or even mod them and change their message, something that I have focused on in previous work (Prax, 2016). This body of research argues that it is not exclusively the game that decides what playing it will look like. Instead, players have the freedom to play and experience games however they want. This leaves us with a paradox: Both of these perspectives make strong arguments but still, in a way, contradict each other. This leads to the frustrating situation where rigorous and important work examining the representation of armed conflict meets the equally important argument that players are free in shaping a game in their play and that it is therefore difficult to draw conclusions about the message of a game.

For example, in recent work about war in games, researchers again arrive at the conclusion that top-down promotion of militaristic values is a too simplistic view (McSorley, 2019). This is because actual player responses cannot be assumed based on an analysis of political economy (Lundedal Hammar & Woodcock, 2019) and that investigations of the interpretations of relevant games by players can produce incongruous results (Jørgensen, 2019). And, it is good to be careful here: exclusive reliance on this approach cannot account for players who play what, according to the analysis of its political economy, should be a pro-wargame. They may walk away with a war-critical experience or, for that matter, the opposite, as Jørgensen's (2019) analysis of players of *This War of Mine* shows (11 Bit Studios, 2014). In this game, player experience civil war from the perspective of a group of civilians who try to survive through winter in a war-torn city. With its depiction of the dark sides of war, including mental breakdowns and starvation, this game is typically seen as very clearly anti-war. However, Jørgensen (2019) still found players who played and understood it differently, rejecting it as 'ineffective', 'trying too hard,' or 'unintentionally funny'. The complexity of player reactions comes through when she explains that one player's 'response is to almost feel provoked by the attempt to promote a serious message through crude mechanics' (Jørgensen, 2019, p. 85). Recently, Hammond and Pötzsch (2019) have stressed the complexity of military propaganda in games:

> Given the long-standing relationship between the industry and the military indicated above, it is entirely plausible to view military-themed videogames as serving some sort of propaganda function in contemporary popular culture.
> Yet this does not necessarily mean that they are ideologically effective or straight-forward: such games offer a more complex mode of address, and elicit more varied player responses, than the term "propaganda" might be assumed to imply.
> (Hammond and Pötzsch, 2019, p. 4)

This is an important line of thinking. The maintenance of the military-entertainment complex in a situation where it is already established enough to deserve this title might not require too much propaganda. It does not need to change anything, but only needs to maintain a hegemonic worldview. In this situation, games can be made to support militarism in the eyes of the players who want to see that message in their games, but could at the same time convincingly claim to have a different message whenever they are critically examined, for example by journalists or researchers. Especially the analysis of issues such as the representation of armed conflict requires a level of care in the interpretation of games. There is a space of uncertainty where it is risky to judge games. A gentle and reflexive approach that makes sure that the researcher is not oversimplifying in either direction is necessary. That said, in the balancing-act between political economy and the military-entertainment complex on the one hand, and the active player on the other hand, this space of uncertainty could become a blind spot for analysis. This blind spot can be taken advantage of by designing games that are part of the military-entertainment complex and support militarism, but that are possible to be played and read differently, and that even plausibly could be argued to be critical of war and warfare. This way they can abuse the complexity of meaning-making in games to find a niche of plausible deniability. They can be pro-war, but have an alternative anti-war reading in the back-pocket. This could be, at the very least, a part of the problem that Hammond and Pötzsch (2019) are discussing above. Both critical game analysis and journalism could benefit from being able to recognize a tagged-on alternative reading without being thrown off by it. As a proposed solution, this chapter presents the concept of 'Designed Ambivalence', to enable critical approaches to handle complexities of meaning making in games about armed conflicts.

Defining Designed Ambivalence

In this chapter, I will present a definition and operationalization of *designed ambivalence*. The aim of *designed ambivalence* as a concept is to enable an understanding the blind-spot in the analysis of the representation of armed conflict in games, and to be able to see if that blind spot is used to disarm criticism. It will be based both the notion of *ambiguity by design* and by the discussion of the representation of war in games journalism and the games community.

Ambiguity in Design

From the perspective of the design research, a related concept is that of *ambiguity in design* (Gaver et al., 2003). In this classic of HCI research, Gaver et al. (2003) propose that ambiguity is a virtue in design because it allows designers to lift up issues without having to take responsibility towards resolving them. 'it [ambiguity] allows the designer´s point of view to be expressed while enabling users of different sociocultural backgrounds to find their own interpretations' (Gaver et al., 2003, p. 1). Gaver et al. (2003, p. 8) conclude that 'ambiguity is a powerful tool for designers to raise topics or ask questions while renouncing the possibility of dictating their answers'. Their chapter contains tactics for emphasizing ambiguity in design. A critical point and a danger they see is that renouncing the possibility of dictating answers, even within a frame of ambiguity in design, might instead mean renouncing the responsibility for how a certain text or design can be read. The representation of armed conflict is most certainly not the core area of application for the work of Gaver et al. (2003) and a quite extreme topic at that. However, at its core ambiguity in design is about offering grey tones and nuances in the representation of the world and then inviting the user to make up their own mind based on the its moral complexity.

Ambivalence, in *Merriam-Webster*, is defined as 'simultaneous and contradictory attitudes or feelings (such as attraction and repulsion) toward an object, person, or action' (*Merriam-Webster*: ambivalence; www.merriam-webster.com/dictionary/ambivalence). Accordingly, designed ambivalence means that something, in the case of this chapter a game, is designed to engender simultaneous and contradictory attitudes. This is conceptually different from ambiguity in design because it does not create a corridor of different interpretations or varying grey tones. Instead, something can be considered to have designed ambivalence if it supports competing, contradictory, and polarizing interpretations without productively joining them. In the case of the representation of armed conflict specifically, this means that designed ambivalence could be a relevant frame if a game represents violence and its consequences in warfare in a way that could be read as ravelling in destruction and glorifying the military on the one hand, or alternatively as a representation of the horrors of war that is meant to dissuade people from supporting it. In short, if a text communicates two competing extremes, but no grey tones or middle-ground, that would indicate designed ambivalence.

Designed Ambivalence in Online Culture

An example from the discourse about the representation of armed conflict in games in broader online culture that both serves as an example for why *designed ambivalence* is relevant here, and that offers a succinct formulation of the problem is the meme called '*Wow Cool Robot*'.[3] The meme shows a drawing of a Gundam robot suit on the left and the face of a fan looking at the robot from the right. The fan says 'Wow!! Cool Robot!!!'. At the same time, a shot coming out of the robot's gun goes over the head of the fan. The shot contains the message 'WAR IS BAD'. This meme is saying that stories like Gundam, one of the most successful Japanese manga- and anime series (and multi-media franchise) that features giant militaristic robot suits in space warfare, are at their core about the horrors of war, but that the fans of Gundam do not realize this because they are excited about and distracted by the aesthetics of the fighting robot. The message that 'WAR IS BAD' is both literally and figuratively going over their head. This meme exculpates media texts from their possible contribution to pro-war propaganda. It further decouples the content of a medium that is produced as part of a military-entertainment complex from pro-war messages. Instead, it positions such media as critical of war and stresses the responsibility of the audience who is missing the critical point of the text and is only misreading it as pro-war. Applied to the topic of this chapter the meme could be understood as a warning to researchers not to miss the actual, critical and, nuanced message of a game. This argument needs to be taken seriously. As mentioned above, it is absolutely possible that games that are trying to be part of a critical conversation about warfare are instead stigmatized, based on prejudice about games as being without substance, or possibly because of expectations of games as pro-war. Here, we are right at that blind spot of analysis. It is difficult to propose a critical perspective on a game, or the way it is representing conflict, because it is always possible that the issue does not lie with the game but that the analysis is missing the point and misreading the game.

In a situation like this, the concept of *designed ambivalence* should be helpful for analysis. It reveals that the view presented in the meme is advancing polar opposites without middle-ground or grey tones, because the reader of the game is portrayed as either understanding or ignorant, and the resulting views on the game are at odds with each other. The argument is not that discussions around the representation of warfare are complex and need nuanced approaches, but that critical approaches are missing the inherently ironic point of the text. This perspective completely removes the responsibility of the texts/games produced in a military-entertainment complex and makes critique impossible. An iteration of *Wow Cool Robot* (Figure 9.1) offers yet again an interesting perspective on this dynamic that is useful for the development of *designed ambivalence*. The meme in Figure 9.1 states that the people who believe in what the original version of

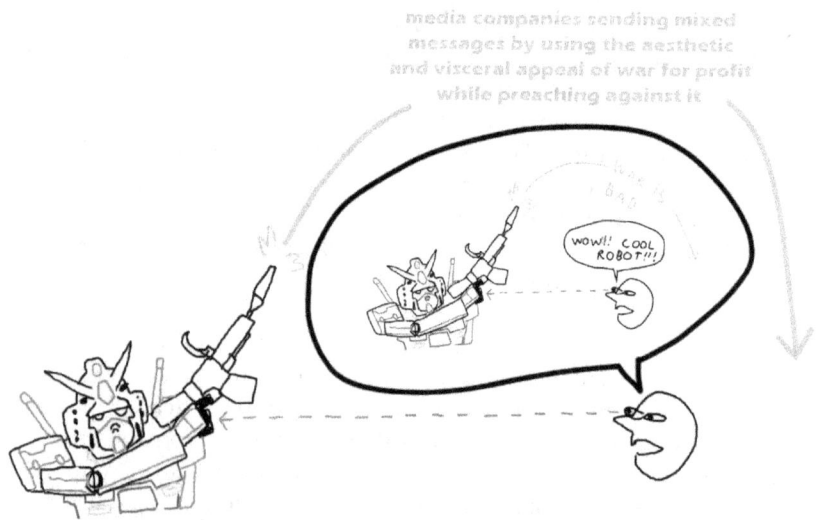

Figure 9.1 A development of the 'Wow Cool Robot' meme widening the frame to the political economy of conflict representations in cultural industries (Oberonn, 2018).

the meme described above is stating are themselves missing an important point that is going over *their* head, namely that 'media companies [are] sending mixed messages by using the aesthetic and visceral appeal of war for profit while preaching against it'. Games that are using the visceral appeal of war could qualify as a more complex kind of propaganda that Hammond and Pötzsch (2019) are writing about. They would serve their propaganda function while at the same time preserving the possibility to dodge criticism by means of including elements that could support an ironic or subversive reading that opposes war and warfare. The meme in Figure 9.1 could act as a kind of receipt for creating a wargame that hits the (blind-) spot of being immune to reflexive and careful criticism by using *designed ambivalence*.

The meme offers a reason for designing this way. The point is not that there is a cabal of evil game designers sitting somewhere planning to promote war through designing games. Instead, it poses that this way of designing simply maximizes the possible audience. This motivation maps to the political economy perspectives in research. The argument of political economy as an analytic frame is that games become pro-war because this makes financial sense in the existing system of cultural production. It positions this way of making games and presenting armed conflict as a consequence of the same economic and imperial system that is at the core of the criticism of political economy in general.

Definition and Operationalization

The core of the concept of *designed ambivalence* is that it is a way to design games to purposefully avoid critical analysis of the way the game is representing armed conflict. This is done through, and I am borrowing the formulation from the meme, 'sending mixed messages by using the aesthetics and visceral appeal of war for profit while preaching against it'. However, this could still refer to ambiguity in design where mixed messages could indicate an attempt to include nuances and alternative ways for the player to explore the complexities of the topic. In order to clarify the difference for the definition of *designed ambivalence*, this will be changed to '*sending contradictory messages by using the aesthetic and visceral appeal of war for profit while preaching against it*'.

As a last element in order to clarify what nuances and grey tones in the representation of armed conflict could look like, I am using the analysis of wargames by Dyer-Witheford and De Peuter (2019). Both the dehumanization of the opponents and the lack of a discussion of the meaning and consequences of violence have been shown in their analysis, and in games there is frequently no visibility of the wounded, of PTSD, or even of the long-term political consequences of the player's actions in the conflict. A game that sincerely claims to be using drastic depictions of warfare to avoid real tragedies will show the humanitarian cost of war. This offers us a final element of designed ambivalence: The absence of the representation of the humanitarian consequences of armed conflict.

In summary, *designed ambivalence* can be defined like this:

> Designed ambivalence is a way of designing the representation of armed conflict in games so that it resists a critical analysis by sending contradictory messages and supporting conflicting interpretations of the game. Instead of offering nuance and grey-tones, these games omit the real, human, consequences and costs of warfare and use the aesthetic and visceral appeal of war for profit while preaching against it.

In order to test the defined version of *designed ambivalence* the analysis will approach games with this set of questions:

1. Does the game represent armed conflict in a way that sends contradictory messages and supports conflicting interpretations?
2. Does it use the aesthetic and visceral appeal of war while preaching against it?
3. Does it offer nuance and grey tones to support the discussion of armed conflict?
4. Does it show or does it omit the human consequences of costs of warfare?

Reflexive Note

In reality, the question of what it means to be militarist, to 'support war', or to be against war and the military are more complex that this chapter can discuss. The military can, for example, be supported and strengthened specifically because one does not want war. With the complexity of the issue at hand it needs to be possible to communicate positive messages about the military or its function as well. On the other hand, given global imperialist power that is upheld by warfare and the reliability of the developed world, and specifically its technology industry on the spoils of these wars in terms of rare natural resources and cheap labour, this argument might itself need to consider the notion of the military-entertainment, and maybe more directly the military-industrial complex. The fact that Swedish universities and research, including mine, are partly funded by profits from the weapons industry is not lost on me. It is important to reflect on one's own position as a researcher and given that I am typing this chapter on a laptop that most likely contains conflict minerals while working in institutions that benefit from permanent war-economy, this means that I am also benefiting the *designed ambivalence* in the representation of armed conflict.

Analysis

In this chapter I am showing the usefulness of *designed ambivalence* through analyses of a set of relevant games. The analysis of games is predominantly concerned with how the games play. That means that both audio-visual presentation, narrative, and procedural gameplay are relevant. While procedural expression, interactivity, and rule systems are specifically important for games as a media form, this chapter is not interested in establishing any kind of hierarchy for media properties of games.

The analysis primarily uses auto-ethnographic play where the researcher themselves plays the relevant games. The cases that have been chosen for analysis have been specifically selected to show the breadth of how armed conflict is represented differently. In order to see if the notion of *designed ambivalence* can make a contribution, it makes sense to look at some of the games that other authors have analyzed previously to see if there are any possible differences produced by using this theoretical lens. Using previously analyzed games means that I cannot claim to have approached these titles without pre-conceptions any longer because I have read about them before in relevant games research. That said, I am trying to be reflexive of my biases, and to take into account Jørgensen's (2019) point that one playthrough and one player cannot get all the possible readings of a game. On the other hand, being aware of how previous researchers have interpreted a given game offers me the possibility to consciously look for alternatives and specifically ambivalence in the way a game can be interpreted.

Further research could, if *designed ambivalence* is shown to be a useful frame, use methods like close readings of games to look at what kind of techniques the game or designers deploy to create ambivalence.

The games that I will be analyzing for this chapter are:

- *Call of Duty: Modern Warfare 2* (Infinity Ward, 2009)
- *Spec Ops: The Line* (Yager Development, 2012)
- *This War of Mine* (11 Bit Studios, 2014)

Trigger warning: This analysis contains descriptions of the atrocities that are part of the analyzed games.

Call of Duty: Modern Warfare

One of the most controversial representations of armed conflict in recent years, the 'No Russian' level of *Call of Duty: Modern Warfare* (Infinity Ward, 2017) is in a sense a textbook example for testing the frame of *designed ambivalence*. The level starts with the player and a number of Russian 'terrorists' opening fire on civilians in front of a security check at an airport, killing them. Throughout the level, the player character and the terrorist group he tries to infiltrate shoot their way through the airport, fighting police, and either killing or scaring away civilians. The level ends when the leader of the group, when killing the player character, reveals that he had been aware of his under-cover mission the entire time and had even required it and the presence of an American soldier for his plan to work. The act of terror is a means of starting the war that the rest of game is about. Mechanically the player is not required to shoot at the civilians in any way while playing through the level. That said, the civilians are still being shot by the terrorists that are part of the group that the player character is working with.

The way the game is constructed offers two polar opposites in the possible readings. The game can be seen as depicting horrible violence as a spectacle, maybe a novelty. The alternative reading could be that the game warns against geopolitical meddling of the US. It could be read as saying that the ends do not justify the means, and that doing horrible things for some kind of greater good can rapidly collapse as a valid excuse. Other versions of these critical readings hope that getting to players feel disgust and shock at their own actions will get them to think about the realities where things like this might happen (Sterling, 2009), or point generally in the direction of games as art productively engaging even with extreme issues like this one (Campbell, 2013). Both kinds of readings do make sense to some extent but they offer no real middle-ground for interpretation. These different perspectives are contradictory and conflicting.

The next questions would be if these readings offer nuances and grey tones, and present information about the consequences and cost of war and warfare. This could be an entry point for a real conversation about geo-politics, terror, motivations for violence, or the role of imperial powers. The journalistic discussion of the recently remastered version of the game on *wirded.com* comments specifically on the way this level and its gratuitous violence are in fact not presented with any discussion of consequences or impact:

> Nothing about the level has any broader impact on the way the game feels to play. It just feels crass and stupid; what sort of undercover agent embeds in a terrorist group to not stop them from doing mass murder, anyway? The sequence is disturbing without having any clear reason to exist. It was, of course, controversial upon release, and the remaster includes an option to skip it, which feels like an admission that it was never that necessary to begin with.
>
> (Muncy, 2020)

This game, or more specifically this level that has been analyzed here, can be seen as using the aesthetic and visceral appeal of war while preaching against it. The discussion in both research (Campbell, 2013) and journalism shows that there really was a conversation about exactly this question when the game launched. That discussion could have benefited from the concept of *designed ambivalence*. This analysis would conclude with that *Call of Duty: Modern Warfare* (Infinity Ward, 2017) represents a case of *designed ambivalence*.

Spec Ops: The Line

Spec Ops: The Line (Yager Development, 2012) looks, from the outset, similar to *Call of Duty*, but could at the same time be seen as an opposite. The game is explicitly taking inspiration from *Heart of Darkness* (Conrad, 1899) and *Apocalypse Now* (Coppola, 1979). It is a third-person shooter where the player takes control of an elite US soldier sent into a war-torn Dubai. However, about in the middle of the game, the player is on a mission to rescue civilians and is confronted with a large group of well-armed opponents in a base between them and the mission target. The only option, in order to progress, is to use a white phosphorous mortar to clear out the enemy base. In order to do that, the player uses a mortar to fire a camera into the air and then, from the very abstract and distanced view of the airborne camera, aim the phosphorous strikes. This view initially distances the player from the effect of the weapon they are using, which is comparable to napalm. However, after having hit the entire enemy base the player needs to walk through the remains of the base and is directly confronted with the consequences of their actions. Soldiers are screaming, crawling towards the player, mortally burned and unable to fight, the in-game camera showing their faces and their suffering. After having nearly traversed the entire base, the player character realizes that he hit the group of civilians he had meant to rescue. He walks towards the horrific scene of burned civilian corpses, including a dead mother who in vain had attempted to protect her baby with her body.

The eyes of the player character dart forward and back as he attempts to un-see what is in front of him. The player character has already before showed signs of PTSD and psychosis, and this event pushes him over the edge. From here on out, the player character suffers from increasingly intrusive hallucinations, including playing an entire level for the second time while the player character is aware that he had done this before. At the end of the game, the player has the choice to let the player character commit suicide, to kill the rescue team that comes to pick him up, or to come with them and go home. When, in the latter alternative, a soldier asks how the player character survived all that he replies: 'Who said I did?'

This game features the visceral appeal of war. Large sections of the game are not considerably different from other shooter games and it clearly shows atrocities and the horrors of warfare. The game is a commercial release, aiming to make money. The *Spec Ops* franchise was not on the same level as *Call of Duty*, but it was still a known name and aimed for commercial success. However, the way these horrors are depicted are not in the same way supporting contradicting interpretations. As an example, the game is setting up the white phosphorous scene as ethical from the start and deliberately distances the player through the use of the airborne camera to show them the results of the horror that they have just now unleashed. The player has no other option than to use the weapon if they want to continue the game (and in the mind of the player character rescue civilians) but at the same time, what they have to do to continue is atrocious.

After shooting the weapon, the player is forced to confront the consequences of their actions directly. The game even forces the player character to slow down to a walk while traversing the burned camp, full of charred and dying soldiers that cry for help in vain. When I played it the first time, without having seen it before, I was shocked, mostly because the game was doing something that I was not expecting. The contrast of the disembodied view of the airborne camera while killing, and the direct confrontation with the results, has lasting impact. I was mostly shocked that I had, just recently, happily and easily brought this horror over people in the game. The end of the scene with the dead civilians is worse in the sense that the picture is even more horrible, but it is not having the same impact because killing civilians is not something I as a player consented to or knowingly did. However, that could also be a point about the collateral damage of warfare. It could lead to a discussion of how we wage war, how we detach ourselves and even our soldiers from the consequences of their actions using technology and visualization like airborne cameras. There are no clear answers here, but there are grey tones and nuances, even added insight through interactivity and play, added to the conversation about the atrocities of war. In any case, the game does not omit the costs of warfare and it does show the human consequences. Even the mental health of the player character does not recover from this and he can end the game committing suicide. He, in more than one way, dies in that desert.

Morwood (2014) in his analysis of *Spec Ops* sees this as an example 'to show how an ostensible wargame is capable of turning players against war or, at least, encouraging them to contemplate its consequences' (Morwood, 2014, p. 107). I would agree with his assessment. In a sense, this game is doing what most other games only claim to do. It does set the player up for a harsh look into the mirror by getting them to first do horrible things in the taken-for-granted normality of shooter games, to then unexpectedly show the human costs of these actions. This game can be an example of a more honest engagement with the human costs of war. It certainly uses the aesthetic and visceral appeal of war while preaching against it, but it does not use the possibility of an anti-war interpretation for plausible deniability. This analysis shows that the definition of *designed ambivalence* can handle difficult cases and that the different steps of the operationalization work. In this example, the game does use the visceral appeal of war, but it also presents the human costs of warfare and it offers a nuanced argument. Designed ambivalence can thereby be a category/concept/lens or perspective that is useful for discussing the relationship between player action and political economy.

This War of Mine

This War of Mine (11 Bit Studios, 2014) is known for representing the horrors of war. In the game, the player is responsible for, and experiencing the world through, a small group of civilians who try to survive inside a half-ruined house during a civil war. The people in the house that the player can control on missions to collect resources like food and other supplies experience stress and can suffer due to mental health. Besides this, as mentioned above, Jørgensen (2019) has found players that had other readings of the game. In my play-though, playing the game twice in a row, I can see what her point is. Already in the first play-though I resorted to using the wiki pages for the game to in a sense shield myself as the player and the people in the house from the worst possible circumstances. I did not kill or steal from people if it could be avoided. The moral and ethical dilemmas were a part of the reason for that. There is a location in the game where an elderly couple is protected by their son in a small apartment building. In the first play through I left them in peace and just scavenged what I could without disturbing them because they posed no threat and it would have felt wrong to kill them. That said, the other reason for this kind of play is the mood system in the game. The mood system influences the state of the playable characters and doing things they regard as wrong an immoral can make them depressed and even broken. Broken characters can be consoled and recover, but this takes resources and time that would otherwise be needed to secure the house and collect resources. A broken character does not function any longer and can die without help. In this way, *This War of Mine* includes mental health as a core game-play feature.

However, on the second play through I used the information from the wiki to make sure that I could play with Roman as one of the people in the house early on. Roman is a deserter with combat training which means that he, for the most part, can kill without experiencing depression. Using him I ended up killing close to the entirety of the town, looted everything, and stockpiled guns and resources. I was aware that I was subverting the game by playing that way.

This means that while it is possible to play the game in a way that foregrounds a different kind of engagement with armed conflict, doing this requires effort and is still visibly running counter to the intended way to play the game. Looking at this game through the lens of *designed ambivalence* shows that the game does come down clearly on the side of being critical towards armed conflict. It can be subverted in play, but has to be done on purpose. Is not offering contradictory messages and while it uses, in a way, the visceral appeal of war, it so clearly shows consequences of warfare and its horror that I would argue it can be seen as a clear example of a game that is critical of warfare.

Summary of Analysis

In summary, it can be said that *designed ambivalence* as a category was useful for analyzing these titles. It structured the conversation about how these games represent armed conflict and makes it possible to say something about the games that resonates with how others have been writing about them and which helps to take a step out of the blind spot of political economy and game studies. Especially, the ways in which the last two examples could be discussed and analyzed using the concept of *designed ambivalence* led to a more in-depth engagement with the text and managed to accommodate different ways to play. These cases where chosen to be difficult cases. That the analysis reflected that and showed that these games were not using *designed ambivalence* means that the concept does not return false positives in an area where the aim is to think twice and be conservative with judging games.

Discussion

As mentioned earlier, one of the advantages of both the way political economy and the *Wow Cool Robot* meme approach *designed ambivalence* is that it does not try to blame game designers. Games are not understood to have been made by evil designers or even military propagandists. The argument that designers can choose to implement designed ambivalence does not mean that they build propaganda or hide militarist dog whistles in their games on purpose. The point is not that this is about hiding militarist messages in plain sight. Instead the argument is that maintaining a military-entertainment complex does not seem to need clear and unambivalent messages. Especially in a culture that already is saturated by messages that support armed conflict, keeping the normalization of military conflict one of the viable options might be enough for the discursive continuation of the military-entertainment complex. Instead, what pushes games to represent armed conflict ambivalently are market logics: Representing armed conflict this way makes it possible to sell to everybody: no matter their politics, there is a possible reading of the game that will work for them. Designed ambivalence means that game producers do not, in fact, need to decide. They can have their cake and eat it too. For political economy research into games this means that this approach highlights a mechanism by which market and production logics can influence the content and messages of games.

That being said, this approach does not completely release designers and game producers from responsibility. While *designed ambivalence* is here understood as a consequence of economical logics that should be valid for media beyond games, working with the subject matter of armed conflict could be seen to carry with it a certain responsibility for the more diffuse and distributed cultural effects. *Designed ambivalence* does normalize the portrayal of war in a way that marginalizes the discussion of the real human consequences of warfare. This might create an environment where games that are more sincerely critical of war are met with resistance. The way *Spec Ops: The Line* represented warfare has been seen as unorthodox, even though it does what the other games are just pretending to do. It does show the horrors of war in a way that at least makes it possible to convincingly argue that it means to prevent future atrocities. I would like to just take a second to point this out: showing the real, human, cost of war is the exception! Taking *designed ambivalence* as something to be avoided in design would mean aiming for representing the costs and consequences of armed conflict in a more realistic fashion. It would mean offering nuances and grey tones around conflict, instead of one straight and one critical reading that are opposed to each other. As a final consideration, the notion of *designed ambivalence* in a way concerns itself with the vulnerability of media analysis to plausible deniability, to manipulation, and to lies. This might also be a topic of growing importance in an environment of post-facts and fake news.

Conclusion

This chapter offers the definition and operationalization of *designed ambivalence* as a means to address a blind spot in between research that focusses on the political economy of game design on the one hand and work that stresses the importance of player activity in meaning-making on the other hand. It is meant to address the situation in which Hammond and Pötzsch (2019, p. 4) at the same time see it as 'entirely plausible to view military-themed video games as serving some sort of propaganda function in contemporary popular culture' but also state that these games are not necessarily 'ideologically effective or straight-forward'. *Designed ambivalence* is developed based on these perspectives. The definition of *designed ambivalence* and its operationalization can support the analysis of how games represent polarizing issues like armed conflict and it can help researchers to make sense of seemingly incongruent and opposing results. *Designed ambivalence* is here understood as a consequence of the production of games for profit in the military-entertainment complex and as a means of making it possible to sell to a broader target audience by offering competing interpretations for the atrocities represented in the game. The proposed frame of *designed ambivalence* for the analysis of armed conflict in games does this by arguing that games do not need to be either effective or straightforward to fill a function in a media system that is a part of the military-entertainment complex. This way of understanding the connection between the political economy of games and their content does not see propagandists behind these ambivalent representations of armed conflict. It instead understands *designed ambivalence* as a way for business-savvy developers to sell to both sides of the political isle through tapping into the aesthetics of war and maintaining plausible deniability. This ambivalent representation of armed conflict is understood as a consequence of the production of games as cultural commodities. Unmasking the use of designed ambivalence as a strategy is necessary for critical game analysis and can even be useful for the conversation in games journalism and the wider gaming community.

Notes

1 The notion of the Military-entertainment complex is based on the term 'Military-industrial complex' coined by former US president Eisenhower in his famous warning of the US-American people: 'The total influence – economic, political, even spiritual – is felt in every city, every statehouse, every office of the federal government. . . . Our toil, resources and livelihood are all involved; so is the very structure of our society. In the councils of government, we must guard against the acquisition of unwarranted influence, whether sought or unsought, by the military – industrial complex' (Eisenhower, 1961).
2 'Where Mobutu's Congo had been a cold-war ally against communism in Africa, and Kazakhstan a Soviet weapons depot, both have assumed new roles in a digital economy where cell phones and gaming stations are traded for weapons, which thereby enable warlords to continue processes the reproduce the entire system of production and exchange' (Mantz, 2008, p. 42).
3 Memes are subject to rapid iterations that often modify and reply to each other. Some of the history of this meme is shown here: https://knowyourmeme.com/memes/wow-cool-robot (accessed 11/04/2022)

References

11 Bit Studios. (2014). *This war of mine* [PC]. 11 Bit Studios.
Andersen, R., & Kurti, M. (2011). From America's army to call of duty: Doing battle with the military entertainment complex. *Democratic Communiqué, 23*(1), 45.
Ayres, C. J. (2012). The international trade in conflict minerals: Coltan. *Critical Perspectives on International Business, 8*(2), 178–193.
Barthes, R. (2001). The death of the author. *Contributions in Philosophy, 83*, 3–8.
Campbell, V. (2013). Playing with controversial images in videogames: The terrorist mission controversy in Call of duty: Modern warfare 2. In F. Attwood (Ed.), *Controversial images* (pp. 254–268). Palgrave Macmillan.
Conrad, J. (1899). *Heart of darkness*. Blackwood's Edinburgh Magazine.
Coppola, F. (1979). *Apocalypse now* [Movie]. Omni Zoetrope.
Dyer-Witheford, N., & De Peuter, G. (2009). *Games of empire: Global capitalism and video games*. University of Minnesota Press.
Dyer-Witheford, N., & De Peuter, G. (2019). Armed vision and the banalization of war: Full spectrum warrior. In J. Marchessault & S. Lord (Eds.), *Fluid screens, expanded cinema* (pp. 231–250). University of Toronto Press.
Eisenhower, D. (1961) *Farewell Address*. Both audio recording and written notes available at the Dwight D. Eisenhower Presidential Library, Museum, and Boyhood Home. Retrieved May 31, 2022, from www.eisenhowerlibrary.gov/research/online-documents/farewell-address

Flanagan, M. (2009). *Critical play: Radical game design*. MIT Press.
Gaver, W., Beaver, J., & Benford, S. (2003). Ambiguity as a resource for design. In *CHI '03: Proceedings of the SIGCHI conference on human factors in computing systems* (pp. 233–240). https://doi.org/10.1145/642611.642653
Hammond, P., & Pötzsch, H. (2019). Introduction: Studying war and games. In P. Hammond & H. Pötzsch (Eds.), *War games: Memory, militarism and the subject of play* (pp. 1–14). Bloomsbury Academic.
Infinity Ward. (2017). *Call of duty: Modern warfare 2* [PC]. Activision. (Original work published 2009)
Jørgensen, K. (2019). Understanding war game experiences: Applying multiple player perspectives to game analysis. In P. Hammond & H. Pötzsch (Eds.), *War games. Memory, militarism and the subject of play* (pp. 73–88). Bloomsbury Publishing.
Jørgensen, K., & Karlsen, F. (2019). *Transgression in games and play*. MIT Press.
Lenoir, T. (2000). All but war is simulation: The military-entertainment complex. *Configurations, 8*(3), 289–335.
Lenoir, T., & Lowood, H. (2005). Theaters of war: The military-entertainment complex. In H. Schramm, L. Schwarte, & J. Lazardzig (Eds.), *Collection, laboratory, theater: Scenes of knowledge in the 17th century* (pp. 427–456). Walter de Gruyter.
Lindley, J., & Coulton, P. (2015). Game of drones. In *CHI Play '15: Proceedings of the 2015 annual symposium on computer-human interaction in play* (pp. 613–618). ACM. http://dl.acm.org/citation.cfm?id=2810300
Lundedal Hammar, E. (2020). Imperialism and fascism intertwined: A materialist analysis of the games industry and reactionary gamers. *Gamevironments, 13*, 317–357.
Lundedal Hammar, E., & Woodcock, J. (2019). The political economy of wargames: The production of history and memory in military video games. In P. Hammond & H. Pötzsch (Eds.), *War games: Memory, militarism and the subject of play* (pp. 52–66). Bloomsbury Publishing.
Mantz, J. W. (2008). Improvisational economies: Coltan production in the eastern Congo. *Social Anthropology, 16*(1), 34–50.
McSorley, K. (2019). Playing in the end times: Wargames, resilience and the art of failure. In P. Hammond & H. Pötzsch (Eds.), *War games: Memory, militarism and the subject of play* (pp. 37–51). Bloomsbury Publishing.
Mortensen, T. E., Linderoth, J., & Brown, A. M. (2015). *The dark side of game play: Controversial issues in playful environments*. Routledge.
Morwood, N. (2014). War crimes, cognitive dissonance and the abject: An analysis of the anti-war wargame Spec ops: The line. *Democratic Communiqué, 26*(2), 107–107.
Mukherjee, S. (2018). Playing subaltern: Video games and postcolonialism. *Games & Culture, 13*(5), 504–520.
Muncy, J. (2020, May 9). Call of duty: Modern warfare 2 is still an infuriating relic. *Wired*. www.wired.com/story/revisiting-call-of-duty-modern-warfare-2/
Oberonn, C. (2018, July 22). Concept: The 'wow! cool robot!' meme [Blog]. *Charlesoberonn*. https://charlesoberonn.tumblr.com/post/176153174336/concept-the-wow-cool-robot-meme-but-you-go
Prax, P. (2016). *Co-creative game design as participatory alternative media*. [Doctoral thesis, Informatics and Media, Uppsala University]. www.diva-portal.org/smash/record.jsf?pid=diva2:923235

Robinson, N. (2012). Videogames, persuasion and the war on terror: Escaping or embedding the military – Entertainment complex? *Political Studies, 60*(3), 504–522. https://doi.org/10.1111/j.1467-9248.2011.00923.x

Seiwald, R. (2020). Play America great again. Manifestations of Americanness in Cold War themed video games. *Gamevironments, 13*. https://doi.org/10.26092/elib/406

Šisler, V. (2008). Digital Arabs: Representation in video games. *European Journal of Cultural Studies, 11*(2), 203–220.

Sterling, J. (2009). Why I will support Modern warfare 2. *Destructoid.* www.destructoid.com/why-i-will-support-modern-warfare-2/

Tanenbaum, T. J. (2013). How I learned to stop worrying and love the gamer: Reframing subversive play in story-based games. *DiGRA Conference, 7*.

Trammell, A. (2015). *The ludic imagination: A history of role-playing games, politics, and simulation in Cold War America, 1954–1984.* [Thesis, ProQuest Dissertations & Thesis Global]. Rutgers, The State University of New Jersey.

Wilde, T. (2017, April 28). Don't try to sell Call of duty to us as anti-war. *PC Gamer.* Retrieved April 11, 2022, from www.pcgamer.com/dont-try-to-sell-call-of-duty-to-us-as-anti-war/

Yager Development. (2012). *Spec Ops: The Line* [PC]. 2K Studios.

10 Where Are the White Perpetrators in All the Colonial Board Games? A Case Study on *Afrikan Tähti*

Sabine Harrer and J. Tuomas Harviainen

Introduction

This chapter explores the representation of colonial atrocities in European board gaming by investigating the role of the white perpetrator. While many internationally successful board games explicitly draw on historical colonial themes in their aesthetics and central gameplay premise, a central agent of colonial conflicts seems to be missing, the white perpetrator. Where has he gone (and mostly it is an implied 'him')? This chapter looks at the aesthetic features which allow colonial-themed board games to simultaneously affirm and deny the violent presence of a white perpetrator through their design premise.

We focus this quest on an exemplary case study of *Afrikan Tähti* ('Star of Africa'), a popular Finnish board game from 1951 (Mannerla), which is still widely played across Europe. The game has a history of being accused of portraying colonial violence (e.g. Nummelin, 1997; Ylänen, 2017), as well as defenders who state that it depicts a harmless, if outdated fantasy, suited especially for very young players. Furthermore, within Finland and beyond, especially within Northern European ex-colonial nations like Sweden, Denmark and Norway, *Afrikan Tähti* has been able to establish itself as a household classic. Publishing companies like *Alga*, *BRIO* and *Egmont* have distributed translated versions of the game to Nordic audiences, including *Den forsvunne diamanten* (Norway), *Den försvunna diamanten* (Sweden) and *Afrikas Stjerne* (Denmark).

Given the wide-spread popularity of this simple dice-rolling game, we are especially interested to unpack the main thematic paradox at work in *Afrikan Tähti* as an emblematic example of many colonial-themed board games, namely that it simultaneously depicts and hides white-coded atrocities through abstraction (see Borit et al., 2018; Foasberg, 2016; Robinson, 2014). By being a conceptual rather than realistic simulation of history (as per Chapman, 2016), the game emphasizes this, through its designer's selection on what to present and what to hide. We thereby contribute to a larger project of naming and 'making strange' (Dyer, 1997) casual fantasies of white domination in European board game culture. The idea is that such fantasies can only remain casual if their intrinsic logics of white violence and the dehumanization of racial 'others' remain (wilfully) unacknowledged by a majority of players.

While digital games routinely mediate violence through white male avatars (Passmore et al., 2018; Dietrich, 2013), board games do not need to rely on such directly racialized elements. Instead, they abstract the presence of white violence through the use of pawns, tokens, maps and ludic rituals (e.g. Robinson, 2014) which construct the implied player as someone who would be likely to accept the role of a white supremacist colonizer. We thus suggest that the presence of the white perpetrator in colonial board games emerges in the intersection of colonial rules, ludic materials and rituals carried out with enthusiasm by the players. As pointed out by Salen and Zimmerman (2004), games can be seen as having three levels of rules: operational rules on how to play the game (e.g. 'move your counter a number of steps equal to the dice roll'), constitutive rules that function behind the operational ones (e.g. the concepts of 'money' and 'trade') and implicit rules that are not marked down anywhere but the players nevertheless take into account (e.g. 'no peeking'). In *Afrikan Tähti*, the white perpetrator is present on all three levels.

Board Games as White Spaces

In this chapter we approach board games from a perspective of Critical Whiteness Theory (CWT), as part of those practices, materials and institutions designed to systematically benefit white people (Dyer, 1997; Lorde, 1984). Since whiteness is an ideological framework invented and perpetuated since colonial times, its circulation through board games is neither surprising nor is it the product of malicious intentions by designers or players. It is closely associated with the persistence of colonial tropes in strategy games, which is a long-standing topic in game studies (e.g. Breger, 2008; Lammes, 2003; Mukherjee, 2017; Poblocki, 2002). More recently, postcolonial game scholarship has drawn attention to the importance of maps and cartography in making white privilege playable (Mukherjee, 2017; Murray, 2018), including detrimental effects on players from regions frequently misrepresented by such maps (Mukherjee, 2018). Overall, there is a growing consensus that leaving patterns of white supremacy and colonial values in games unchecked comes at the cost of harming an increasing number of non-white and non-Western players, who are othered, stereotyped and thus alienated from 'white' gaming spaces (e.g. Gray, 2012; Harrer, 2018; Mukherjee, 2018; Nishi et al., 2015; Passmore et al., 2018).

In board games like *Risk*, *Puerto Rico*, *Vasco da Gama* and *Afrikan Tähti*, existing geographies and territories are appropriated through the lens of coloniality and whiteness. This is done by representing these territories as empty places to be 'cultivated' through 'sophisticated' playful involvement

(López et al., 2019). From a CWT perspective, the eruption of colonial violence in these settings is a matter of white self-representation, and more precisely the ludic staging of civilizing activities historically performed by white Europeans.

Adding to the existing discussion of how colonial violence pushes marginalised players into positions of 'subaltern play' (Mukherjee, 2018), we explore the complementary discourse of joyful attachment to white supremacist values through European board game design and play. We do so while considering the spatial nature of whiteness (Bell, 2017) and its 'invisible' properties to white designers and players (Dyer, 1997). Part of the violence enacted through white self-representation is what cultural scholar Anne McClintock describes as the imperial *conversion* project (McClintock, 1995). Attempts to systematize human life according to Enlightenment standards was 'dedicated to transforming the earth into a single economic currency, a single pedigree of history and a universal standard of cultural value – set and managed by Europe' (McClintock, 1995, p. 34). This logic applies to European style board games featuring colonial themes as well. They convert the complexity of colonial history into a single playable currency, a single set of mechanics and universal aesthetics of gameplay – set and managed by European board game designers.

A significant trend in colonial board games has been that they hide or even erase the violence of the situation (Borit et al., 2018; Foasberg, 2016; Robinson, 2014). For example, exploitative or even slave-labor based production gets abstracted to mere economic decisions, as in the case of *Puerto Rico* (2002), *Goa* (2004), just as was done in pre-*Afrikan Tähti* games such as *Diplomacy* (1939), *Jeu des Échanges: France – Colonies* (1941), and *South American Pictorial Travel and Trading Game* (1942). In addition to game mechanics, linguistic choices often function to disavow the cruelty of European colonial violence: *Puerto Rico*'s rules, for example, use the word 'colonists' (rather than the more appropriate 'enslaved people') to refer to the brown tokens working on colonized land. A central exception to erasing violence can of course be found in games of conquest such as *Risk* (Lamorisse, 1957), where the focus is on military conflict. Yet even there, the racial dimension of military conflict remains unacknowledged.

As Wilson (2015) points out, many players of colonial games are primarily interested in the mechanics of the game and may thus consider the theme less important. From a CWT perspective, this must be treated with suspicion, since players' conscious interests say little about the unconscious dimension of whiteness as a societal structure. In fact, to claim mechanical over thematic importance may be a deflection strategy for players who want to avoid difficult discussions about coloniality in games. In the case of *Afrikan Tähti*, which is generally held to have very poor mechanics, as demonstrated by, for example, its reviews on BoardGameGeek, it is further implausible that people would play it for its mechanical design alone.

Methodology

In this chapter, we perform a close reading (e.g. Bizzocchi & Tanenbaum, 2011) of *Afrikan Tähti* and the way it has been perceived by players within the last decade. While our main focus is on the reading of three major design aspects – *game board, mechanics,* and *character design,* we also reviewed international user comments on the game's BoardGameGeek site[1] (n= 185) and comments on a recent social media debate initiated by the Finnish comedian Ilkka Kivi on Facebook (n=352). Rather than comparing multiple games, the goal of our analysis is to investigate how ideological features of coloniality and whiteness, especially as they pertain to violence, persist below the threshold of conscious play or design.

Our close reading method is grounded in the understanding that games are kinaesthetic, in that they establish a dynamic connection between mechanics, aesthetics, themes, and the players' bodies (e.g. Keogh, 2014). This understanding is inspired by a cultural studies approach to games as pedagogical sites with a normative, hegemonic function (e.g. Harrer, 2022; Seidl, 2008). More specifically to whiteness, this means that we approach *Afrikan Tähti* as a 'racial project' whose design pushes towards maintaining the hegemonic racial order (Leonard, 2003) by engaging players in a multimodal experience of rules, aesthetics and themes.

Applying Critical Whiteness Theory (CWT) to board game studies, we expect that whiteness manifests itself through its *invisible* properties in European board games (Dyer, 1997). We contend that this is a theory which has been critiqued for its limitations, especially in how it recentres whiteness as a point of reference. After all, whiteness is only invisible to those who inhabit it, while it is blatantly visible to racial minorities (Ahmed, 2004). However, this concern exactly mirrors our limitations as white European researchers attempting to study white supremacy in a European game. Rather than expecting this to yield comprehensive results, we do so following an ethical imperative to *make whiteness strange* by making it visible (Dyer, 1997).

We are aware of the paradoxical nature of such a proposition. On the one hand, as white researchers with roots in Austria and Finland, two countries which have benefited from European colonial activity, we are the beneficiaries of historically grown structural advantages like white European privilege (Rastas, 2012). Being fluent in and able to use the particular lingo of white European game studies enables us to perform a particular kind of 'critical discourse' which gets recognized within certain game studies circles.

However, from the perspective of CWT, this creates the paradox of what Sara Ahmed has termed the 'performativity' of critical whiteness (Ahmed, 2004). At the same time of critiquing white dominance, we cannot help but confirm whiteness as dominance and whiteness as norm via our presence and standpoints (Harding, 1992) as white authors. This is especially problematic when considering that this article deals with ludic representations of Africa, while our epistemologies and methodologies are steeped in a Eurocentric, and thus structurally racist worldview. This limits and contextualizes how we can productively make sense of a game like *Afrikan Tähti* as a cultural artifact. We can aim at unpacking what the game does to casually perpetuate white supremacist values. What we cannot do is speak to its impact on racial minority players

By acknowledging these limitations via our racialized positionality as white researchers, we mobilize what Ahmed calls the 'myth of transcendence' in whiteness studies: By admitting our limitations via our 'bad' racist socialization, we declare ourselves 'good'. Ahmed critiques this self-reflexive turn in whiteness studies as a fantasy because the conditions are not in place that would allow such declarations to do what they say. Under current conditions, any declarations of whiteness prevent, rather than facilitate the kind of critical transformation desired by critical discourse.

Our ambition with this chapter must be seen in the light of this paradoxical tension between 'making strange' acts of white- and European coded violence in *Afrikan Tähti* while doing so from a standpoint which benefits from current racial hierarchies. The goal is both to reflect on our collective white European complicity in accepting atrocities committed by our ancestors to become whitewashed and glorified by games, and to craft a language of accountability which can be usefully expanded in similar future studies (see Harrer & Laiti, in press).

Maps, Mechanics and Bodies in *Afrikan Tähti*

Kari Mannerla was 19 years old when he finalized the design of *Afrikan Tähti* in 1949. Little did he know that almost 70 years later, his simple dice rolling game would not only be among the most popular games in the Nordic region[2] but would have gained cult status among its Finnish audience who unanimously hail it as part of Finland's cultural heritage.[3] At the same time, *Afrikan Tähti* is very explicitly a game about colonial conquest and exploitation. The players start by receiving funds and placing their token on one of two North African cities on a distorted African map from where they begin their scramble for the titular 'Star of Africa' diamond. This happens by taking turns rolling the dice, moving their pawns deeper into the African continent, and paying to loot tokens from the board: These tokens elicit various effects, ranging from disappointment (empty tokens), monetary enrichment (gems), assault (white cowboy bandits stealing a player's funds) or simply 'luck' (a horseshoe or visa which allows players to leave the continent in the end). Once a player has discovered the 'Star of Africa', it becomes their mission to bring it to 'safety' back in the North, and thereby a very clearly implied colonizing Europe that is the actual starting and return point. All other players attempt to plunder the rest of the continent in an attempt to find a lucky token which will make them the winner instead if they make it 'home' first.

At first glance, the entanglement of Finnish national identity with a game about plundering colonial Africa seems odd. After all, as part of its national self-narrative, Finland likes to stylize itself as an outsider to European colonialism, insisting on its "exceptionalist" status which seems to alleviate it from suspicions around structural racism and discrimination (Rastas, 2012). As Anna Rastas argues, this discourse of white Finnish exceptionalism substantiates rather than dissipates the existence of white supremacist values at the core of Nordic self-narratives.

In the section ahead, we discuss *Afrikan Tähti* as a symptom of structural racism, not only as a relic of its time and the way Europeans like Kari Mannerla desired to see Africa in the 1950s, but as a demonstration of how Europeans in the 2010s still desire to *unsee* their own involvement in colonial atrocities. Mannerla himself critiqued the game map's inaccuracies in his older years, but did not challenge the appropriateness of turning colonial conquest into a game theme. In 2005 he even published a similar game set in South America, clearly showing that the colonial aspects of the game were not a problem to him. 70 years later, players endorse the game for a different reason, namely for its function as an intergenerational bonding object among presumably white Finnish families, as reported by several reviewers on BoardGameGeek. The project of making *Afrikan Tähti* strange using CWT requires us to pierce this surface of national nostalgia and face the heart of game design. This is where we find the white perpetrator.

White Violence through Ludic Mapmaking

> So geographers, in Afric maps,
> With savage pictures fill their gaps,
> And o'er unhabitable downs
> Place elephants for want of towns.
>
> —Jonathan Swift, On Poetry: A Rhapsody[4]

Map making and cartography have been described as powerful tools of imperial control (McClintock, 1995) and a key component in the colonial construction of gaming spaces (Mukherjee, 2018). European colonial maps of Africa have historically served not only to neutrally sketch 'discovered' territories, but to declare symbolic ownership over these territories from a Eurocentric perspective. Jonathan Swift's lines above satirically call out the failings of geography by pointing to the cartographic convention of filling colonial unknown spots with fantastical, 'savage' beasts. Thus, 'savagery' is a direct result of cartography, a symptom of European embarrassment over ignorance (Neill, 2002). Much of this is contained in the design of *Afrikan Tähti*'s game board, which adopts the visual language of colonial-style cartography to make 'Africa' palatable to white European players.

When it comes to the presentation of African geography, the map highlights 32 places, equally represented by red dots and referred to as cities in the rules. Upon closer inspection, these 'cities' in fact include references to nations, regions, and landmarks as well, occasionally using outdated colonial terminology. This conflation of different geographical phenomena and names from different points in time under a single visual category signifies how little geographical accuracy matters to the game. The map prioritizes the perpetuation of colonial names, most perniciously 'Slave Coast' and 'Gold Coast', which come with connotations of intergenerational trauma and long-lasting harm on African economy and society. There are no compelling historical reasons for using this nomenclature,[5] besides presenting these places from a sanitized white supremacist perspective which frames atrocity as adventure. Both locations' names are further emphasized by the rules: The value of any gem found at 'Gold Coast' is doubled, while finding an empty marker at 'Slave Coast' forces the player to miss three turns, while being temporarily[6] 'held as a slave'.

There are two locations which visually stand out and hold the special function of start and end points: Tangier and Cairo. It is significant that these cities are located in the North, and thereby define the direction of ludic expansion southwards. As we will expound in the next section, this direction attributes positive experiences to the North ('home', 'safety' and 'success'), while classifying in-land expeditions towards the South as risky, invoking the logics of the so-called 'Scramble for Africa'. On the visual level, Tangier and Cairo are represented by comparatively large illustrations of the Grand Mosque (Tangier) and the Giza Necropolis (Cairo), marking them as civilizations. Compared to this 'civilized' North, Central and South African regions are crammed with stereotypical imagery of primitive peoples and wildlife roaming the jungle. The relegation of African presence to the decorative level represents it as passive and frozen in time. African peoples are literally 'stuck' on the board, which contrasts them to the active, mobile players moving their tokens across the board and taking from the board. This mimics what McClintock has called *panoptical time*, the colonial viewpoint from which European activity is treated as the pinnacle of human civilization, while Indigenous, Black people and People of colour are imagined in a state of perennial pastness (McClintock, 1995; cf. López et al., 2019). It also minimizes the documented history of precolonial African politics, for example the existence of kingdoms, empires, statelets, principalities, city-states and acephalous societies (Iweriebor, 1982), and the structural resistance of Africans to colonial rule (Asiwaju, 1974; Brantley, 1981). At the time the game was released in the early 1950s, 177 million Africans were living on the continent, a fact which seems surprising when looking at the map.

Besides geographical features and nomenclature, the game board geography is structured by ludic elements. Next to the red 'city' markers, these are in-land travel routes, sea- and air routes, the latter allowing long-distance travel. These travel routes spread equally across the continent, underscoring the lack of concern for real-world circumstances (e.g. Cape Verde is an island country which cannot be accessed by land). The suggestion is that European movement was equally possible across all African regions, a contention that is historically false. As mentioned, European attempts at establishing control were frequently crossed by local resistance tactics, such as migration or non-compliance with forced labor (cf. Asiwaju, 1974). In the game, such resistance is abstracted and externalized via the arbitrary 'chance' mechanic of the die. How far each player is allowed to move each turn is externally determined. However, unlike in history, progression of movement through Africa, however slow, is always guaranteed. In the interest of providing a balanced travel experience, a 'safari' on rails, all places are made equally accessible to the implicitly heroic European player.

Whether this succeeds or not is itself contested. On BoardGameGeek, several players express their dismay about the dice mechanics as too simplistic (e.g. 'Pretty stupid random dice rolling' (R20), 'Marginal choices to be made' (R25)). This tendency can be interpreted in two ways: First, it might mean that the players uttering the critique wish to see the complexities of colonial exploitation problematized and presented in a more nuanced light. However, in our sample, the complaints about 'simple gameplay' never contain a reference to the game's politics. This suggests a second reading. Players would appreciate a more sophisticated representation of white privilege; one that would empower them to experience white superiority in a deeper way than a simple dice roll can.

Unlike other colonial themed games, especially computer games which represent unexplored regions through *fog of war* (Lammes & Smale, 2018; Mukherjee, 2018), all relevant places in *Afrikan Tähti* are visibly known. This constructs a notion of European manifest destiny: It is not only guaranteed that we progress with each move, we are also guaranteed to *find* the treasure, sooner or later. Such it is written in the rules.

Old Mechanics of New Imperialism

While the previous section explored how *Afrikan Tähti's* map is designed to present Africa in terms of a white supremacist playground, it is important to look at the way players are invited to enter, explore, and exploit this map. This starts with the tedious ritual of setting up a game by putting the 32 'city' markers face down on the African map and receiving 300 pounds from a nebulous bank. The players then put their pawns on either of the two starting cities, Tangier and Cairo. Rolling their dice, the players make their way into the continent, using their finances to cover air and boat travel, and to flip 'city' tokens in the hopes of finding the Cullinan Diamond. This can be a long process, since tokens can contain a variety of items, including gems which are exchanged for money, white bandits with cowboy hats (who take their money), or nothing at all. Once a player has found the Diamond, their objective is to take it to 'safety' in Tangier or Cairo. If they do so, they win, unless a fellow player with a horseshoe (or in later versions, a visa) manages to reach the North before them.

There are three dimensions of this gameplay which are salient in characterizing white colonial violence. As mentioned, the overall gameplay premise of competing over African soil by raiding and looting its resources is highly evocative of the 19th century European 'Scramble for Africa'. Both in the game, and in history, the reason for this invasion is purely economic (e.g. Iweriebor, 2002; Oyebade, 2002). When the players receive money from an undisclosed source without explanation, they are neither supposed to question its purpose nor origin, nor are they to second-guess their rule-given entitlement to invade and take from the African continent. The game does not challenge players to ask *whether* to exploit Africa, but only *how* to do so most efficiently in the light of European competition. Much in line with nationalist agendas during New Imperialism, the game stresses the importance of inter-imperial fights: How can players plan their budget more carefully than their opponents? Who gets to find the Diamond first? Can the finder be stopped? This fixation on game economics captures well the effect of greed inherent in white expansionist power fantasies. From the moment the game starts, Africa only exists as an exploitable surface and an exotic backdrop. The real objective is gaining dominance over other *Europeans* around the Nordic summer cottage table, often a parent, childhood friend, or significant other.

Besides the unquestioned finances players are given to procure the diamond, the mechanics of *taking resources* are worth a closer inspection. When a player reaches a 'city' they can pay to flip the marker and take it from the board. This mechanic abstracts and sanitizes the violent mining and looting practices established during New Imperialism. Simulating a colonial attitude, players are neither interested in what they precisely pay for, nor whom they pay when they 'flip' a marker. Likewise, if the player is out of money, they may roll a die to see if they may flip the marker, in a manner referring also to prospecting, but in this case completely without compensating anyone. Rolling the dice here is a sanitized representation of the brute force exerted by European explorers to enhance their economic 'luck' at all cost.[7] The flipping mechanism furthermore emphasizes the locust-like nature of the players: When a marker is removed, the location becomes unworthy of visiting again to everyone, as all potential resources from it have been removed. This makes the situation a scramble for territory and route planning, in which the players try to effectively reserve as much unexplored territory as possible for themselves.

On an affective level, these dynamics steer players' attention to the potential profits of looting, while its consequences for the increasingly depleted African continent are disregarded. The excitement over how looting might positively (gems) or negatively (bandits) affect individual wealth has the players' full attention and is among the most commonly reported memories associated with the game. That said, given that there are 32 markers, flipping and taking are repetitive actions which characterize European invasion in terms of a mundane, even boring, activity. In fact, among player reviews, the simplicity of this luck-based mechanic is a common reason for complaint, while also named as a factor which seems to make the game suitable for very young children. This contrast is expressed in reviews 33 and 20: 'Played very much in my childhood, but it is too simple nowadays' (R33); 'Pretty stupid random dice rolling, but in my childhood I loved this. My children still like this for some reason' (R20). R52 speculates that the 'reason' might be entertainment: 'I quite liked this game as a child, particularly as you could add your own treasures and hazards into it. Wouldn't play with adults, but could go for a round to entertain kids.'

The recurrent attitude that *Afrikan Tähti* is a children's game is indicative of a widely held belief that games are pure mechanics rather than politically charged artifacts. Many users acknowledge the pedagogical function of the game but seem to disregard what children might learn about colonization, the relationship of Europeans with the African continent, or whiteness as a historically grown position of entitlement with violent consequences worldwide.

While a small number of users on BoardGameGeek acknowledge that *Afrikan Tähti* might be better suited as a discussion starter about colonialism than an actual game,[8] many more, especially users from Finland characterize the game solely in its role as a national 'classic' whose iconic status compels them to keep up the proud family tradition of playing it with small children. The 'classic' theme is repeated in reviews which emphasize that 'most Finns know' the game (R17, R35), 'like' it (R68) or own (R147) it. Such reviews focus on the collective 'responsibility' to embrace the game, not because of its design or gameplay experience but because of its 'classic' status among a community of Finnish players. This is epitomized in a user self-identifying as Finnish on BoardGameGeek and who writes that *Afrikan Tähti* is 'the Finnish classic that most Finns like. I'm not an exception' (R10). Here, liking the game is framed as inescapably Finnish. If one does not desire to be 'an exception' one ought to adhere to this taste. Importantly, this focus on collective belonging to a (national) taste community effectively removes any focus from the game's actual contents, themes, or history. What counts is group cohesion and attachment to a shared emotional experience.

This is in line with what Anna Rastas has called a 'selective amnesia' of 'Finnish exceptionalism' (Rastas, 2012). Because Finland has not officially participated in New Imperialism and established colonies of its own,[9] it must be presumed innocent and therefore spared uncomfortable conversations around pervasive coloniality. What we glean from user comments which combine a dismissal of *Afrikan Tähti's* mechanics with a recommendation to play it with young children is this insistence on white innocence (Wekker, 2016) and exceptionalism. We suggest that under the condition of structural racism pervading society, this selective forgetting of problematic historical contexts coupled with a selective remembering of fond childhood memories is itself a form of white perpetration. It is symbolic violence in the form of tolerating intolerance towards stereotyped and dehumanized minorities. The forgetting is invested in the idea that whiteness cannot – under any circumstances – be associated with evil. Toni Morrison has compared this to a state of "neurosis", whereby the delusion of white supremacy must be kept alive at all cost (see Oh, 2019).

What she suggests is that white supremacy has not only harmed the colonized (e.g. Fanon, 1961), but also those fashioning themselves as colonizers through a neurotic reframing of violence as innocence (Morrison, 1993; Wekker, 2016). Although individual players cannot be held accountable for the existence of the larger Nordic project of racist amnesia, our continued investment in it still contributes to the harm against those who do not have the luxury of selective forgetting because they do not access games from a place of whiteness.

Colourful Pawns and the Disavowal of Whiteness

This takes us to the question of racial identity, and how the representation of bodies, both in the game, and through players participating in the game, renders *Afrikan Tähti* a white racialized space (Bell, 2017). CWT has argued that all space is racialized, and that due to the dominance of white ideology in most social spaces in the west, white space mostly remains unseen by whites (Bell, 2017; Dyer, 1997). In *Afrikan Tähti*, the players are represented by pawns of different colours, which, rather than race, represents how the players wish to see themselves: As raceless, neutral beings moving on an equally neutral board. At the same time, the game premise troubles this assertion by framing players' presence in Africa in terms of a well-known story of the glorified explorer, whose racial identity (white) is equally well-known to us.

This puts the pawn in a paradoxical position, illustrating the dynamics of whiteness: Players are expected to play as white superior colonizers while simultaneously denying the reality of race. This was expressed in a Finnish Facebook user comment which treated the 'racelessness' of plastic pawns as an indication that associations to race and racism did not really exist in the game: 'Do the rules say that the game is only for white men, or on what basis do you claim that only they explore in the game? In my understanding, the game offers many tokens of different colours. So the problem actually was just that you have prejudices in your head.' (Second author's translation from Finnish). According to this logic, racism needs to make itself seen, for example, by explicitly excluding players of colour in the rules rather than 'merely' symbolically dehumanizing them. However, racism as an ideology precisely maintains power through not being seen and acknowledged. This is because it positions white identity as an unmarked default treating whites as 'colourless' individuals, while other racial identities are seen and categorized (Dyer, 1997, p. 45).

One way to see the implicit whiteness of player tokens is in how racial others are depicted on the African map: The racist illustrations of Black peoples dancing in front of primitive cottages, and hunting elephants and snakes with prehistoric spears, have been criticized as deeply racist (e.g. Ylänen, 2017). What we would like to add, however, is that as much as defining others, these illustrations also define the white self as a superior point of view from which racism is created and maintained. In his work on *Orientalism* (1978) Edward Said has described this dynamic of constructing the white ('occidental') self through the invention of an 'oriental' other. The Orient is a fantasy invented for the sake of 'authorizing views of it . . ., ruling over it' (Said, 1978, p. 38). Similarly, *Afrikan Tähti*'s illustrations of Africa authorize a view on it which simultaneously establishes the viewers as civilized rulers of this 'fantastical' place. This produces violence through the imagined superiority of white people entitled to look down at other races, deriving joy from enacting rituals of invading and looting, and consuming distorted images of the other.

The only instance where whiteness is directly represented is through the faces of the bandits, which are occasionally encountered when flipping the 'city' markers. These are the only non-player opponents in the game, and their threat to the players is merely economic, never deadly. Locals are explicitly present in gameplay only in the form of one single element: a static, marked point where, if the player lands on it, he is 'captured by Bedouins, and needs to roll each turn to see if he is released. Two functionally identical 'pirate' points also exist, near St. Helena, but the pirates' ethnicity is not defined. Rather than acknowledging the history of local resistance to European invasion, the game resorts to a whitewashed version of colonial adventure commonplace for popular media at its time. Monumental racist films like *The Birth of a Nation* (Griffith, 1915), *Lawrence of Arabia* (Lean, 1962), and the *Tarzan* series (since 1918) use white actors to present both white heroes and non-white enemies, usually in blackface. The seemingly arbitrary decision to place white Hollywood cowboys in Africa is likely owed to this convention.

According to Anne McClintock, historical documents of colonization are often documents of white male paranoia and megalomania, for instance in the way they displace conquest through the feminization and othering of territory (McClintock, 1995, p. 27). The cowboys are an object of white fear since they are a displacement of Black resistance-made manageable through whiteness. This is how the game reveals its attachment to white supremacist values most poignantly: In its inability to admit to the *reality* of Black African resistance to European colonization, and its commitment to the historical lie of unchallenged white supremacy. Irrespective of Mannerla's design intentions, the existence of white robbers as the only source of (manageable) danger in Africa states a clear message. Rather than admit that there have always been local forces which not only resisted, but in many cases actively defeated European colonizers (such as in the case of Ethiopia), the game would rather implant a set of white fictional cowboys.

The Persistence of the White Perpetrator: Conclusive Thoughts

We suggest that rather than portrayed directly in the form of evil or malicious wrongdoing, the white perpetrator in *Afrikan Tähti* emerges from three interlocking design features pertaining to maps, mechanics, and character design, which have been perceived as 'charming' (R64, R99, R165) by several reviewers on BoardGameGeek. On the level of map making, the game latches on to Eurocentric conventions of geography which continue a tradition of symbolic violence by disrespecting Africa's diverse topography and self-determined nomenclature. The African map is commodified according to white supremacist expectations, becoming nothing more than an exotic backdrop to what many users treat as a children's games.

On the mechanical level, the 'coin flipping' mechanic both abstracts historical atrocities by presenting them in terms of luck based economic progress for the European colonizers, and minimizes the role of local resistance to the colonial project. By putting the focus on commercial domination and the competition with others, the game reenacts the 'glory' of New Imperialism, while denying its dehumanizing aspects. In fact, dehumanization, and the repetition of race logics is performed, but never admitted, through character design, and the choice to simultaneously deny the whiteness of player characters while providing stereotypical illustrations of African peoples on the game board.

This implicitly bolsters the players' self-image as non-racialized (and therefore white) individuals and links the status of *Afrikan Tähti* as a Finnish family game classic directly to white nationalism. Importantly, this is a link which is never explicitly made by players. While some users said they use the game to teach colonial history to their children, most comments highlighted the 'Finnishness' of the game, some admitting that the only reason they play the game today is its status as a national cultural heritage and beloved family object. Childhood memories and nostalgia are named as common reasons why users feel obliged to play *Afrikan Tähti* with their children. Further, while a frequent complaint concerns the simple gameplay mechanics, none of these complaints revolve around the lessons small children might learn about European-led expeditions in 19th century Africa.

Overall, *Afrikan Tähti* demonstrates how historical board games have contributed to the whitening of board game spaces through a combination of offensive colonial game elements and their collective sanctioning through a language of nationalist nostalgia and family values. While gamer audiences have become more diverse since the game was released in 1950s, the selective stylization of *Afrikan Tähti* as a part of Finnish national self-identity indicates the ongoing denial of colonial cruelties. Post-*Afrikan Tähti*, the white perpetrator has remained an invisible leitmotif in gaming culture. As long as board games package the illusion of terra nullius, manifest destiny, and domination through colonization as a power fantasy rather than a catastrophic consequence of white megalomania, he will remain alive and kicking.

Acknowledgements

We would like to thank Johanna Granvik, Simon Nielsen, the Games and Society research group at Game Design Department Uppsala University, and the book editors for their valuable suggestions and comments. This research is supported by the Academy of Finland funded Center of Excellence in Game Culture Studies (CoE-GameCult, 312395), and the Austrian Science Fund (FWF) supported Hertha Firnberg Project T1222-G.

Notes

1 We reviewed all user comments from the following site which were written between 2010 and 2020, excluding those which did not provide a rating and at least two words in the comment section: https://boardgamegeek.com/boardgame/5130/afrikan-tahti. Considering a decade worth of comments on the game was supposed to highlight themes and priorities in the way players have made sense of the game over time.
2 See, for example 'Afrikan Tähti täyttää 50 vuotta', *Kauppalehti.fi*, 12.09.2001, p. 42.
3 This cannot only be demonstrated in the online comments, many of which refer to it as 'classic', even when giving the game a low rating (e.g. 'Legendary Finnish board game. Dull as fcuk.', 4/10 (Dec 2016)). *Afrikan Tähti* has also been included in the permanent exhibition of the Finnish Museum of Games, due to its iconic status as a Finnish family game: http://vapriikki.fi/en/pelimuseo/pelit/.
4 The entire poem can be accessed online: www.online-literature.com/swift/3515/
5 A common reasoning by players is that the game is a relic of its time and therefore cannot be expected to be geographically accurate. However, in the early 1950s when the game was designed, other place names were already in use. Viable alternatives would have been Abidjan ('Gold Coast'), and Benin ('Slave Coast').
6 This presentation of slavery as a temporary inconvenience rather than a systemic institution which has led to intergenerational trauma and wide-ranging social injustices is a symptom of the privileged position from which 'enslavement' is here imagined. For those players who use *Afrikan Tähti* for educational reasons, the 'Slave Coast' mechanic offers two potential lessons about racism: First, racial injustice relies on the commitment of white people to deny the structural impact of racism, such as in the suggestion that enslavement equals temporary inconvenience. Alternatively, the mechanic lends itself to explaining 'white fragility' (DiAngelo, 2018) which describes how white people experience instances of minor racial stress (like being temporarily held in a place) as major injustice ('enslavement'). We suggest that the potential frustration small white children may feel while held captive can thus be a useful conversation starter on the crucial differences between occasional prejudices held against white people versus slavery as an institution invented by white colonizers.

7 An infamous example from history is Belgium's King Leopold II whose economically motivated atrocities in the 'Congo Free State' during the late 19th and early 20th century included forced labor, the systematic severing of limbs, and the killing of approximately 10 million Congolese people.
8 One reviewer in particular commented on how *Afrikan Tähti* 'shows the colonial view on Africa', including the problematic imperative to exploit and leave Africa. They then suggest that the game might be used in pedagogical settings: 'Great if you want to problematize on colonialism or show how "we" viewed Africa in the 1950s, which can lead to a discussion about so many topics. So actually, it's a great game, not in itself but as a start for a discussion' (R36)
9 Anna Rastas points out that 'the idea that Finland is innocent in relation to colonialism is largely built on the fact that Finns never established any colonies for themselves. But how could they (we) have done that? Finland was part of the Swedish realm until 1809, and after that, a Grand Duchy of Finland in the Russian Empire before becoming an independent state in 1917' (Rastas, 2012, p. 3).

References

Ahmed, S. (2004). Declarations of whiteness: The non-performativity of anti-racism. *Borderlands*, *3*(2). https://webarchive.nla.gov.au/awa/20050616083826/www.borderlandsejournal.adelaide.edu.au/vol3no2_2004/ahmed_declarations.htm

Asiwaju, A. (1974). Anti-French resistance movement in Ọhọri-Ije (Dahomey), 1895–1960. *Journal of the Historical Society of Nigeria*, *7*(2), 255–269.

Bell, M. (2017). *Whiteness interrupted: Examining the impact of racialized space on white racial identity*. [Doctoral Dissertation, Syracuse University, ALL], 769. https://surface.syr.edu/etd/769

Bizzocchi, J., & Tanenbaum, T. (2011). Well read: Applying close reading techniques to gameplay experiences. In D. Davidson (Ed.), *Well played 3.0: Video games, value and meaning* (pp. 262–290). ETC Press.

Borit, C., Borit, M., & Olsen, P. (2018). Representations of colonialism in three popular, modern board games: Puerto Rico, Struggle of empires, and Archipelago. *Open Library of Humanities*, *4*(1), 17. https://doi.org/10.16995/olh.211

Brantley, C. (1981). *The Giriama and colonial resistance in Kenya, 1800–1920*. University of California Press.

Breger, C. (2008). Digital digs, or Lara Croft replaying Indiana Jones: Archaeological tropes and 'Colonial Loops' in new media narrative. *Aether: The Journal of Media Geography*, *11*, 41–60.

Chapman, A. (2016). *Digital games as history: How videogames represent the past and offer access to historical practice*. Routledge.

DiAngelo, R. (2018) *White fragility: Why it's so hard for white people to talk about racism*. Beacon Press.

Dietrich, D. (2013). Avatars of whiteness: Racial expression in video game characters. *Sociological Inquiry*, *83*(1), 82–105.

Dorn, R. (2004). *Goa: A new expedition* [Board game]. Z-man Games.

Dyer, R. (1997). *White*. Routledge.

Fanon, F. (1961). *The wretched of the earth*. Penguin.

Foasberg, N. (2016). The problematic pleasures of productivity and efficiency in Goa and Navegador. *Analog Game Studies*, *3*(1). http://analoggamestudies.org/2016/01/the-problematic-pleasures-of-productivity-and-efficiency-in-goa-and-navegador/

Gray, K. (2012). Deviant bodies, stigmatized identities, and racist acts: Examining the experiences of African-American gamers in Xbox Live. *The New Review of Hypermedia and Multimedia, 18*(4), 261–276.

Griffith, D. W. (Director) (1915). *The birth of a nation* [Film]. David W. Griffith Corp.

Harding, S. (1992). Rethinking standpoint epistemology: What is "strong objectivity?" *The Centennial Review, 36*(3), 437–470.

Harrer, S. (2018). Casual empire: Video games as neocolonial praxis. *Open Library of Humanities, 4*(1), 1–28.

Harrer, S. (2022). Beyond digital shoulder pads and sublime settings: What Monika Seidl's visuality method can teach us about critical games education. In A. Ganser, E. Lechner, B. Maly-Bowie, & E. Schörgenhuber (Eds.), *Caring for cultural studies*. V&R Unipress.

Harrer, S., & Laiti, O. (in press). Outside the racist nostalgia box: Rethinking Afrikan tähti's cultural depictions. *Journal of Games Criticism, 5*(A), Surviving Whiteness in Games.

Iweriebor, E. (1982). State systems in pre-colonial, colonial, and post-colonial Nigeria: An overview, Africa. *Rivista trimestrale di studi e documentazione dell'Istituto italiano per l'Africa e l'Oriente, 37*(4), 507–513. www.jstor.org/stable/40759619

Iweriebor, E. (2002). The psychology of colonialism. In T. Falola (Ed.), *The end of colonial rule: Nationalism and decolonization*. Carolina Academic Press.

Jeu des Échanges: France – Colonie [Board game] (1941). Office de publicite et d'impression (France).

Kaltenborn, H. V. (1939). *Diplomacy* [Board game]. Trend Game Company.

Keogh, B. (2014). Across worlds and bodies: Criticism in the age of video games. *Journal of Games Criticism, 1*(1), 1–26.

Lammes, S. (2003) On the border: Pleasure of exploration and colonial mastery in *Civilisation III Play the World*. In *Proceedings of the 2003 DiGRA international conference: Level up* (Vol. 2). http://www.digra.org/digital-library/publications/on-the-border-pleasure-of-exploration-and-colonial-mastery-in-civilization-iii-play-the-world/

Lammes, S., & de Smale, S. (2018). Hybridity, reflexivity and mapping: A collaborative ethnography of postcolonial gameplay. *Open Library of Humanities, 4*(1), 1–31. https://doi.org/10.16995/olh.290.

Lamorisse, A. (1957). *Risk* [Board game]. Hasbro.

Lean, D. (Director) (1962). *Lawrence of Arabia* [Film]. Horizon Pictures.

Leonard, D. (2003). "Live in your world, play in ours": Race, video games, and consuming the other. *Studies in Media & Information Literacy Education, 3*(4), 1–9.

López, L., de Wildt, L., & Moodie, N. (2019). 'I don't think you're going to have any aborigines in your world': Minecrafting terra nullius. *British Journal of Sociology of Education, 40*(8), 1037–1054. http://doi.org/10.1080/01425692.2019.1640596

Lorde, A. (1984). *Sister outsider: Essays and speeches*. Random House.

McClintock, A. (1995). *Imperial leather: Race, gender, and sexuality in the colonial contest*. Routledge.

Mukherjee, S. (2017). *Videogames and postcolonialism: Empire plays back*. Palgrave Macmillan.

Mukherjee, S. (2018). Playing subaltern: Video games and postcolonialism. *Games & Culture 3*(5), 504–520.

Murray, S. (2018). The work of postcolonial game studies in the play of culture. *Open Library of Humanities, 4*(1), 13. https://doi.org/10.16995/olh.285

Neill, A. (2002). Swift and the geographers: Race, space and merchant capital in Gulliver's travels. In *British discovery literature and the rise of global commerce*. Palgrave Macmillan.

Nishi, N., Matias, C., & Montoya, R. (2015). Exposing the white avatar: Projections, justifications and the ever-evolving American racism. *Social Identities, 21*(5), 459–473.

Nummelin, J. (1997). Imperialismin neljä unta ja painajainen. Afrikan tähden diskursiivista muodostumista. *Kulttuurintutkimus, 14*(2), 34–40.

Oh, I. (2019). Watch Toni Morrison Explain the "Profound Neurosis" of Racism. *Mother Jones*. www.motherjones.com/politics/2019/08/watch-toni-morrison-explain-the-profound-neurosis-of-racism/

Oyebade, A. (2002). Colonial political systems. In T. Falola (Ed.), *Colonial Africa, 1885–1939, vol. 3 of Africa*. Carolina Academic Press.

Passmore, C., Birk, M., & Mandryk, R. (2018, April 21–26). The privilege of immersion: Racial and ethnic experiences, perceptions, and beliefs in digital gaming. In *Proceedings of the 2018 CHI Conference on Human Factors in Computing Systems (CHI '18)*. Association for Computing Machinery, Paper 383. https://doi.org/10.1145/3173574.3173957

Poblocki, K. (2002). Becoming-state: The bio-cultural imperialism of *Sid Meier's Civilization*. *Focaal, 39*(1), 163–177.

Rastas, A. (2012). Reading history through Finnish exceptionalism. In K. Loftsdottir & L. Jensen (Eds.), *Whiteness' and postcolonialism in the Nordic region* (pp. 89–103). Ashgate.

Robinson, W. (2014). Orientalism and abstraction in Eurogames. *Analog Game Studies, 1*(5). https://analoggamestudies.org/2014/12/orientalism-and-abstraction-in-eurogames/

Said, E. W. (1978). *Orientalism*. Penguin.

Salen, K., & Zimmerman, E. (2004). *Rules of play: Game design fundamentals*. MIT Press.

Seidl, M. (2008). Über himmlische schwerter, schulterpolster und sitzende avatare – Geschlecht, raum und körper in computerspielen. In K. Mitgutsch & H. Rosenstingl (Eds.), *Faszination computerspielen: Theorie, kultur, erleben*. Braumüller.

Seyfarth, A. (2002). *Puerto Rico* [Board game]. Ravensburger.

South American pictorial travel and trading game [Board game] (1942). Parker Brothers.

Wekker, G. (2016). *White innocence: Paradoxes of colonialism and race*. Duke University Press.

Wilson, D. (2015). The Eurogame as heterotopia. *Analog Game Studies, 2*(7). http://analoggamestudies.org/2015/11/the-eurogame-as-heterotopia/

Ylänen, H. (2017). Kansakunta pelissä. Nationalismi ja konfliktit 1900-luvun alun suomalaisissa lautapeleissä. *Ennen ja Nyt, 17*(1). https://journal.fi/ennenjanyt/article/view/108787

Part IV
Alternative Ways of Representing Conflicts in Games

11 Narrative and Mechanical Integration

Playing with Interpersonal Conflicts in *Life Is Strange*

Fatima Jonsson and Lina Eklund

Introduction

It all starts in the future. Our choices to come already bearing fruit. Maxine 'Max' Caulfield, an aspiring photographer is trapped in a storm on a high cliff overlooking the ocean. A giant tornado is quickly moving toward her, decimating an entire town on its way. A sailboat flies through the air and smashes against a lighthouse. As Maxine turns and runs, the screen blurs and in the next scene, she finds herself in class at the prestigious Blackwell Academy. Maxine (hereby called Max) is the main protagonist in the award-winning video game (Pötzsch & Waszkiewicz, 2019) *Life Is Strange* (DontNod Entertainment, 2015) where players navigate teenage social life in the fictional sleepy coastal town of Arcadia Bay, Oregon. As the game continues, it shows a panoramic shot of a school hallway filled with youth enacting the social minefield we have come to know from film and television as symptomatic of the US school experience. Max mysteriously gains the ability to rewind time and through this supernatural power the player, as Max, engage in interpersonal conflicts, learns from these, and goes back in time to do things differently in order to save Arcadia Bay from impending disaster.

Much previous research on representations of conflicts in video games have focused on the war/military nexus (Jørgensen, 2016; Pötzsch & Hammond, 2016; Sterczewski, 2016; van den Heede et al., 2018; van Zwieten, 2011). This may be due to the fact that games and war have always stood in close relationship to one another (Pötzsch & Hammond, 2016) and physical violence is often a staple in these types of conflict. In her study of the wargame *Specs Ops: The Line* developed by Yager Development (2012), Jørgensen (2016) argues that conflicts are rarely questioned and often understood as the primary means of player agency. The convention for solving conflicts is glorified violence (Jørgensen, 2016). Research on interpersonal violent conflicts in games have looked at racial and gendered conflicts (DeVane & Squire, 2008) and violence against nonhumans in 'friendly' games (van Ooijen, 2018) such as *Stardew Valley* (Baron, 2016). However, the domination of violence as a means of solving conflicts in

DOI: 10.4324/9781003297406-16

games is not universal. For example, in the role-playing game *Fallout* (Interplay Inc., 1997) players could win by talking to the final boss rather than resort to violence. The antiwargame *This War of Mine* (11 Bit Studios, 2014) counteract and denaturalize violent interventions as players take the perspectives of civilians. However, research on video games has yet to explore alternative representations of conflicts and experiences beyond dominant narratives and interactions of violent conflicts as the primary means of player agency.

To begin to fill this research gap we engage in an in-depth case study of representations of mostly nonviolent and everyday interpersonal conflicts in the single player game *Life Is Strange* (hereby abbreviated *LiS*), that is, conflicts arising in interaction between two or more persons. As the game is about navigating social relationships between friends, high school students, stepfamily members, students, and teachers, *LiS* is a suitable case to analyze interpersonal conflicts set in an 'everyday' setting. We delimit ourselves to representations of interpersonal conflicts within the game, and exclude social interactions between players (Taylor, 2006).

In analyzing the game, we look at the underlying principles that organize players' actions, in other words the game mechanics, the methods invoked by agents for interacting with the game world (Sicart, 2011), as well as the narrative drawn on in translating the mechanics to players. As the narrative and game mechanics both support player involvement and gameplay experiences, we here consider these two key frames of what constitute a video game (Linderoth, 2015), not separated but interrelated. We analyze two core game mechanics in *LiS*, *the temporal rewind* mechanic and *the multiple choice* mechanic, their interplay with each other as well as the narrative. By focusing on the interplay of innovative game mechanics and a powerful narrative our aim with this chapter is to show how these key design elements can be leveraged to provide more nuanced and complex representations and player experiences of social conflicts beyond violence and battles.

Conflicts in Games

Games in themselves, it has been argued, build on conflict, where rules create artificial conflicts for the player and the narratives explain the presence of these conflicts, validates them and in a sense hides the fact that they are artificial (Juul, 2005). Yet, when it comes to research on representations of conflict in video games, much attention has been given to representations and discourses in wargames. Games model armed conflicts such as the Second World War and the Vietnam War as confrontations between major military powers, and have been shown to depict morally unambiguous combat in which negative aspects of violent conflict are filtered out (van den Heede et al., 2018). These types of violent conflicts in video games have almost exclusively been portrayed from an American or

Western perspective (Breuer et al., 2011; Pötzsch & Hammond, 2016). An example of this is the first-person shooter game *Medal of Honor* (Danger Close, 2010), that naturalizes violent interventions (van Zwieten, 2011), and where the US military are framed as heroes while Afghani combatants are framed as terrorists. Wargames represent a militaristic, masculinist, Western geopolitical frame of violence, where western bodies are abstracted and continually respawned – target bodies are disassembled and disappear. This has the effect of depoliticizing the violence inherent in war (Salter, 2011).

The depoliticizing of violence can be understood as rhetoric, which constructs messages or 'arguments about the way systems work in the material world' (Bogost, 2010, p. 47). This refers to the process when a [video]game introduces a computational representation of a cultural process such as conflict, and through this, the game talks about how that process is thought to function in the world (van Ooijen, 2018). Or to paraphrase van Ooijen (2018, p. 174): the way a game implements conflict says something about how conflict is thought to be carried out.

Interpersonal Conflicts

In this study, we focus on mainly non-violent interpersonal conflicts. Such a focus does not imply that interpersonal conflicts do not contain violence. We are thus interested in how conflicts in the interpersonal, micro level of person-to-person interaction are made playable and meaningful. In other words, conflicts that occur between individuals on a regular basis and which players most likely will have had concrete experiences of. An interpersonal conflict can be defined as 'a dynamic process that occurs between interdependent parties as they experience negative emotional reactions to perceived disagreements and interference with the attainment of their goals' (Barki & Hartwick, 2004, p. 8). There are thus three elements to an interpersonal conflict: 1) disagreement (cognitive); 2) negative emotions (affective); and 3) interference (behavioral) (Barki & Hartwick, 2004). According to this definition, interpersonal conflict exists only when all of its three components are present in a situation. For us, this means that interpersonal conflicts in games, like those we are studying here, can be defined as *a dynamic process where game characters (NPCs and/or Protagonist) display negative reactions to disagreements and interference with attainment of their goals represented through game mechanics and/or narrative elements.*

We also draw on George Simmel's ideas on conflict as a social form. Simmel, the classical sociologist, argued, at the turn of the last century, that conflict is a type of sociation (2011). In sociation, opposing views meet and can be resolved, and thus conflict can also lead to change (Simmel, 2011). In conflict, individuals and groups interact on the social stage and through this interaction engage with each other. While the frequent narrative framing of conflicts in games, as solvable through violence, has had a lot of criticism, conflict in itself does not always have to be negative. Conflicts also have the inherent potential to create unity. As long as we are in conflict, we are interacting with the person we are in conflict with, even if we might not like them. If any empathy for the interactional partner exists, there is conflict with the potential to resolve it, rather than indifference where we cease to care at all about the person or even recognize their existence (Simmel, 2011).

Life Is Strange

Life Is Strange is an episodic narrative adventure game in five episodes. The game was released in 2015 and is available on Windows, Playstation 3 and 4, and Xbox. Its success has been described by a game reviewer in the magazine Rolling Stone Australia as '[*LiS*] unique blend of a high school drama and supernatural powers was a fascinating combination that won over critics and gamers alike' (Guetti, 2021).

Previous studies have engaged with the game from a feminist perspective (Rakkomkaew Butt & Dunne, 2017), a queer perspective (Drouin, 2018), existentialism (de Miranda, 2018), moral engagement (Dechering & Bakkes, 2018), and the politics of the game (Pötzsch & Waszkiewicz, 2019). As stated, our focus is rather on how interpersonal conflict is represented through game mechanics and narrative. We look specifically at the rewind and multiple choice mechanics duo (Kleinman et al., 2018). Multiple choice gives players several options to interact with NPCs and objects in the game, and ultimately to influence the way the narrative unfolds. But, as stated by Dechering and Bakkes (2018), choices are not only deemed meaningful in how they present different options, as a choice must also have consequences. The game developers underscore the consequences of actions and player actions. As the introduction load screen state:

> *Life is Strange is a story-based game that features player choice, the consequences of all of your in-game actions and decisions will impact the past, present and future. Choose wisely . . .*

In *LiS*, choices have consequences for how Max's relationships with NPCs unfold. For example, if the player constantly chooses to be kind to the suicidal NPC Kate, these actions will shape Max's relationship with Kate and the way the player can or cannot interact with Kate throughout the game. As rewinding often reveals additional dialogue or action choices, the rewind mechanic and multiple choice are closely linked.

The ability to rewind time is not unique to *LiS*, and a growing number of games utilizes the rewind mechanic. It gives the player the ability to return to a previous specific point in the storyline and/or gamestate, and from there attempt to replay the game to achieve a different outcome or to experience the game differently (Kleinman et al., 2018). In *LiS*, rewinding is indicated by a rotating swirl on the screen, and displays any notable events which have occurred, such as a conversation or interaction with an object or an NPC. Besides supporting a narrative function, the rewind mechanic also supports a game level functionality, as the rewind function lets Max keep her memories and inventory while everyone else as well as the game environment reverts to a previous state. As such, the rewind mechanic gives advantages as the player can use previous information and insights learnt in conversations with NPCs, to change the same conversation, and earlier decisions. The game supports other game mechanics, such as puzzle mechanisms, but as these have less impact on the focus of our study, we have chosen not to include these.

Method

We applied close playing, a qualitative method similar to close readings in literature studies (Bizzocchi & Tanenbaum, 2011). A close reading is a detailed examination, deconstruction and analysis of a specific media text (Bizzocchi & Tanenbaum, 2011). Both authors played through all (five) episodes in November and December 2019. One of the authors played the game on a mobile phone, and the other author on a PC. When undertaking a close playing, we maintained two different levels of cognitive attention (Bizzocchi &Tanenbaum, 2011). On one level we engaged in the game in an authentic way, to absorb the game without any preconceptions. On the other hand, we had to stay distanced from our experiences, to bring objectivity to the observation of our experience. While playing, we simultaneously coded (by note taking) all instances of interpersonal conflicts we encountered. The coding was compared and discussed after each completed chapter as our games sometimes diverged due to the consequences of our actions. In a dataset we coded: chapter, name of characters involved in the conflict, environment/setting where the conflicts took place, conflict situation, interactive and non-interactive elements, resolution of the conflicts, gender of participants. Furthermore, we coded conflict characteristics: physical violence or verbal disputes, and characters emotions/reactions during the conflict. We identified around 100 instances of interpersonal conflicts. After completing all chapters, we examined this coding and applied the analytical lens of interpersonal conflict as explicated above. Through this we drew out and grouped common themes and patterns in the interpersonal conflicts we observed. Below we present our analysis of these themes. We discuss the two main game mechanics, the interplay between game mechanics and narrative, the use and limits of interpersonal conflicts, and the consequences of playing with interpersonal conflicts.

Results

Playing with Interpersonal Conflicts

One of the game's key scenes plays out in the girls' bathroom at school. Here the player, as Max, witnesses her estranged childhood friend Chloe Price, a working class, rebellious type who has dropped out from high school, get into a heated argumentation with Nathan Prescott, a spoiled upper-class student. Chloe, who needs money, threatens Nathan to tell his family that he sells drugs to kids in school. Nathan yells to Chloe to leave his family out of it and that he is sick of being controlled by others. In this heated conflict, Nathan pulls a gun on Chloe, fires a shot and Chloe falls down dead. At this point, Max, who is hiding in the bathroom, discovers that she possesses the supernatural power to rewind time as she reaches her hand out in desperation. She suddenly travels back in time to before this tragic event happened, and find herself again in the lecture room with her teacher and classmates. The player can thus return to the bathroom and intervene in the conflict between Chloe and Nathan. By hitting the fire alarm, this spooks Nathan who runs away before taking out his gun, saving Chloe. The player is thus able to intervene in the deadly interaction and change the devastating outcome of Chloe's death. Violent conflicts are to some extent part of the game's narrative, but the rewind and possibility to interact with objects allows player to interrupt, defuse, and undo violent interpersonal conflicts and harm.

The second key game mechanic of relevance for our analysis is *multiple choice*. Max engages in interactions featuring conflicts with NPCs, uses their arguments to learn and change the outcome of the interactions, often in order to avoid, diminish or solve conflicts rather than step into them. In the excerpt below we can see how the rewind and multiple choice mechanics interact together to create the particular gameplay that *LiS* puts center stage.

Excerpt 11.1 Conversation with Juliet, School hallway

Line	Interactions, bullets indicate player options, **bold** indicate the choice taken by the player
1.1 1.1	Max: Hey, Juliet, is everything cool? Juliet: Oh, yes, Max. I've locked Dana in the room because we're 'cool'. *Player options:*
1.3	• **What did she do?** • She's your friend.
1.4 1.5 1.6	Juliet: What didn't she do? Dana's been sexting with my boyfriend. Max: Ouch. How did you find out? Juliet: Uh, why do you care? Why are you even asking me? You never talk, just zone out with your camera.

Line	Interactions, bullets indicate player options, **bold** indicate the choice taken by the player
1.7	Max: That's why I'm talking to you now.
1.8	Juliet: What's my last name?
	Player options:
1.9	• **Juliet Patson.**
	• Juliet Mason.
	• Juliet Olson.
1.10	Juliet: That was truly sad. Thanks for your concern, 'Max Caulfield'. By the way, Juliet Watson.
	Rewind (the player rewinds time to start the conversation over)
2.1	Max: Hey, Juliet, is everything cool?
2.2	Juliet: Oh, yes, Max. I've locked Dana in the room because we're 'cool'.
	Player options:
	• What did she do?
	• She's your friend.
2.3	• **Juliet Watson, be nice.**
2.4	Juliet: I'm flattered. I didn't even think you knew my name at all.
2.5	Max: Uh. Of course I do.
2.6	Juliet: Thanks . . . I locked Dana in because she was sexting Zach, my boyfriend. Unbelievable.

In the segment above we see how the game offers the player to change the outcome of a conversation and conflict by being more attuned to Juliet's feelings. At first Juliet is hostile and uncooperative, claiming that Max does not care about her, proved by the fact that Max does not know her last name and she shuts down Max's attempt at helping (see line 1.1–1.10). The two characters disagree (1, cognitive), display negative emotions (2, affective), and Juliet stops Max learning more about the situation (3, behavioral); as a player it is clear that we are engaging in an interpersonal conflict. By using rewind, the player is able to defuse the conflict before it starts, by using the knowledge and experience from previous actions she now possesses (see Line 2.1–2.6). This leads to Juliet moving away from a locked door, allowing the player to enter. In this excerpt we see how Max, in a conflict with Juliet, learns about her needs, and through rewind uses the knowledge learned from the argument to interact with Juliet and foster a budding friendship.

Today, this narrative form of reversing time is incorporated into many video games (Kleinman et al., 2020), but also in other media formats such as films, perhaps made most famous in the film *Groundhog Day* (Ramis, 1993). In the film, the main character replays the same day over and over and learns an important life lesson along the way. In the game, on the other hand, it is Max, controlled by the player, who learns. In *LiS* the player can shape Max's personality, making her more or less antagonistic, and, as we shall see, choose the form the final ethical lesson of the game takes. Max improves and learns from interactions and relationships in the present in order to grow up and make herself ready for the future. Although *LiS*'s narrative suggests that past life editing would not improve our existence, the rewind mechanic still allows you to make social mistakes, to learn from these, and do better.

Making Interpersonal Conflicts Meaningful

One of the goals of the game is to unravel the mystery of the missing student Rachel Ambers as Max reconnects with her childhood friend Chloe. In a classic crime story manner, we find clues by talking to people and traversing the environment. Blackwell Academy, where most of the gameplay activities take place, is filled with interpersonal conflicts, made narratively relevant through the character's social group belongings such as social status, gender, and social class belongings. In particular, the game narrative draws on recognized forms of sexualized violence – verbal and physical – against women, such as slut shaming, and uses these themes to explain many of the interpersonal conflicts that the player engages in.

Excerpt 11.2 Max and Kate talk in Kate's room

Line	Interactions, bullets indicate player options, **bold** indicate the choice taken by the player
1.1	Kate: So Max, can I ask you a question? And please be honest.
1.2	Max: Absolutely Kate, anything.
1.3	Kate: I need to find out if Nathan Prescott helped me . . . or hurt me after that party. Should I go to the police? *Player Options:* • Go to the police.
1.4	• **Look for proof.**
1.5	Max: If you do that, they won´t believe you. You're on video grabbing all the guys and they´ll use that against you.
1.6	Kate: But I know I was drugged.
1.7	Max: That's what you have to prove, not them. I'm just telling you how the cops and school will look at this. The video doesn't exactly back you up . . .
1.8	Kate in tears: You make me feel so hopeless. . . . Thanks Max. (Kate looks away and down).
1.9	Max to herself: She did not like what I had to say. But we need more proof of what happened. ***Rewind (the player rewinds time to start the conversation over)*** *Player Options:*
2.1	• **Go to the police.** • Look for proof.

Line	Interactions, bullets indicate player options, **bold** indicate the choice taken by the player
2.2	Max: Yes, you should definitely go to the police, Kate. I totally believe every word you say. Nathan Prescott is truly dangerous.
2.3	Kate: Bless you, Max. I will go to the police . . . and also Principal Wells. With you as my back-up witness, they'll have to take us seriously now.
2.4	Max: Back-up witness? Well, I mean, I believe you and everything, but . . . we're still just spoiled punk students to the cops and faculty . . . I just think we need to be very careful here . . .
2.5	Kate: Why? Careful of what?
2.6	Max: Nothing . . . except the Prescotts are a powerful family. I hope this won't backfire on us, that's all. Even though that rich bastard has earned some serious bad karma. He'll get it . . .
2.7	Max (thinking): Time out, Max. You actually told Kate to go to the police and the Principal . . . after getting a scary text threat. Now the police will definitely drag you into this shit.

In excerpt 11.2, Kate Marsh, a bullied student and a friend of Max's, asks Max for advice on what to do when a viral video of her kissing strangers at school party is spread on social media. In line 1.1. a distraught Kate asks Max for advice as Max is the only one she can trust. Kate asks Max to be honest as she suspects that she has been drugged by Nathan Prescott, who claims to have only helped her. The player has two options, to tell Kate to go to the police and report that she was drugged during the party, and likely sexually abused, or to look for proof. The first option is perhaps the 'right' choice, in light of the game's critique of sexual policing and sexualized violence against women. On the other hand, the second option; looking for proof makes sense as it gives voice to a common experience of victims of sexual violence of not being believed. If Max, out of concern, tries to convince Kate to look for proof Kate will feel hopeless, and the interaction ends in conflict. The game, in Max's voice, tells the player what consequences this choice had (line 1.9, 'she did not like what I had to say'). The player can finish this interaction in conflict, which will have dire consequences later on, or rewind time and try again. By choosing, 'Go to the police' (line 2.1), the player can avoid a conflict with Kate. Kate's response is gratitude as Max supports her (line 2.3). Max ends the interaction by explaining to the player that she helped Kate, but the consequences will be trouble for herself (line 2.7). This can be read as a comment that helping others, the right thing to do, sometimes comes at costs for the individual.

The first choice (lines 1.1–1.9) contains disagreement and negative emotions, both visible in the excerpt, as well as interference, as the player convinces Kate to act contrary to her own desire. The disagreement between Max and Kate is narrative grounded in often debated gendered intergroup conflicts between men and women, which makes the conflict understandable and believable. Real-world intergroup conflicts – where various social groups are in conflict with each other on the social arena – is a powerful narrative resource that render interpersonal conflicts in *LiS* meaningful. The intergroup conflicts deal with difficult themes such as bullying (between groups of popular and unpopular students), sexuality, class-hierarchies, and gender, and motivates players to engage in interpersonal conflicts in order to traverse the game. In reality, many interpersonal conflicts stem from things such as past events where people have a history that causes problems or incompatible personalities, things which are perhaps harder to represent in games as it takes more effort and time to make them relatable.

The Limits of Interpersonal Conflicts

As the game progresses, Max can make peace with much of her opposition in the game. Through conflict with authority figures such as the security guard at school or the popular girl, Max can create consensus and understanding and make friends out of foes. However, as in many games of choice, the player has some agency over this and players can choose to smooth out or escalate conflicts between Max and NPCs. Excerpt 11.3 is an example of how the player is given the options of escalating or defusing conflict between Max and the popular girl Victoria. In a previous scene, Max can choose to get back at Victoria and make fun of her in front of others. If so, then Max´s room will be vandalized and a conflict with Victoria escalate.

Excerpt 11.3 Max's room

Line	Interactions, bullets indicate player options, **bold** indicate the choice taken by the player
1.1	*Previous player options:* • **Made fun of Victoria** • Didn´t make fun of Victoria
1.2 1.3	'CRAPPY ARTIST FILTHY WHORE' will be written on Max's mirror and the photo of Victoria covered in paint will be stolen. Max's stuff will be scattered near her bed. <div align="center">**ALTERNATIVE EVENT**</div>
2.1 2.2 2.3	*Previous player Options:* • Made fun of Victoria • **Didn't make fun of Victoria** *Max's room will be untouched.* *Max gets dressed at her closet.*

The narrative frames a conflict between Max and a bully and, as we see in excerpt 11.3, the *multiple choice* mechanic provides players the option to bully back or so to say take the high road. The conflict option is punished later in the game as Max´s room will be vandalized (line 1.2–1.3).

The conflict will thus take different directions depending on the player's decision, and shows that if you decide to escalate the conflict with the opponents, you will be punished, but if you decide not to (line 2.1–2.3), the game continues.

There is one key exception in the game, however, where the player is given no options. This is in those extreme situations when Max interacts with 'The evil'. In the game it is represented, aptly for the themes of the game, by an abusive, white, middle-class man in an authority position.

Excerpt 11.4 The Bunker, Max has been captured by the main villain, Mr. Jefferson

Line	Interactions, bullets indicate player options, **bold** indicate the choice taken by the player
1.1	*Max wakes up lying on the ground in an underground bunker with her hands tied, while Mr. Jefferson takes pictures of her.*
1.2	Jefferson: This angle highlights your purity, see? The slightly unconscious model is often the most open and honest. No vanity or posing just . . . pure expression. *Jefferson moves Max's leg*
1.3	Jefferson: Oh Christ . . . Look at that perfect face.
1.4	*Max tries to move her head. Jefferson smacks her back into position.*
1.5	Jefferson: *(shouting)* Hold that stare there! *(angrily)* Stay still!
1.6	*Jefferson continues to take pictures.*

The boss and main villain in the story, the art teacher Mr. Jefferson does not see the young women he drugs and abducts as potential interaction parties; he lacks empathy. In excerpt 11.4, we see that Mr. Jefferson sees the potential to exploit and has lost perspective on his victims as humans (line 1.1–1.3) by the way he treats Max. When Max tries to move her head, she is physically and verbally beaten (1.4). The game describes Mr. Jefferson as evil and it is impossible to engage in interpersonal conflict with him. Following Simmel's notion, conflict requires the recognition of the other party as the opposition. Therefore, the game does not offer players to rewind and there are very limited options to interact with Mr. Jefferson. The relationship between the young women and Mr. Jefferson in the bunker, could be understood as what Simmel characterizes as indifference. We are indifferent to something with which we have no empathy or understanding for. The potential for change, for a new consensus to be reached through conflict is thus lacking. The game here ties into perceptions of intragroup conflicts and who has and has not got power in society. Mister Jefferson represents some of the ways power intersects with unequal relationships of gender, race and age, and Max the many ways it does not.

In the game, as shown in the example, Max ends up not engaging in and solving conflicts to complete this part of the game. The gameplay experience turns from dealing with interpersonal conflicts to overcoming the environment in different ways. Puzzle mechanics come into play in the last chapter of the game, from having been less used before. When the game turns away from managing interpersonal conflict, the rewind mechanic is no longer available, and instead other game mechanics step in and contribute to the gameplay experience. The narrative makes it impossible to continue playing the game through the multiple choice/rewind mechanic combination. Here we see that how we perceive conflicts, represented in the narrative partly by referring to intergroup conflicts, shapes which game mechanics can be drawn on. This illustrates the way that game mechanics and narrative are dependent on each other.

The Impossible Choice/Conflict: Save the Girl or Save the World, the Tragedy of Lesbian Love Stories

In the end we are again at the beginning. As it should with tales of time travel. As the tornado approaches, set to rip Arcadia Bay apart, Max, standing at the lighthouse looking out over the town, faces the final choice in the game.

Excerpt 11.5 Lighthouse, final choice

Player options:
- Sacrifice Chloe
- Sacrifice Arcadia Bay

While players might come with the assumption that a game is something that can be won, as interpersonal conflicts are made playable in *LiS*, we cannot win. It is perhaps not even desirable to assign winners in interpersonal conflicts. Or, as Simmel (2011) might express it, is it understanding and empathy through conflict that is the goal? This contributes to an understanding of interpersonal conflicts, in the sense of a rhetoric (Bogost, 2010) about the way conflicts work in the material world, as not about winning but about morally informed choices. Max can either go back and undo her own action to save Chloe in the bathroom at the start of the game, or leave with Chloe and let Arcadia Bay and everyone in it perish. The end choice becomes a final ultimatum. Suddenly no rewind is available: we cannot have our cake and eat it. We as players must choose. Unfortunately, our choice lines up with a long history of unhappy endings for same sex love stories, something the game has been critiqued for. Important for our analysis, the ending contradicts the idea that we can 'win' in a game. This end is not about winning but about choosing between personal desires and what is best for the community. We can choose Chloe of course, but then we have to condemn all other characters we have met in the game.

In most games, conflicts can be won and the game form can even be said to trivialize them and reward excessive violence or killing in specific ways.

LiS, however, states that interpersonal conflicts cannot be won, and in the end no rewind is possible. As in real life. However, sometimes not having to make hard choices is what draws people to fiction. Indeed, a fan-made, alternate ending where the player gets to save both Cloe and Arcadia Bay has 2.5 million views on YouTube (Nick at Arcadia Bay, 2017). Considering that the game sold 3 million copies this is a popular alternative canon.

Concluding Discussion

In Simmel's theory, conflict has the potential to lead to compromise, to new thoughts, new states (Simmel, 2011). Through conflicts in society, we move forward. Conflict, according to Simmel, is thus not negative; it has the potential to bring parties together. In this chapter, we have shown that conflicts in games can create engaging gameplay. In the coming-of-age drama of *LiS*, the representations of interpersonal conflicts have a clear purpose. Max evolves and matures as a social human being through the interpersonal conflicts she engages in, when navigating the social minefield of an American high school. As the game progresses, Max grows up by learning how to navigate social relationships and life, mainly by managing or mitigating interpersonal conflicts.

In *LiS*, the rewind mechanic allows players to learn about NPCs through conflict, and these lessons can, after rewinding, be used to foster understanding and create social relationships, a common narrative not only in games but also in movies. Yet, the game allows players to try, and redo, to test out the consequence of various actions and paths. Rewind in combination with multiple choice allows the player to learn from previous experiences and mistakes, and by leveraging these experiences, the player can make more informed decisions. As such, the game mechanic combination can be seen as an ethical design mechanism that supports players to regret and adjust former decisions and action based on experience. The game can thus enable us to explore our relations to others and the ethical values we use to guide interactions, something video games often lack (Sicart, 2013). As *LiS* enables us as players to experience and learn from conflicts, listen to the opinions and positions of others, there is potential for empathy. These lessons can, after rewinding, be used to foster understanding for the opponents and lead to new states and thoughts.

Here we have explored how it is not only violent conflicts that can make for engaging gameplay experiences, but how disagreements regarding opinions and beliefs can also do this. As a player, as in real life, you can make the wrong decision and actions, hurting or helping yourself and others. The game allows us to navigate through social relationships, and by showing interest in and acknowledging other peoples'/characters' feelings, players can gain friends and have allies on their journey towards the end of the game. Paying attention to people and getting to know them can reward the player by progress. However, considering interpersonal conflicts the stuff of games also suggests that interactions have to be characterized by a mutual recognition of interaction parties. If conflict and ethical decisions is the focus of the gameplay experience, player's relationships with NPCs cannot be characterized by indifference. *LiS* is a telling example of a video game where empathy is not designed away but is rather underscored in the design. It is supported by the game mechanics multiple choice and rewind as well as the narrative, as Max needs to understand the opponents' opinions, perspectives, and emotions to progress in the game. Characters are thus not anonymous and abstract, whether they are close friends to Max or her bullies. They are given emotions like frustrations, anger, worries, and anxieties, and as such they are personalized and relatable. Aptly, there are no scores or points in *LiS* and the game is not in a common-sense way 'winnable', but the player can make it to the end and experience the full story.

Not all interpersonal conflicts in *LiS* are constructive – there are also representations of violent conflicts with deadly outcomes. In these, players are encouraged to act on the conflict or to undo the scene, to avoid violence. In the game interpersonal violence is mainly performed by male characters. While conforming to traditional notions of femininity and masculinity, this limits the player's repertoire to non-violent interpersonal conflicts. Considering that the game sometimes draws on stereotypical notions of femininity and masculinity, it is no surprise that the main character is a woman, adhering to ideas of the interpersonal as the domain of women. Still, players, however they identify get to play with the interpersonal care work the game simulates. Whenever a conflict escalates into violence, Max loses her agency and ability to act. This happens when Max meets the last boss, Mr. Jefferson. The interaction with the last boss cannot be characterized as conflict as the game indicate that evil cannot be interacted with. We engage thus not in conflict but in indifference (Simmel, 2011). Indeed, indifference characterizes many wargames as we as players are forced to engage in battles and conflicts with anonymized opponents where the design provides no room for seeing the other (see also Salter, 2011). In war it is said that most soldiers shoot to miss – conflict does not have to be devoid of empathy. However, wargames do not often allow for empathy, and it is often designed away.

In *LiS*, through the interplay of certain game mechanics and the overall narrative, players can explore and learn, even experience the opinions and positions of others in a rather risk-free environment. Pötzsch and Hammond (2016) argue that games are useful tools to emulate a variety of possible scenarios and challenges, and to enable a largely risk-free and repeatable experimenting in more or less realistic settings. However, Consalvo et al. (2019) note that there are limits with the magic circle as players create self-imposed boundaries when engaging with games.

Making interpersonal conflict the core challenge in a game supports a conflict worldview rather than a consensus one, acknowledging that social or personal change comes through conflict. Conflicts represented in the narrative and game mechanics can be designed to construct interpersonal conflicts as ways to create understanding, even if not consensus, despite differences. In this study, we have provided examples of promising ways of framing, designing, and thus experiencing interpersonal conflicts in video game through narrative framing in combination with multiple choice and rewind game mechanics. Social life is complex, characterized with interpersonal conflicts and ethical dilemmas to navigate through. Games could draw on this complexity in order to create more ethically grounded and complex game experiences.

Acknowledgment

Opening sentence inspired by: 'It all starts in a sanitized environment.' (Against procedurality by Miguel Sicart).

References

11 Bit Studios. (2014). *This war of mine* [PC, Mobile]. 11 Bit Studios.

Barki, H., & Hartwick, J. (2004). Conceptualizing the construct of interpersonal conflict. *International Journal of Conflict Management, 15*(3), 216–244. https://doi.org/10.1108/eb022913

Baron, E. (2016). *Stardew valley* [IOS]. ConcernedApe.

Bizzocchi, J., & Tanenbaum, J. (2011). Well read: Applying close reading techniques to gameplay experiences. In D. Davidson (Ed.), *Well played 3.0: Video games, value and meaning 3* (pp. 289–315). ETC Press.

Bogost, I. (2010). *Persuasive games: The expressive power of videogames*. MIT Press.

Breuer, J., Festl, R., & Quandt, T. (2011). In the army now: Narrative elements and realism in military first-person shooters. In *Proceedings of DiGRA 2011 conference: Think design play, 6*. DIGRA. http://www.digra.org/digital-library/publications/in-the-army-now-narrative-elements-and-realism-in-military-first-person-shooters/

Consalvo, M., Busch, T., & Jong, C. (2019). Playing a better me: How players rehearse their ethos via moral choices. *Games & Culture, 14*(3), 216–235. https://doi.org/10.1177/1555412016677449

Danger Close. (2010). *Medal of honor* [Video Game]. EA Interactive.

Dechering, A., & Bakkes, S. (2018). Moral engagement in interactive narrative games: An exploratory study on ethical agency in The walking dead and Life is strange. In *FDG '18: Proceedings of the 13th international conference on the foundations of digital games*, Article 23. Association for Computing Machinery (pp. 1–10). https://doi.org/10.1145/3235765.3235779

de Miranda, L. (2018). Life is strange and 'games are made': A philosophical interpretation of a multiple-choice existential simulator with copilot Sartre. *Games & Culture, 13*(8), 825–842. https://doi.org/10.1177/1555412016678713

DeVane, B., & Squire, K. D. (2008). The meaning of race and violence in Grand theft auto: San Andreas. *Games & Culture, 3*(3–4), 264–285. https://doi.org/10.1177/1555412008317308

DontNod Entertainment. (2015). *Life is strange* [Video Game, PC and Mobile]. Square Enix.

Drouin, R. A. (2018). Games of archiving queerly: Artefact collection and defining queer romance in Gone home and life is strange. *Alpahville: Journal of Film and Screen, 16*, 24–37.

Guetti, A. (2021, September 17). With 'Life is strange: True colors' out now, Rolling Stone goes inside the game that has helped its biggest fans discover their true selves. *Rolling Stone.* https://au.rollingstone.com/culture/culture-features/what-life-is-strange-fans-love-about-the-franchise-29841/

Interplay Inc. (1997). *Fallout* [Platform]. Bethesda Softworks.

Jørgensen, K. (2016). The positive discomfort of Specs ops: The line. *The International Journal of Computer Game Research, 16*(2).

Juul, J. (2005). *Half-real: Video games between real rules and fictional worlds.* MIT Press.

Kleinman, E., Caro, K., & Zhu, J. (2020). From immersion to metagaming: Understanding rewind mechanics in interactive storytelling. *Entertainment Computing, 33*, 100322. https://doi.org/10.1016/j.entcom.2019.100322

Kleinman, E., Carstensdottir, E., & El-Nasr, M. S. (2018). Going forward by going back: Re-defining rewind mechanics in narrative games. In *FDG '18: Proceedings of the 13th international conference on the foundations of digital games*, Article 32. Association for Computing Machinery. https://doi.org/10.1145/3235765.3235773

Linderoth, J. (2015). Creating stories for a composite form: Video game design as frame orchestration. *Journal of Gaming and Virtual Worlds, 7*(3), 279–298. https://doi.org/10.1386/jgvw.7.3.279_1

Nick at Arcadia Bay. (2017). *How to save Chloe and Arcadia Bay – Life is strange* [Video]. YouTube. www.youtube.com/watch?v=c3kZ138J_1M&t=395s

Pötzsch, H., & Hammond, P. (2016). Special issue – War/game: Studying relations between violent conflict, games, and play. *Game Studies, 16*(2). http://gamestudies.org/1602/articles/potzschhammond

Pötzsch, H., & Waszkiewicz, A. (2019). Life is bleak (in particular for women who exert power and try to change the world): The poetics and politics of life is strange. *Game Studies, 19*(3). https://munin.uit.no/handle/10037/18066

Rakkomkaew Butt, M.-A., & Dunne, D. (2017). Rebel girls and consequence in life is strange and the walking dead. *Games & Culture, 14*(4), 439–449. https://doi.org/10.1177/1555412017744695

Ramis, H. (Director). (1993). *Groundhog day* [Movie]. Columbia Pictures.

Salter, B. M. (2011). The geographical imaginations of video games: Diplomacy, Civilization, America's army and Grand theft auto IV. *Geopolitics, 16*(2), 359–388. https://doi.org/10.1080/14650045.2010.538875

Sicart, M. (2011). Against procedurality. *Game Studies, 11*(3).

Sicart, M. (2013). *Beyond choices: The design of ethical gameplay.* MIT Press.

Simmel, G. (2011). *Georg Simmel on individuality and social forms.* University of Chicago Press.

Sterczewski, P. (2016). This uprising of mine: Game conventions, cultural memory and civilian experience of war in Polish games. *International Journal of Computer Game Research, 16*(2).

Taylor, T. L. (2006). *Play between worlds: Exploring online game culture.* MIT Press.

van den Heede, P., Ribbens, K., & Jansz, J. (2018). Replaying today's wars? A study of the conceptualization of post-1989 conflict in digital 'war' games. *International Journal of Politics, Culture, and Society, 31*(3), 229–250. https://doi.org/10.1007/s10767-017-9267-5

van Ooijen, E. (2018). The killability of fish in *The Sims* 3: Pets and Stardew Valley. *The Computer Games Journal*, 7(3), 173–180. https://doi.org/10.1007/s40869-018-0055-x

van Zwieten, M. (2011). Danger close: Contesting ideologies and contemporary military conflict in first person shooters. In *Proceedings of DiGRA 2011 conference: Think design play*, 6. www.digra.org/wp-content/uploads/digital-library/11312.17439.pdf

Yager Development. (2012). *Specs ops: The line*. 2K Games.

12 The Most Intimate Conflict of All

Marriage as Conflict in Digital Games

Jakub Majewski and Piotr Siuda

Introduction

Familial, and marital conflicts represent perhaps the very smallest type of conflict under consideration in this volume. Nonetheless, their small scale belies their tremendous importance: the influence of marital conflicts on mental, physical, and family health is well documented. Individual mental well-being, higher rates of depression or eating disorders are associated with marital conflicts. The same with poorer health in general, as hostile behaviors during conflict relate to alterations in immunological, endocrine, and cardiovascular functions (Whitson & El-Sheikh, 2003).

Given this importance and the centrality of conflict to the gameplay mechanics of most digital games (Salen & Zimmerman, 2004), one might assume a range of games building their gameplay around marital conflicts. In fact, it seems quite uncommon, and games do not tackle this topic as often as expected. This fact, when considering the prevalence of marital conflicts, may at first seem surprising. However, when the issue is more closely considered, the absence of marital conflicts is unsurprising given the current state of game technology and the risk-aversion inherent to big-budget digital games. Game writers continue to bemoan the relative triteness of game narratives and the unwillingness for game developers to take risks with more difficult topics. When such topics are explored, it is typically not in big-budget 'blockbuster' releases of the so-called triple-A games, but rather in smaller games produced by independent studios where low production costs allow developers to take relatively greater risks (Bateman, 2021). Besides, the complex and intimate, personal nature of marital conflict makes it a particularly difficult subject for digital games to approach. Emotional engagement and depth of player characters are acknowledged as weaknesses in digital game narratives. In his discussion of the player-avatar relationship, Chris Bateman (2021), notes that though there is a range of ways in which the player-avatar relationship can be framed, one of the most common, and most powerful is the avatar-as-mask model. In this model, popular especially in first-person games, players are given a role, but not a defined character. Other models described by Bateman also tend to

DOI: 10.4324/9781003297406-17

sideline or limit character depth. The rule appears to be: the deeper and more defined the player character becomes, the harder it becomes for players to comfortably occupy this role. Without a strong central character, it then becomes difficult to depict marital conflicts except as limited spectacle for the player to observe, but not to participate in.

In this chapter, we examine these challenges of depicting marital conflict in games and examine some case studies of how particular games try to sidestep them. In order to better contextualize this discussion, we first briefly lay out the fundamental characteristics of marital conflicts as such. Next, we examine the broader context of romance in games, along with existing literature around this topic. The picture that emerges from this initial analysis is one of a medium that, much like other forms of entertainment, frequently explores the formation of romantic relationships, but rarely delves into the complexities of long-term relationships. Where long-term relationships do appear, they are all too often employed purely as a gameplay mechanic to provide both a goal (i.e., the formation of marriage) and a reward to the player (the benefits of being married). Very little interest is being given to exploring the actual relationship underpinning the marriage in question.

Additionally, we employ strategies borrowed from textual game analysis to drill down into a selection of case studies involving one aspect of romantic relationships, namely conflict within marriage. Textual analysis as applied to games calls for a holistic, qualitative examination of the object of study (Fernández-Vara, 2015). While most such analyses concentrate on just some aspects of the game, it is critical to examine these aspects in context, providing an overview of the game as a whole.

We chose five titles to study marital conflicts in games. Of these, *Façade* (Mateas & Stern, 2005), *The Novelist* (Hudson, 2014) and *Firewatch* (Campo Santo, 2016), delve deepest into the subject matter, with *Façade* and *The Novelist* especially placing a marital conflict at the center of both gameplay and narrative. In turn, *Firewatch* uses the subject extensively in the first part of the game, but then pushes the issue into the background. The remaining two titles chosen for study, *Grand Theft Auto V* (Rockstar North, 2013), and *Gone Home* (Fullbright, 2014) are given less attention here, as their depictions of marital conflict are less significant.

Marital Conflict: A Short Characteristic

Considering the topography of marital conflict, its sources range from psychological and verbal, and physical abusiveness to personal characteristics and behaviors, incompatible goals, wishes, and expectations. For example, spouses may complain about perceived inequity in labor division or finances with marital dissatisfaction strongly related to marriage power struggles (Fincham, 2003). Also, problems arise with sexual dissatisfaction, spousal extramarital sex, problematic drinking, or drug use with all of these being predictive of divorce. The chances of a split-up increase with reports on greater severity of problems (Gottman, 1993). Thus, the sources of these may vary, making marital conflicts a complex issue, especially since problems multiply, and spouses reciprocate negative behavior (Fincham, 2003). At the same time, marital conflicts tend to be frequent and stable, as longitudinal research on overt disagreements shows (e.g., Birditt et al., 2010).

The complex nature of the presented conflict is also evident when looking at the investigations of how marriages succeed and fail. The inability to resolve the conflict may result from poor problem-solving behaviors of spouses. However, this behavior cannot be examined in isolation, as researchers agree that it is necessary to consider both personal resources (including people's cognitive processes) and spouses' assessments of problem, for example, perceived problem difficulty (Bell et al., 1982). The marital conflict is thus personal, especially given not all conflicts are overt, and can go undetected by one of the partners or have minimal impact on them (Fincham, 2003). This usually results in marital dissatisfaction of one or both spouses, and hidden problems.

In sum, marital conflict is complex in nature, with many blind spots waiting to be studied. For example, researchers focus on how contextual variables modify conflict behavior and outcomes. The nonmarital and marital context seems to be of equal importance here. Considering only a few examples, one can indicate how external stressors, negative life events (e.g., illness, work problems, etc.), social support received, or patterns in people's attachment or commitment may shape conflicts (e.g., Fincham, 2003). This complexity, as we later show, makes marital conflicts a particularly difficult subject for digital games to approach.

Digital Games and Romance

Romance have always been one of the driving themes in narratives irrespective of medium. Digital games are no exception, with romantic subplots appearing in adventure games (e.g., the Runaway series; Pendulo Studios, 2001–2012), action games (e.g., the Uncharted series; Naughty Dog, 2007–2017), space shooters (e.g., the Wing Commander series; Origin Systems, Inc., 1990–2006), role-playing games (e.g., the Mass Effect series; BioWare, 2007–2017), strategy games (e.g., the StarCraft series; Blizzard Entertainment, 1997–2016), and even puzzle games, especially so-called hidden object puzzle adventures (e.g., *Hidden Runaway*; Pendulo Studios, 2012). There are also more specifically romance-oriented interactive visual novels (Prósinowski & Krzywdziński, 2018), and so-called dating simulators (Brathwaite, 2006).

While games frequently involve romance, they rarely engage in matters of sexuality (e.g., Brown, 2015). It has thus been argued that romance in games follows a traditional model based on fairy tales, defaulting to heterosexual monogamy (Consalvo, 2003). Much like in fairy tales, the digital game hero (typically male) usually only 'gets the girl' (typically female) at the conclusion of the storyline. Nevertheless, romance in digital games has long been an object of study. These topics can be examined from two very different perspectives, depending on whether the focus of interest are the players themselves and their activities, or game content and player interactions with this content.

Player-Centric Studies

The former perspective revolves especially around relationships in MUD and MMO games, best exemplified by Brown's (2015) study of erotic roleplay. Brown's focus is not romance narrative or gameplay as written and implemented by the game's creators. She rather concentrates on the cultural and social aspect of the encounter between players, the mediation of this encounter through virtual avatars, and the place such virtual romances occupy within the broader structures of online game culture. A side branch of the player-centric research approaches are studies of the relationship between players and their avatars (Waggoner, 2009).

Straddling the middle ground between the study of players and the study of game content is research on player-produced content, that is, game mods and the motivations of the players who produce them (e.g., Sotamaa, 2010). Unsurprisingly, some mods veer in the direction of implementing or modifying relationships (Howard, 2019), and large websites exist to aggregate such content (Majkowski, 2019). While these are beyond the scope of the present study, one can indicate player mods do not tend to add any significant complexity to relationships beyond what already exists in games (Howard, 2019; Majkowski, 2019).

Content-Centric Studies

The second perspective is research focused on game content as designed and implemented by the game's creators. Research in this area uses content analysis or game textual analysis to explore the depiction of romance and sexuality in games. Here, the emphasis is thus on the relationship between the player, again mediated through an avatar, not with other players but rather with computer-controlled NPCs (non-player characters). Also, the focus is on the relationship between NPCs, which shifts the player into the role of a mere witness.

One of the first studies of relationships and sex depictions in game content was Brenda Brathwaite's *Sex in Video Games* (2006). This wide-ranging study explores the depiction of sex, design issues and controversies around sex; it falls short, however of exploring relationships in games outside of their sexual aspect. Indeed, one of the notable aspects of research in this area is a tendency to focus on sexual content rather than relationships. This tendency was already visible in early game studies (e.g., Consalvo, 2003) and remains popular today (see, e.g., Wysocki & Lauteria, 2015). Nonetheless, some studies have also emerged that explore relationships, including marriage, beyond the merely sexual aspects, delving more deeply into the role and nature of romantic relationships in games (e.g., Howard, 2019; Prósinowski & Krzywdziński, 2018; Waern, 2010).

One of the first book-length studies exploring relationships in games is the Polish-language work *Cyfrowa Miłość: Romanse w Grach Komputerowych* (*Digital Love: Romance in Computer Games*) by Prósinowski and Krzywdziński (2018). This study can best be described as an exploratory overview, with the authors reviewing a range of games across a broad spectrum of game genres. They cover adventure games, visual novels, mobile games, and simulations, and finally the role-playing game (RPG). The RPG is a genre that stands out in this area, providing numerous examples – so much so, that the authors further break this genre down into several subgenres as well as game series. The RPG game, and especially its subgenre, the open-world RPG, typically grants the player significant agency to create and develop their own character, as well as building their relationships with the rest of the game world (Majewski, 2018). This can include or in some cases does include the possibility of entering a romance, sexual relationship (e.g., the Mass Effect series), and in some cases even forming a marriage (Prósinowski & Krzywdziński, 2018). Among games that allow players to enter marriage or a long-term relationship, Prósinowski and Krzywdzinski mention *The Elder Scrolls V: Skyrim* (Bethesda Game Studios, 2011), *Fallout 4* (Bethesda Game Studios, 2015), and the Fable (Lionhead Studios, 2004–2017) series. Marriage and long-term relationships are also possible in The Sims (Maxis, 2000–2021) series of life simulators.

Ultimately, none of the romances Prósinowski and Krzywdziński identified across different genres devote any significant attention to marital conflict. For most of the examined games, romance is either an immutable part of the game's plot, or an option the player can choose to engage into in order to spice up the game's narrative, or to expand upon the relationships between the player and other characters. The games that do allow marriage or other long-term relationships consider such relations primarily as a gameplay enhancement. For example, in *Skyrim* marriage ultimately only means that when the player occasionally returns to his or her homestead, the typically stay-at-home spouse can provide various benefits from additional income to extra food and a 'well rested' bonus for sharing a bed. Conflict between the player character and the spouse is at best abstract and non-verbal (e.g., The Sims series), but most typically literally nonexistent. This is perhaps most remarkable in the Fable series, which allows the player to divorce their spouse, but not to engage in a marital conflict.

Aside from the examples cited by Prósinowski and Krzywdziński, the 'marriage as an in-game benefit' model is also visible in the Paradox Interactive game series Crusader Kings (Paradox Development Studio, 2004–2020). This grand strategy series puts the player in control of the successive heads of a dynasty over a four-century timespan, and the marital aspect of medieval dynastic politics is a vital game mechanic. For the dynasty to thrive, gain prestige, and arrange beneficial treaties with other feudal lords, the player must carefully arrange marriages not only of their own direct heir, but also of other eligible candidates from their dynasty. These relationships do incorporate conflict, as the game procedurally simulates the ups and downs of the most important relationships at any given time. The game presents the player with role-playing decisions that may even lead to the possibility of assassination by a jealous spouse. However, ultimately, given the repetitively procedural nature of these conflicts and the emotional distance between players and their successive characters, these marriages remain a gameplay mechanic engaged in for direct gameplay benefits, rather than complex relationships. Likewise, conflict is not a genuine clash of characters, but a randomly triggered challenge for the player to overcome.

The same principle can be seen in other games not covered by Prósinowski and Krzywdziński, such as in *Mount & Blade: Warband* (TaleWorlds, 2010). The reason is not difficult to surmise: procedural relationships between the player and a non-player character must necessarily be simple. In *Skyrim*, there are more than 50 characters available to the player to marry, and the players enter these relationships with a character of their own creation, varying in race, ethnicity, personality, and profession. Sexual orientation is up to the player and the game mechanics allow same-sex marriage. The combination of numerous player configurations on one side, and numerous marriageable characters on the other means that from a production perspective, the only way to implement marriage is in a stilted manner that plays out identically regardless of who is involved, with the same dialogues leading up to the marriage, and the same dialogues and interactions between spouses after marriage (The Unofficial Elder Scrolls Pages, 2021). In such circumstances, marital conflict would inevitably be abstract and incomprehensible. It would not be feasible to prepare especially written dialogues for every possible relationship variant, while procedural generation such as was employed in the Crusader Kings series, would necessarily get very complex at this high level of granularity of individual character interactions. At the same time, *Skyrim* did incorporate a system for dynamic quest randomization and the semi-random generation of pre-prepared events to dynamize the game's social fabric (Majewski, 2018). This system could have conceivably been used for marital relationships. The fact that even this very limited level of procedural dynamization was not employed suggests marital relationships are not limited primarily by technology limitations, but by developer priorities.

Overall, most games avoid conflict in their romantic relationships. In RPGs, as noted, marital conflict is an unnecessary and undesirable complication. In other games, where romance is purely a narrative contrivance, conflict is even less desirable, as the challenge for players is to enter a relationship rather than to maintain it. In this model, even if broadly understood marital conflict does emerge, it will not be a key focal point of the game. Nonetheless, in recent years several games have emerged that do place more emphasis on marital conflict as such. These are now examined as case studies.

Marital Conflict in Games: The Case Studies

Façade (2005)

Billing itself as an 'interactive drama' rather than a game, Façade was an experimental collaboration between PhD student Michael Mateas and game developer Andrew Stern. The title is considered an important landmark in artificial intelligence research, while also regarded as a notable game, winning awards and gaining media attention at of its release (Thompson, 2020). As an experiment, Façade was released for free and never commercialized (it remains freely available today: www.playablstudios.com/facade).

Fundamentally, Façade is an attempt to use artificial intelligence to drive an interactive drama structure (Mateas & Stern, 2007). The game is structured similarly to a small-scale theatre play and the story unfolds over the course of a single evening, within a single location and just three characters. The player is a (male or female, depending on player choice) character visiting his longtime friends, the married couple Trip and Grace, after a break of several years. The game takes place entirely within Trip and Grace's apartment, and the core gameplay affords the player only three basic possibilities – to move and look about, to touch items using the mouse cursor, and to converse with Trip and Grace. The latter option is deeply developed using a word parser, that is, software that interprets the player's textual input, allowing the game to respond to a much wider variety of keywords than a typical graphical user interface would allow (for more about parsers, see Aarseth, 1997). Also, the conversations are dynamic, as the three characters are free to move about – e.g., Grace may join, and thus interrupt a conversation between the player and Trip, or a three-way conversation may splinter when someone walks away.

The game does not provide the player with objectives, but as the evening progresses, the player may discover through conversations that Trip and Grace are on the verge of divorce. The player's interactions with the couple are structured in what the developers describe as social games (Mateas & Stern, 2007) that shift as the evening proceeds. The early part of the evening is organized around two simultaneous games. Firstly, the zero-sum affinity game in which the couple seeks to interpret which side the player is on. Secondly, the hot-button game, where commenting on volatile 'hot-button' issues triggers the characters to reveal more information about the underlying conflict while affecting the outcome of the affinity game based on player behavior. Eventually the story may transition into the therapy game, in which the player may or may not help Trip and Grace better understand their marital problems and potentially achieve a breakthrough. The player's deep capacity to influence the ongoing story is notable: the player may set Trip and Grace on the path to reconciliation, or catalyze a final breakup.

The dynamics of the situation are made more complex by the aforementioned affinity game – Trip and Grace can react to the same action or phrase in different ways depending on how they perceive the player's sympathies at a given point. From the player's perspective, much of this process remains intentionally opaque. Although the game's internal systems tally affinity and therapy points for Trip and Grace as well as tracks the player's misbehaviors, these tallies are never exposed to the player. This results in dramatic, unpredictable conversations that are difficult to understand unless the player makes the effort to comprehend the personalities of the interlocutors. However, it must be noted that the limitations of the artificial intelligence and parser capabilities lead also to a different, less desirable unpredictability. As Thompson (2020) notes, the game has become an unexpected favorite among YouTubers, as its sometimes awkward drama can lead to unintentional hilarity.

Whatever the flaws of its artificial intelligence and drama systems, *Façade* integrates marital conflict into its gameplay structures. By leaving it up to the player to extract information from Trip and Grace via conversation and other interactions, *Façade* creates the impression that the player is being drawn into an emergent, dynamic argument, while also slowly revealing information about the deeper, underlying conflict that has divided the couple. Several factors have contributed to the conflict, including criticisms and even outright non-acceptance of each other's hobbies and career choices, family issues, and ultimately personality incompatibilities. These can potentially be resolved, but have been allowed to fester too long in hiding. In this way, *Façade* highlights the long-lasting and complex nature of marital conflicts, which often can stew under the surface – indeed, façade – of a seemingly happy marriage, only to explode as if by chance over something trivial. For example, the player making a chance remark about art brings to the fore a fundamental disagreement between the somewhat anti-intellectual Trip, and his artistically-minded wife.

The complex conflict in *Façade* would present a significant design challenge if the game were to cast the player in the role of one of the spouses, namely the requirement for the player to not only take on a new personality, but also to gain an awareness of the spouses' extensive histories. Such knowledge gaps between the audience and the lead characters are common in films and books, where a lead character will often suddenly reveal facts about their own past, shedding a new light on their earlier actions in the story. While knowledge gaps in non-interactive narratives only pose difficulties if the gap becomes too wide for the audience to understand the story world, in games the knowledge gap is a more formidable challenge, as typically the gap interposes itself between the player and the player's own character. The implication is thus that players cannot fully immerse themselves in their character, as they lack sufficient information about the character's personality and past to properly play the role. Many role-playing games work around this problem by casting the player in the role of an amnesiac character, who is excusably ignorant of the story world (Whitlock, 2012). Other titles reduce the player character to a 'cipher' – a relatively blank persona that players can easily overwrite with their own personality (Heussner et al., 2015). However, such solutions do not easily allow the player character to be party to a marital conflict.

Apart from the knowledge gap, there is also going to be an *affective gap* – the distance between the experience of the player character living through the emotional rollercoaster of marriage and marital conflict, and the player, who is being asked to suddenly step into, and feel a situation that had been years in the making. A game like *Façade* could cast the player as Trip or Grace but could not easily evoke in the player such complex emotions towards their virtual spouse. *Façade* avoids this conundrum by making the player a relatively ignorant bystander. And by noting the player character hasn't seen Trip and Grace in many years, the game actively encourages players to ask questions without feeling that these are questions their character should know the answer to. The problem of the knowledge and emotion gaps is a crucial one to games that engage deeply in marital conflict. *The Novelist* and *Firewatch* employ a different strategy to work around this issue.

The Novelist *(2014)*

The Novelist tells the story of Dan Kaplan, his wife Linda and son Tommy, as they go on a vacation in an isolated house. Kaplan is the titular novelist, struggling to meet the demands of his literary agent to write his next novel in time, while at the same time juggling his familial responsibilities. If *Façade* makes the player a bystander, *The Novelist* goes a step further: here, the player is almost completely separate from the game world and its inhabitants, playing a disembodied presence. It is implied the player is a ghost of some sort, but ultimately this is not referenced in any way in the narrative. As the player moves around the house, it is possible to read diaries, notes and drawings from Dan, Linda and Tommy. It is also possible to hear selected thoughts from each of the Kaplans, as well as view playbacks of their memories. The player does not directly interact with the Kaplans, and they are supposed to remain unaware of his presence.

When the Kaplans arrive at their holiday retreat, Linda reveals they are on the verge of divorce ('the d word'), and Tommy is desperately trying to gain his father's attention. The game, whose complex narrative structure was later described in detail by its creator Kent Hudson (2018) is divided into nine semi-randomly arranged chapters. In each chapter, the Kaplans face a conflict revolving around Dan's limited time. Each conflict is fundamentally structured in the same way: Dan may either concentrate on his novel, his wife, or his son. It is the player who determines what choice Dan will make in the given chapter. In each case choosing one means neglecting the others. However, if the player spends enough time exploring the given chapter, it becomes possible to discover a compromise solution to the dilemma, whereby one additional character's wishes are partially fulfilled. The game's systemic rules thus convey the message that juggling work, marriage and parenthood commitments requires repeated compromises and attention-shifts. If Dan neglects his wife in one chapter, he can make up for this in a later chapter; but repeatedly neglecting her results in disaster.

Like *Façade*, *The Novelist* is fundamentally an experimental game, with Hudson's goal being to explore a form of dynamic storytelling where control over the story is to some extent handed over to the player. The chapters are randomly rearranged in each playthrough, but each chapter will play differently depending on past choices, with Hudson paying special attention to providing systemic exceptions to 'edge cases' (Hudson, 2018). For example, if Dan has been neglecting Tommy for a while, the player will find Linda signaling that she does not wish Dan to fulfil her needs in this chapter – as one might expect from a concerned mother, she wants him instead to concentrate on fatherhood.

The Novelist's procedural story has been criticized as somewhat unconvincing and sometimes poorly written (Franklin, 2014), with the situations faced by the Kaplans at times being contrived and cliché based. At the same time, Hudson recounts many positive messages he received from players who claimed the game allowed them to meditate through the time-relationship-based dilemmas they faced in their own lives. *The Novelist* thus seems to show how games can provide the players with a systemic, reactive framework to work through and meditate on the issues involved within martial conflict. This is due to observing how the game's system reacts to their different choices and despite lacking the narrative and emotional depth to properly convey the complexities of such a conflict.

Firewatch *(2016)*

Façade and *The Novelist* resolved the problem of engaging the player in a marital conflict by sidelining the player, allowing them to explore the roots and resolution of the conflict without having to struggle with a knowledge or emotional gap. *Firewatch* instead tries to provide the player with a deep past for their character, Henry, matching Bateman's (2021) *avatar as invitation to role-play* model of player-avatar relationship. As the game begins, Henry has just set out for a summer job in an isolated tower in a Wyoming national park. Fire lookout towers serve to provide advance detection of forest fires in American national parks (Luckhurst, 2021). Each tower is manned by just one watcher, and in the 1980s when the game is set, their possibilities of contact with the outside world were limited to a walkie-talkie radio set.

At the outset, the game intercuts scenes of the player travelling to his assigned tower, with text-based flashbacks of Henry's relationship with his wife Julia, from their first meeting in a bar, through to her breakdown into early-onset dementia, and finally their separation, when Julia's Australian family decide to take her back home to Australia. Each of the flashback texts typically involves a choice for the player to make, thus making the player an active participant in the formation, development, and difficulties of Henry's marriage, reducing the knowledge gap and providing some sense of emotional buy-in for the player. For example, it is the player that determines how Henry behaved when Julia became ill – whether he exerted all possible effort to take care of her, or if he chose to run away from his problems spending more and more time in bars. Julia is taken back to Australia by her parents regardless of the player's choices, but it is the player that determines whether this was because Henry couldn't take care of her well enough, or if he *didn't want* to take care of her. Consequently, when the player finally arrives at his post and the game begins in earnest, there is a sense of *being* Henry. Having had some control over Henry's choices over several years of his life, players can better identify with the character, and attempt to behave in accordance with their vision of who Henry is.

It is at this point that Julia disappears from the picture. However, while she remains absent, Henry's marital conflict remains a deep influence over the story, that is forming a sort of relationship with Delilah, the occupant of a neighboring lookout tower. If the player allows him or herself to become emotionally immersed in the story, the choices Henry makes will inevitably be based on how the player sees Henry's emotional state. Does Henry still consider himself married, or does he consider the illness-induced conflict between himself and Julia's family to have effectively ended the marriage? Does he seek consolation by getting closer to Delilah, or does he reject her flirtations? Apart from dialogue choices, *Firewatch* provides the player with other, smaller opportunities to grapple with this dilemma. For example, as Henry gets up in the morning in his tower, the player may notice Henry's wedding ring on the table. The ring's removal may potentially be deeply symbolic – did Henry simply remove it for the night, or is he making a statement about his marriage? Though the game never comments on this, the player does nonetheless have a choice – as Henry, the player may pick up the ring and put it back on. Such reactivity is one of the key narrative strategies in *Firewatch*, with the game's dialogues frequently providing alternative lines depending on small choices made earlier in the story (Remo, 2021).

From the perspective of this chapter's topic of marital conflict, *Firewatch* is a borderline case. The story of the marriage depicted in the early stages of the game is not really the story of a marital conflict, but rather the story of a marriage maturing and progressing, only to be disrupted by a major external factor in the form of a debilitating illness (though this illness does result in a conflict between Henry and Julia's family). Overall, the game's narrative strategy of presenting the player character with a deep past and thus facilitating the partial closure of the knowledge–emotion gap between player and character is very notable in the context of the broader depiction of marital conflicts in games. Where a game would like to immerse the player directly in a marital conflict as one of the spouses, the narrative tools employed by *Firewatch* provide one method of doing so in a convincing manner. However, the game also shows the limits of this approach, with the deep history section of the game being told perfunctorily through text screens – a necessity, given the game's small development budget (Remo, 2021).

Grand Theft Auto V *(2013) and* Gone Home *(2014)*

While the previously discussed titles placed some form of marital conflict at the center of their story and gameplay mechanics, other games use such conflicts in a lesser manner, as one element in a bigger story. Two such cases will now be briefly discussed, one is *Grand Theft Auto V* (*GTA V*), to signal that marital conflicts can be present in high-budget AAA games, and the second *Gone Home*, to indicate that marital issues can merely serve as a background.

GTA V can best be described as a crime heist film turned into a game. The Grand Theft Auto series is one of the longest-running, and most financially successful digital game series (Statista, 2021). Situated in a sort of satirical mirror image of America, GTA games revolve primarily around cars and violence, pushing such content to the extreme. Such a setting does not require more than a perfunctory storyline, and this is certainly the case for *GTA V*. The narrative is conveyed using a model where non-interactive cutscenes (Klevjer, 2002) are interspersed at key points in-between much lengthier gameplay sections. The cutscenes provide establishing incidents and an explanation for the player regarding whatever the next mission is, and then leaving the player to play the game.

The narrative of *GTA V* revolves around Michael De Santa, a bank robber who some years prior to the game retired to live under a false name. Michael, already experiencing a mid-life crisis, is pushed to take on one final job, and the rest of the game exploring the consequences of this action, leading the player progressively through bigger and bigger missions. The establishing incident is Michael discovering that his wife is cheating on him. In theory, Michael's relationship with his wife and coming-of-age children is the core of the game, with cutscenes time and again returning to these characters and the perennial conflicts between them. However, it is impossible to treat this narrative seriously as an exploration of marital conflict – the marriage of a retired bank robber and a retired stripper is played here for satirical value, as are the problems faced by their physically adult, but mentally teenage children. The root causes that lead both spouses to cheat on one another are barely signaled.

If *GTA V* turns marital conflict into little more than a satirical joke, *Gone Home* treats the subject seriously but leaves it firmly in the background. The title was developed by an independent studio, Fullbright, which had been established specifically to create personal, narratively driven games. The game casts the player as a character who enters the stage after all the action had already ended – a daughter returning home after a year in Europe, and finding both her parents and her younger sister absent

As the player character, Katie, explores her family's recently inherited new home, the notes and other items she finds necessarily concentrate on her family. The material evidence presents her with a variety of hints concerning a crisis in her parents' marriage. Her mother's hair salon bill ahead of a meeting with a male co-worker suggests at least the possibility of an extramarital affair, while her father's carefully hidden pornographic 'Gentlemen Magazine' suggests he is also sexually frustrated. Conversely, a pamphlet for a marriage counselling retreat with the word 'booked' scribbled on it, serves both as an explanation for Katie's parents' absence in the house upon her return, and as a hint they are determined to work through their marital difficulties. Players do not learn definitively what happened nor what the deeper root causes definitively were. They are left with hints only, such as a backlog of communications between Katie's father and his publisher, suggesting his writing career has been bordering on the edge of failure, and that perhaps his wife was currently the household's primary provider.

Gone Home uses marital conflict not as a core theme, but as background dressing, to flesh out its characters. The same is true of *GTA V*, where marital conflict is shallow and non-interactive – mere motivation for the lead character. Other games not examined here, such as *Everybody's Gone to the Rapture* (The Chinese Room, 2015) and *Tacoma* (Fullbright, 2017), similarly use marital conflict as background dressing. It is indeed likely a range of other similar cases of background marriage and marital conflict could be found, and certainly should not be dismissed. There is a case to be made that even such limited, non-interactive use of marriage as a narrative theme opens digital games up to the possibility of exploring narratives otherwise rarely observed in games (including conflicts much more intimate than others explored in this volume).

Conclusion

Given the preoccupation games have with conflict, one might justifiably expect nuanced portrayals of marital conflict to be present in digital games. This chapter has argued this is far from true – the complex, deeply emotional nature of marital conflict in fact makes such conflicts difficult to convey in games, while their personal, small-scale aspect makes them poor subject matter for high action and adventure. Some games treat the commencement of relationships as narrative or gameplay rewards for players, sparing little attention to depicting the effort required to maintain romantic relationships in the long-term.

With the enormous volume of games available, there are certainly other titles available that contain marital conflicts, for instance the aforementioned *Everybody's Gone to the Rapture* and *Tacoma*. Nevertheless, we find the subject remains rare in games. It is also striking that with the notable exception of *GTA V* – one of the most expensive video games to date (Villapaz, 2013) – the games examined as case studies are indie games. These are a loose category that lacks a single definition, but they can be best described as games developed by small, self-funded teams with the aim of independent publication outside of the more conventional developer-publisher relationship (for more about conventional game development structures, see Kerr, 2006). One of the chief hallmarks of indie games is their unconventionality. They not only tend to employ unique visual styles enforced by the need to make themselves stand out despite a small budget (Juul, 2014, 2019), but also display a great willingness to experiment outside of the usual narrative structures (Bateman, 2021).

Façade, The Novelist, Firewatch, and *Gone Home* are a diverse group of games, but all can be described as experimental, focused on conveying a strong narrative in a unique way within a low budget. Such games choose to stand out not only through gameplay and narrative mechanics, but also through narrative themes, more readily choosing esoteric topics unattractive for big-budget productions. Consequently, while big-budget games will undoubtedly touch upon marriage and marital conflict, for more complex explorations of marital conflict that attempt to best leverage the affordances of the interactive medium, we would do well to pay attention to indie titles. It seems likely that if further mainstream titles containing marital conflict could be identified, they would do so in a manner similar to *GTA V*, limiting the conflict to a purely narrative element beyond the influence of player interactions.

Unusual themes are well served by unusual gameplay mechanics. Thus, the games analyzed in this chapter, apart from the mainstream *GTA V*, employed unique mechanics tailored towards exploring the complexities of marriage and marital conflict mentioned in its short characteristic in this chapter. *Façade* is thus built around a dialogue engine oriented toward the gradual and difficult unveiling of the hidden tensions, and their deeply buried causes. In *The Novelist*, the player becomes a sort of a 'ghost' to surreptitiously explore the needs and thoughts of the protagonists. In both cases, the gameplay concentrates not on action, and not on player development, but on gaining deep understanding of the other characters and helping them resolve their problems. The mechanics thus reinforce the theme of appropriate words and behaviors having the power to resolve marital conflicts, conditional to understanding their causes. Games can also increase awareness of the external context of a marital conflict. For example, in *Firewatch*, the actions of the player make the protagonist reminisce a negative life event as the primary source of the marital conflict. In *Firewatch* it is the illness of one of the spouses, in other games external problems relate to work or sexual life. Notably, *Firewatch* allows deeper exploration of its subject by enabling the player to determine how the protagonist had behaved prior to the game, effectively setting up a bank of memories common to the player and the player character.

Despite indie games touching marital conflicts in more detail, developers face challenges (the mentioned gaps) resulting from the complex nature of such conflicts, as discussed earlier. Resolving these challenges seems crucial not only for entertainment purposes, as games could potentially educate on managing problems marriages face. However, apart from the educational value of the game, a significant issue is the way this kind of conflict pushes at the limits of the game form, posing questions about what kinds of narratives are suitable for digital games. The unusual game mechanics employed by the experimental games described here provide interesting avenues to explore the topic of marital conflict. It also seems, however, as though mainstream game developers at the moment are largely content to limit marital relationships and other romances to achievement-like features, where the successful 'tying of the knot' effectively concludes its in-game utility. Furthermore, it is hard to find any indications that the players of games like *GTA V*, *Skyrim* or *Crusader Kings* perceive the shallowness of marriage mechanics as a problem in need of a solution. The scope of these games makes it questionable whether any potential solution would be sufficiently complex and subtle. Perhaps, then, ultimately the intimacy and intensity of marital conflicts is best left to the tailored efforts of the indie developers?

References

Aarseth, E. (1997). *Ergodic literature.* Johns Hopkins University Press.

Bateman, C. (2021). The avatar and the player's mask. In C. Bateman (Ed.), *Game writing: Narrative skills for videogames* (2nd ed., pp. 379–400). Bloomsbury Academic.

Bell, D. C., Chafetz, J. S., & Horn, L. H. (1982). Marital conflict resolution: A study of strategies and outcomes. *Journal of Family Issues, 1*(3), 111–132. https://doi.org/10.1177/019251382003001008

Bethesda Game Studios. (2011). *The elder scrolls V: Skyrim* [Microsoft Windows, PlayStation 3, Xbox 360, PlayStation 4, Xbox One, Nintendo Switch, PlayStation 5, Xbox Series X/S]. Bethesda Softworks.

Bethesda Game Studios. (2015). *Fallout 4* [Microsoft Windows, PlayStation 4, Xbox One]. Bethesda Softworks.

BioWare. (2007–2017). *Mass effect series* [Xbox 360, Microsoft Windows, iOS, PlayStation 3, Android, Windows Phone, Wii U, PlayStation 4, Xbox One]. Microsoft Game Studios, Electronic Arts.

Birditt, K. S., Brown, E., Orbuch, T. L., & McIlvane, J. M. (2010). Marital conflict behaviors and implications for divorce over 16 years. *Journal of Marriage and Family, 5*(72), 1188–1204. https://doi.org/10.1111/j.1741-3737.2010.00758.x

Blizzard Entertainment. (1997–2016). *StarCraft series* [Microsoft Windows, Classic Mac OS, macOS, Nintendo 64]. Blizzard Entertainment.

Brathwaite, B. (2006). *Sex in video games*. Charles River Media.

Brown, A. M. (2015). *Sexuality in role-playing games*. Routledge.

Campo Santo. (2016). *Firewatch* [Microsoft Windows, OS X, Linux, PlayStation 4, Xbox One, Nintendo Switch]. Panic, Campo Santo.

Consalvo, M. (2003). Hot dates and fairy tale romances: Studying sexuality in video games. In M. J. Wolf & B. Perron (Eds.), *The video game theory reader* (pp. 171–194). Routledge.

Fernández-Vara, C. (2015). *Introduction to game analysis*. Routledge.

Fincham, F. D. (2003). Marital conflict: Correlates, structure, and context. *Current Directions in Psychological Science, 1*(12), 23–27. https://doi.org/10.1111/1467-8721.01215

Franklin, C. (2014). *Errant signal: The novelist* [Video]. YouTube. www.youtube.com/watch?v=8VThsdoxwgc

Fullbright. (2014). *Gone home* [Linux, Microsoft Windows, OS X, PlayStation 4, Xbox One, Nintendo Switch, iOS]. Fullbright, Majesco Entertainment, Annapurna Interactive.

Fullbright. (2017). *Tacoma* [Linux, macOS, Windows, Xbox One, PlayStation 4]. Fullbright.

Gottman, J. M. (1993). *What predicts divorce? The relationship between marital processes and marital outcomes*. Psychology Press.

Heussner, T., Finley, T. K., Hepler, J. B., & Lemay, A. (2015). *The game narrative toolbox*. Focal Press.

Howard, K. T. (2019). Romance never changes . . . or does it? Fallout, queerness, and mods. In *DiGRA '19 – Proceedings of the 2019 DiGRA international conference: Game, play and the emerging ludo-mix*. www.digra.org/digital-library/publications/romance-never-changesor-does-it-fallout-queerness-and-mods/

Hudson, K. (2014). *The novelist* [Microsoft Windows, OS X, Linux]. Orthogonal Games.

Hudson, K. (2018). Dynamic storytelling in the novelist [Video]. *YouTube*. www.youtube.com/watch?v=4ie1NrENMaI.

Juul, J. (2014). High-tech low-tech authenticity: The creation of independent style at the independent games festival. In T. Barnes & I. Bogost (Eds.), *Proceedings of the 9th international conference on the foundations of digital games*. www.fdg2014.org/proceedings.html

Juul, J. (2019). *Handmade pixels: Independent video games and the quest for authenticity*. MIT Press.

Kerr, A. (2006). *The business and culture of digital games: Game work and game play*. SAGE.

Klevjer, R. (2002). In defense of cutscenes. In F. Mayre (Ed.), *Proceedings of computer games and digital cultures conference*. Tampere University Press. www.digra.org/digital-library/publications/in-defense-of-cutscenes/

Lionhead Studios. (2004–2017). *Fable series* [Xbox, Microsoft Windows, macOS, Xbox 360, Xbox One, Xbox Series X/S]. Xbox Game Studios.

Luckhurst, T. (2021). *Fire lookouts: The US Forest Service lookouts watching for fires* [Video]. BBC. www.bbc.com/news/world-us-canada-57626403.

Majewski, J. (2018). *The elder scrolls V: Skyrim and its audience as a world-building benchmark for indigenous virtual cultural heritage*. Bond University.

Majkowski, T. Z. (2019). Dragonborn is for porn: The intertextual semiotics of the TESV: Skyrim fan made pornographic modifications. In *DiGRA '19 – Abstract proceedings of the 2019 DiGRA international conference: Game, play and the emerging ludo-mix*. www.digra.org/digital-library/publications/dragonborn-is-for-porn-the-intertextual-semiotics-of-the-tesv-skyrim-fan-made-pornographic-modifications/

Mateas, M., & Stern, A. (2005). *Façade* [Microsoft Windows, macOS]. Procedural Arts.

Mateas, M., & Stern, A. (2007). Writing Façade: A case study in procedural authorship. In P. Harrigan & N. Wardrip-Fruin (Eds.), *Second person: Role-playing and story in games and playable media* (pp. 183–207). MIT Press.

Maxis. (2000–2021). *The Sims series* [Microsoft Windows, Mac OS, PlayStation 2, GameCube, Xbox, Game Boy Advance, Nintendo DS, PlayStation Portable, Java ME, BlackBerry OS, Bada, PlayStation 3, Xbox 360, Wii, Nintendo 3DS, macOS, PlayStation 4, Xbox One, iOS, Android, Windows Phone]. Electronic Arts.

Naughty Dog. (2007–2017). *Uncharted series* [PlayStation 3, PlayStation Vita, PlayStation 4, Android, iOS, PlayStation 5, Microsoft Windows]. Sony Interactive Entertainment.

Origin Systems, Inc. (1990–2006). *Wing Commander series*. Origin Systems, Electronic Arts.

Paradox Development Studio. (2004–2020). *Crusader Kings series* [Microsoft Windows, macOS, Linux, Xbox Series X/S, PlayStation 5]. Paradox Interactive.

Pendulo Studios. (2001–2012). *Runaway series* [iOS, Windows]. Dinamic Multimedia.

Pendulo Studios. (2012). *Hidden Runaway* [iOS, Windows]. BulkyPix.

Prósinowski, P., & Krzywdziński, P. (2018). *Cyfrowa miłość: Romanse w grach wideo*. Wydawnictwo Libron.

Remo, C. (2021). Interactive story without challenge mechanics: The design of firewatch [Video]. *YouTube*. www.youtube.com/watch?v=RVFyRV43Ei8.

Rockstar North. (2013). *Grand theft auto V* [PlayStation 3, Xbox 360, PlayStation 4, Xbox One, Microsoft Windows, PlayStation 5, Xbox Series X/S]. Rockstar Games.

Salen, K., & Zimmerman, E. (2004). *Rules of play: Game design fundamentals*. MIT Press.

Sotamaa, O. (2010). When the game is not enough: Motivations and practices among computer game modding culture. *Games & Culture*, 5(3), 239–55. https://doi.org/10.1177/1555412009359765

Statista. (2021). All time unit sales of selected games in Grand Theft Auto franchise worldwide as of May 2021. *Statista*. www.statista.com/statistics/511784/global-all-time-unit-sales-grand-theft-auto/

TaleWorlds. (2010). *Mount & blade: Warband* [Microsoft Windows, Android, macOS, Linux, PlayStation 4, Xbox One]. Paradox Interactive.

The Chinese Room. (2015). *Everybody's gone to the rapture* [PlayStation 4, Microsoft Windows]. Sony Computer Entertainment.

The Unofficial Elder Scrolls Pages. (2021, November 24). *Skyrim: Marriage*. The unofficial Elder Scrolls Pages. https://en.uesp.net/wiki/Skyrim:Marriage

Thompson, T. (2020). The story of Facade: The AI-powered interactive drama. *Gamasutra*. www.gamasutra.com/blogs/TommyThompson/20200423/361473/The_Story_of_Facade_The_AIPowered_Interactive_Drama.php

Villapaz, L. (2013). 'GTA 5' costs $265 million to develop and market, making it the most expensive video game ever produced: Report. *International Business Times*.

www.ibtimes.com/gta-5-costs-265-million-develop-market-making-it-most-expensive-video-game-ever-produced-report

Waern, A. (2010). "I'm in love with someone that doesn't exist!!" Bleed in the context of a Computer Game. In *DiGRA Nordic '10: Proceedings of the 2010 international DiGRA Nordic conference: Experiencing games: Games, play, and players, 9.* www.digra.org/digital-library/publications/im-in-love-with-someone-that-doesnt-exist-bleed-in-the-context-of-a-computer-game/

Waggoner, Z. C. (2009). *My avatar, my self: Identity in video role-playing games.* McFarland & Company.

Whitlock, K. (2012). Traumatic origins: Memory, crisis, and identity in digital RPGs. In G. A. Voorhees, J. Call, & K. Whitlock (Eds.), *Dungeons, dragons, and digital denizens: The digital role-playing game* (pp. 135–152). Continuum.

Whitson, S., & El-Sheikh, M. (2003). Marital conflict and health: Processes and protective factors. *Aggression & Violent Behavior, 3*(8), 283–312. https://doi.org/10.1016/S1359-1789(01)00067-2

Wysocki, M., & Lauteria, E. W. (Eds.). (2015). *Rated M for mature: Sex and sexuality in video games.* Bloomsbury Academic.

13 All Smoke, No Fire
The Post-mortem of Conflicts in the 'Walking Simulator' Genre

Jakub Majewski and Piotr Siuda

Introduction

It is common for digital games to position their players as active participants within a conflict (Schell, 2015). The exact nature of such scenarios differs from game to game as the diverse chapters in the presented volume demonstrate; what can be safely asserted, however, is that for most games, conflict occurs in the present tense, forming a central part of the game mechanics.

But what if a game chooses to tackle a conflict only in the past tense, removing it entirely from the sphere of game mechanics, and instead only portrays it in the game's narrative? This is in fact what happens in a variety of disparate games that have come to be known as *walking simulators*. The term 'walking simulator' may appear dismissive, and indeed it was originally pejorative in meaning (Consalvo & Paul, 2019). It refers to games that seemed to lack any substantial gameplay mechanics (Clark, 2017) and revolving around the experience of exploring a setting to gradually discover a story depicted purely through the environment and its affordances such as notes and audio recordings. Conflicts in walking simulators like *Dear Esther* (The Chinese Room, 2012), *Gone Home* (Fullbright, 2014), *Everybody's Gone to the Rapture* (The Chinese Room, 2015) and *Tacoma* (Fullbright, 2017) are thus all smoke, and no fire. These conflicts are mere ashes inviting the player to discover who started the fire, how it burned and how it was finally put out. In this sense, walking simulators arguably circumvent the narrative limitations Jesper Juul (2001) had argued to exist in games due to their forward-oriented chronological structure. Walking simulators eschew cutscenes and other devices described by Juul (2004) that other games employ to complicate the relationship between the chronology of play and chronology of the narrative. In the walking simulator, play time and event time are synchronous, and narrative complications only exist in traces of events past.

This chapter discusses the depiction of conflict in the walking simulator genre, arguing that far from eschewing conflict, walking simulators provide an alternative way for digital games to depict conflict. By turning to the past tense, walking simulators renounce conflict as a game mechanic, but

DOI: 10.4324/9781003297406-18

in exchange facilitate a slower, contemplative exploration of the conflict in post-mortem. This makes walking simulators well-suited for the examination of complex multifaced conflicts with unclear protagonists and antagonists.

Walking simulators present a wide variety of conflicts, including interpersonal, intrapersonal, intergroup or intragroup conflicts (Cox, 2003; Rahim, 1985). Interpersonal conflict occurs between people and arises from many individual differences, such as personalities, values, perceptions and other differences. Meanwhile, intrapersonal conflict is experienced by a single individual, when his or her own goals, values or roles diverge. More broadly, intrapersonal conflict is between incompatible tendencies the person must discriminate between. When unable to cope with the conflict, one may express a range of behavioral strategies such as apathy, boredom, excessive drinking or destructive behavior (Cox, 2003). Intergroup conflict occurs among members of different communities and groups, for example, work departments, companies, political parties, nations, while intragroup conflict within these groups and communities. The sources of those two types of conflict may vary, involving differences in viewpoints, ideas and opinions, or perceived interpersonal incompatibility of group members (Cox, 2003).

To explore conflict in walking simulators, the chapter first presents a brief discussion on the role of conflict as a game mechanic in digital games, contextualizing the walking simulator in the broader discussion of the limits of what construes a game. Subsequently, the chapter focuses on two pairs of walking simulators, specifically 1) *Dear Esther*, and *Everybody's Gone to the Rapture*, and 2) *Gone Home*, and *Tacoma* to describe how these games depict and characterize conflicts in their narratives and environments. While many walking simulators exist, these two pairs of games were chosen due to the strong acclaim in this genre gained by their developers, The Chinese Room and Fullbright respectively (Hinkle, 2014; Yin-Poole, 2017; Consalvo & Paul, 2019).

Methodologically, the games are examined employing textual game analysis. Fernández-Vara (2015) lays out game analysis as a method for holistic and qualitative examination. She highlights the need for such an analysis to examine the game aspects under analysis in a broader context of the whole game and its development history. While in the two decades of game studies, numerous quantitative and qualitative approaches to the examination of games have been developed (for other methods, see especially Consalvo & Dutton, 2006; Miller, 2008; Lankoski & Björk, 2015), textual game analysis is still a relatively young methodology. Fernández-Vara's (2015) textbook serves as the first major attempt to systematically approach the subject. However, textual game analysis also extensively borrows from film analysis (e.g., Bordwell & Thompson, 2013). This is especially significant when exploring walking simulators, whose emphasis on telling a story via the environment is clearly related to the concept of mise-en-scène in theatre and film. As Bordwell and Thompson (2013) explain, mise-en-scène, or putting-on-stage, is the process of arranging what will appear on the stage or the film screen, and how it will be lit and framed. Such decisions allow the creators to convey additional meaning and build or subvert audience expectations through the environment in which the action takes place.

The Mechanics of Conflict in Games and the Limits of Gameness

In an early landmark study of game design theory, Salen and Zimmerman (2004) posited that conflict is one of several fundamental characteristics of games, without which a game indeed could hardly be called a game. Salen and Zimmerman's definition was based upon a review of existing definitions of games, including such foundational works as Huizinga's *Homo Ludens* (1949), Roger Caillois' *Man, Play, and Games* (2001), and pioneer digital game designer Chris Crawford's *The Art of Computer Game Design* (1984).

Only three of the eight definitions discussed by Salen and Zimmerman explicitly invoked conflict, but all the remaining definitions were fundamentally compatible with conflict as a core game feature. Similarly, leading game scholar Jesper Juul does not explicitly include conflict in his own definition of the game as a 'a rule-based formal system with variable and quantifiable outcomes, where different outcomes are assigned different values, the player exerts effort in order to influence the outcome, the player feels emotionally attached to the outcome, and the consequences of the activity are negotiable' (Juul, 2005, p. 36). Nonetheless, as he explores in depth each of the six components of this definition, it becomes clear that his definition of player effort and player attachment to outcomes presupposes conflict in the game. According to Juul, then, a game can be distinguished from the more amorphous concept of play by the fact that it can be lost, with the player being happy to win, and unhappy to lose.

It is worth noting that the concept of losing is not the same as that of failing to complete something – indeed, losing presupposes completion. As game scholar Espen Aarseth (1997) notes, there are many traditional texts that are challenging to read through, and are at times described as 'labyrinthine', implying that it is possible to get lost in them – yet this is fundamentally different to the effort required of the player to work through an interactive text. Aarseth puts forward the idea of ergodics, with ergodic literature requiring a non-trivial effort to traverse the path to completion. Ergodics does not necessarily assume conflict, and indeed many of the works Aarseth defines as ergodic are not games, but rather interactive literature where the reader must try to traverse the text, but the text does not necessarily do anything to stop the reader. It is only when this opposition does emerge, when the text switches from passive to active opposition that the reader becomes a player, the interactive work becomes a game, and it becomes possible to lose.

Thus, conflict, whatever form it may take, provides the uncertainty of outcome central to Juul's (2005) definition of games, and a vital feature for engaging gameplay (Schell, 2015). However, not all games involve conflict, because – as Juul paradoxically notes – not all entities we call games fit the definition of games. Juul illustrates the limits of his and other definitions in the form of 'borderline cases' – works that are widely considered to be games, even though they fail to fulfil all six aspects of his definition. Examples include the open-ended simulator *SimCity* (Maxis, 1989) due to the absence of an end state, games of chance such as casino machines that require no effort, and so on. Even further out beyond borderline cases, Juul notes the existence of various phenomena that are sometimes conflated with games, though they are distinctly not games by Juul's, or indeed almost any definition. In this category Juul places freeform play, noble (i.e. rule-bound) war, and notably – hypertext fiction, a category encompassing Aarseth's ergodic literature. Juul's argument for hypertext fiction not constituting a game is that such works have a fixed outcome that cannot be changed by the player (no losing state), and there is no player attachment to the outcome. The player may or may not like the ending, but the impossibility of achieving any other ending makes emotional attachment a null point.

Disagreements over what constitutes a game are not purely academic. Such disagreements are indeed common among players. Consalvo and Paul (2019), who are critical of the value of definitions such as Juul's (2005) due to their exclusionary tendencies, discuss the history of players, critics, and even game developers disqualifying particular types of games (or not games . . . ?) based on various criteria. Such criteria are not always objective or related to any existing definition of games – just as often, they are arbitrary, emotional, or political. A game may be dismissed by gamers and gaming media because it is perceived to have been optimized towards financially exploiting players. This is evident in the case of numerous Facebook-based and free-to-play games. Another reason for disqualification could be the developer's pedigree – i.e. lack of connections to the 'proper' game industry – as with the casual game companies Zynga and King. Most importantly, games may be dismissed for their relative lack of difficulty and/or attempts to appeal to a casual audience either through the targeting of a simpler technology such as mobile phones, or through the focus on simpler, less demanding mechanics.

Juul (2010) traces the history of so-called casual games and their players, arguing such games arose simply through the process of the game industry learning to make games for a broader, non-specialist audience. Juul points out as a post-script that this change is alarming to some gamers from the specialist, 'hardcore' group, as well as to some developers, who fear that complex hardcore games will be simplified to appeal to the casual audience. This thread is taken up by Consalvo and Paul (2019), who discuss how factors such as length, target platform, and perceived difficulty lead critics and/or audiences to loudly and even aggressively dismiss a game, often also criticizing its developers. One somewhat unique 'victim' of such attitudes is the walking simulator genre.

The Walking Simulator – A Nongame?

The walking simulator arose out of the first-person shooter genre. Its technology and interface remain to this day fully grounded in first-person games, employing the same game engines, the same perspectives, and the same control interfaces. At the same time, the walking simulator was fundamentally a negation of the first-person shooter – an attempt to 'strip down a game to the point where it becomes an immersive, compelling world that players step into' (Consalvo & Paul, 2019, p. 110). Fundamentally, the *only* thing the player can do in a walking simulator is walk around a particular location, look at the environment, and pick up items to inspect them, read their contents, or to activate audio cues. The walking simulator can be seen as connected to adventure games (Adams, 2014), with the similarities especially visible in *Myst* (Cyan, 1993) and its modern descendants like *Obduction* (Cyan Worlds, 2016).

However, where adventure games like *Myst* typically introduce varied gameplay mechanics in the form of puzzles, mini-games, or interactive dialogues, walking simulators contained no such elements. The emphasis instead is on what Champion (2008), in another context, refers to as hermeneutic richness. The environment and its artefacts may convey to some limited extent a passive kind of cultural presence, which Champion compares to the archaeological concept of 'trace'. The gameplay here thus occurs in the player's mind, as he or she tries to first detect and identify all relevant traces in the game's environment, then collate and interpret these traces into a coherent story. As the case studies will show, walking simulators typically refuse to provide full disclosure, leaving sufficiently many pieces missing to allow multiple interpretations of their contents.

The controversy around walking simulators is notable because of the division between gameplayers and game critics on whether they should be rejected. While the rejection of Facebook or mobile games tended to unite game critics and journalists with gameplayers, the walking simulator gained acceptance and even acclaim on the part of game journalists, while generating substantial ire among hardcore gamers (Clark, 2017; Consalvo & Paul, 2019). There is a connection to be made here between the rise of walking simulators and the so-called GamerGate controversy. Arguably, the ire that parts of the hardcore gamer audience levelled against game journalists spilled over into an almost-ritual dislike of walking simulators based on the fact that they are perceived to be the 'darlings' of the game journalists (Clark, 2017). Consalvo and Paul (2019) note the 'cottage industry' that has sprung up around criticizing walking simulators, especially ones whose narrative contains so-called progressive themes, such as the female-centric, lesbian-themed *Gone Home*.

As noted previously, the very term 'walking simulator' was originally pejorative in meaning, though it has long since outgrown such connotations. Conversely, while walking simulators are often praised as a unique new game genre (Ballou, 2019) and as innovative forms of game design (Consalvo & Paul, 2019), it would be impossible to align this genre with most classic academic definitions of games. The walking simulator's lack of conflict and lack of variable player outcomes places it outside the bounds of both Salen and Zimmerman's (2004) and Juul's (2005) definitions. Arguably, walking simulators have more in common, in terms of structure and affordances, with hypertext fiction as described by Aarseth (1997) than with games. Yet, ultimately, there is also widespread agreement that whatever the definition of game may be, walking simulators are games (e.g., Ballou, 2019; Clark, 2017; Consalvo & Paul, 2019).

A deeper exploration of issues around game definitions would lead to the question about the sensibility and utility of strict word definitions, and to philosopher Ludwig Wittgenstein's (1968) analogy of 'family resemblances'. Wittgenstein, in his exploration of the difficulty of defining words, used the word 'game' as a key example of a word that is applied to numerous phenomena that seem to have no single unifying trait. However, upon closer examination, those phenomena can be seen to be related through a family continuum of traits (for a game studies exploration of the implications of a Wittgensteinian approach to game definitions, see Arjoranta, 2014). The concept of family resemblances relates to the idea of games as 'composites' put forward by Linderoth (2015). As Linderoth argues, the oft-discussed tension between gameplay and narrative can be dissipated if games are regarded as a composite form in which different frameworks can coexist. The tension between the gameness and simultaneous lack of gameplay in walking simulators is thus dissipated by noting the features, such as exploration mechanics, they share with games. Ultimately, for our purposes, we must simply note the specificity of the walking simulator as a game that refuses to employ conflict-based game mechanics. In spite of this, walking simulators can and do depict conflicts, though typically in past tense. Four examples of such depictions will now be discussed, divided into two pairs – The Chinese Room's *Dear Esther* and *Everybody's Gone to the Rapture* being one pair, while Fullbright's *Gone Home* and *Tacoma* being the other.

Case Studies of Conflict in Walking Simulators

Dear Esther *(2012) and* Everybody's Gone to the Rapture *(2015)*

Dear Esther stretches the concept of conflict to the extreme of the intrapersonal (Cox, 2003), that is, a person's own internal struggles. The game is frequently invoked by journalists and scholars as the protoplast and in some sense the archetype of the walking simulator (e.g., Pickard, 2016; Ballou, 2019; Consalvo & Paul, 2019).

Originally developed as a research project at the University of Portsmouth by lecturer Dan Pinchbeck, and subsequently redeveloped for commercial release, *Dear Esther* was an experiment in telling a story through the environment. Exploration was not merely the core mechanic; it was the only mechanic. *Dear Esther*'s setting is a desolate island off the shores of Scotland, devoid of human characters or interactable wildlife: there is literally nothing to interact with here. Apart from the natural landscape, the environment also contains man-made elements such as shipwrecks, a lighthouse and a shepherd's shelter, allowing the player to gain some (very limited) insight into the island's former human inhabitants from their material traces. However, the core of the story is delivered in the form of off-screen narration; the nameless narrator reads fragments of letters he had written to his wife, Esther. The letters, delivered in fragments triggered at various points on the island, are intentionally oriented more towards symbolism and poetry than description (McMullin, 2014). They simultaneously reveal a forward-moving story of the narrator's final days on the island, culminating with his implied suicide, and two backstories.

The first of these is the story of the island, its 18th century inhabitants and their encounters with an explorer, Donnelly, whose book the narrator relies on. The other story is the story of the narrator himself, especially the aftermath of the car accident that resulted in Esther's death. Conflict never comes to the fore in these letter fragments – it is always just around the corner, an implicit possibility and tension that never materialized. The narrator visited Paul, the driver responsible for Esther's death, but there was no confrontation; in the distant past, the visiting explorer Donnelly is said to have hated the materially and spiritually impoverished shepherds on the island, but if any substantial disagreement emerged in this relationship, the narrator does not reveal it. Finally, the narrator himself appears to be struggling against himself, either trying to make up his mind whether to commit suicide or striving to overcome the physical debilitation of an injury to jump off the island's tallest point – but these struggles are open to interpretation and couched in poetry.

The game establishes the post-mortem pattern of storytelling so typically employed by later walking simulators: everything here seems to be happening in the past. Even the letters read out by the narrator have already been written, with the implication that, though the story of the narrator's suicide seems to unfold in the present as the player moves through the island, it is in fact a past event, with the player and the narrator being two separate characters.

Many narrative works, such as murder mysteries, concern themselves with what happened before the present-tense story begun; this kind of storytelling also appears in many digital games, such as the first-person shooter *Bioshock* (2K Boston, 2007). However, such works do usually include a present-day story – the detective must overcome present obstacles to catch the murderer, for instance. The pattern established by *Dear Esther* is that of no interaction with human characters, and no present-tense conflict: the storytelling concentrates on uncovering the past, not influencing the present.

Everybody's Gone to the Rapture builds on where *Dear Esther* left off. Like its predecessor, *Rapture* does not ground its player as a specific character – players move about the world as a human being, but with no explanation who they are, and indeed no explanation why they are there. Also, *Rapture*'s narrative implies the world has literally just ended, with humanity wiped out by an inexplicable alien entity.

Unlike *Dear Esther*, however, *Rapture* contains a large cast of characters. The game is set in a small, idyllic English village in the 1980s, a careful recreation of the English countryside (Yin-Poole, 2017) and a plot straight out of a low-budget science fiction film. A husband-and-wife pair of scientists, Kate and Stephen, working at the astronomic observatory in the village have detected a strange pattern of lights, which seems to be alive. Somehow, they have managed to cause the light-based entity to enter the village and start subsuming people into itself by burning them to ash.

When the player enters, these events have already taken place: the village is deserted, leaving only the environment for interaction. Phones and radios, when activated, trigger the playback of past conversations – some from before the catastrophe, and others during its progress, tracking the scientists' attempts to understand and stop what was happening. Material remains also hint at past events, with stalled or wrecked cars and trains typically being arranged in such a way as to reveal what had caused them to stop functioning.

The main way of communicating the past conflicts with the player in *Rapture*, however, comes in the form of vignettes re-enacting events from the past. The vignettes revolve mainly around conversations between the village inhabitants, and while the characters involved are visually unclear – essentially just luminous silhouettes – their voices are fully understandable. Most of the vignettes concentrate on events from the last hours before and during the rapture-event, some of them depict instead conversations from days, weeks, or months before. In these vignettes, the role of the alien being is in many ways understated – most of the time, the vignettes concentrate not on the alien threat, but on characters' reactions to ongoing events, and myriad small interpersonal conflicts that emerge in the face of an unknown but deadly threat.

Not all conflicts revolve around the rapture events. A significant subplot is constructed around the scientist Kate Collins: a triple outsider in this rural community: firstly, as a scientist, secondly as an American, and thirdly, as an African American. Several vignettes depict Kate and Stephen as they attempt to integrate into the community, and the intrapersonal, interpersonal, and intragroup tensions that emerge.

The depiction of these various conflicts in vignettes gives players a broader view, being privy to conversations that show how the same events looked from various perspectives. However, the information given to the player is limited, with pieces intentionally left out to allow a broad range of interpretations. *Rapture* never attempts to explain how the player accesses these vignettes, nor why these conversations are available while others are not. Furthermore, unlike the linear *Dear Esther*, *Rapture* puts the player in a relatively open world, making it possible for the player to 'complete' the game without discovering all story fragments. Overall, the storytelling model employed in *Rapture* is even more unconventional than *Dear Esther*; while the gameplay remains as simple as in all walking simulators, *Rapture* is challenging by virtue of the effort it demands of its audience to firstly seek out story fragments, and secondly to reconstruct a mental picture of a multitude of characters bound in a complex network of relationships, and the full range of conflicts: intrapersonal, interpersonal, intragroup, and, if the light entity is considered, also intergroup (for a sense of the complexity of *Rapture*'s interwoven stories, see Hamilton, 2016).

Gone Home *(2014) and* Tacoma *(2017)*

Fullbright's two walking simulators are in many ways the opposite of The Chinese Room's games. Rather than an extensive, open and natural setting, *Gone Home* takes place entirely within a single (albeit large) house, while *Tacoma* on a space station. Rather than a story told almost purely through audio, in *Gone Home* most of the story is instead told through the material environment, while *Tacoma* weaves together both methods. Rather than an unidentified observer, the player in both cases is assigned a concrete role: there is a story to the player-character's presence.

Gone Home's narrative structure and the tools employed to deliver that narrative is strongly connected to conventional games. Like *BioShock*, *Gone Home* favors diegetic measures: the bulk of the story is told in letters, notes, post-its, journal entries and other material objects that exist physically in the world. The player is cast as Katie Greenbriar, an American college girl returning home after a gap year spent travelling in Europe. However, she finds her home mysteriously deserted, with both her parents and her younger sister Samantha absent. To further complicate matters, her home is not in fact her home – while Katie was away, the Greenbriar family had moved into a new home, recently inherited from Katie's father's deceased uncle Oscar.

Since the game is set in 1995, the comparative poverty of intercontinental communication means Katie is completely unfamiliar with the new home, as well as being out of touch with the day-to-day goings-on in her family. Thus, the game's narrative opening justifies the player's unfamiliarity with both the milieu and its absent occupants, providing diegetic motivation that unifies Katie and her player in a desire to explore. Additionally, the recent move justifies the house being full of out-of-place items, bringing to the surface old and forgotten secrets and trivia. For instance, a torn, 23-year-old letter from uncle Oscar to Katie's father Terrence hints at some past event that caused a permanent rift between the two until Oscar's lonely death in this house. The game intentionally uses the environment and early story fragments to encourage players to expect a typical haunted house story, only to gradually dispel this notion through the rest of the story. Individual story fragments inform the player about a network of interconnected intrapersonal and interpersonal struggles in the Greenbriar family. A cold disapproval for Terry's career choices from his father, a sequence of letters cataloguing Terry's failures and successes as a pulp science fiction author and electrical appliance reviewer, a workplace friendship threatening to bud into a romantic affair between Katie's mother, Janice, and one of her co-workers, and so on.

Gone Home concentrates, however, on one person in particular: Katie's younger sister Samantha. Sam's story is told through a rich panoply of text-based sources – her journal being the most important, but also letters, notes left hanging around the house as 'notices' to her parents, school assignments and other creative outputs. Sam's story is privileged as the only one where the developers choose to break the limits of diegetic environmental storytelling. At specific points and places in the house, the player will hear Sam's voice reading out relevant entries from her journal; though the player does ultimately find this journal at the game's conclusion, the way these entries are delivered ahead of this discovery is extradiegetic. Sam's story is that of a troubled teenager, whose life has been disrupted by the move to a new house and new school, who has evidently had for years struggled in her relations with her parents, and who has become entangled in a same-sex relationship with Lonnie, a girl who has become her only friend in the new school. The same-sex relationship caused a further degeneration in Sam's relations with her parents. However, by the time the player as Katie returns home, this most recent conflict has unexpectedly concluded: while Katie's parents are away at a marriage counselling retreat, Sam ran away from home with Lonnie, leaving no way to trace them.

The sources documenting *Gone Home*'s characters and intrapersonal and interpersonal conflicts are often constructed carefully as palimpsest with multiple layers of meaning. In some cases, as with one of Sam's homework assignments, there are literally multiple layers of information – the text of the assignment itself, and the teacher's comment to 'see me!' at the bottom. In other cases, the story is in the material used for the note, its location, or its state. Thus, a wastepaper bin in Sam's room contains a school disciplinary referral for her friend Lonnie. The fact that this note, which Lonnie was required to return to school signed by her father, is instead found crumpled in a bin in her friend's room reveals what Lonnie did with the note. Damage to textual sources can thus be used to hint at a character's emotional state and actions.

Tacoma builds on the methodology from *Gone Home*, but also integrates into its toolbox the storytelling methods from The Chinese Room's *Everybody's Gone to the Rapture*. Like in *Gone Home*, a lot of the story is told through material items: papers, photos, book covers, but also varied digital files accessible through computer screens. However, *Tacoma* also provides itself an excuse to depict character vignettes not dissimilar to *Rapture* – except, as seems typical for Fullbright, more strongly justified diegetically. The player in *Tacoma* is cast as Amy Ferrier, a data retrieval specialist who has been dispatched to the abandoned space station Tacoma with the mission to retrieve artificial intelligence (AI) data from the station, along with the main processing module of the station's central AI. As Amy enters the station, she is informed that everyone on the station is monitored and always recorded. These recordings can be accessed and replayed in the form of *Rapture*-like vignettes showing holographic depictions of the six members of Tacoma's crew. They are depicted in various situations as the station experiences an emergency triggered by a meteor impact that has severely limited the oxygen supply. The player's role as a data retrieval specialist encourages her to be inquisitive and watch and listen to all the vignettes, even when they show crew members in intensely personal interactions. Like *Gone Home*, *Tacoma* is structured semi-linearly: the order in which the player accesses different station sections is prescribed, ensuring the story of the station's crew is gradually revealed in a much more orderly and conventional fashion than *Rapture*, though with room for small divergences.

At *Tacoma*'s core is a science fiction story of futuristic corporate conflict. As the player explores the station and encounters more and more story fragments, she not only sees the varied personal stories of the station crew, but also discovers how the crew has been pushed against their will into a far broader intergroup conflict of a political nature. The Venturis Corporation which owns the station has been trying to push through the repeal of an international accord banning automated, unmanned space stations, the accord preventing Venturis from developing its new investment. When Venturis' boss consulted the corporation's strategic AI searching for a solution, the AI proposed to arrange an accident at Tacoma, which, by causing the death of the station crew, would demonstrate the dangers of requiring stations to always remain manned. Ultimately, the station's own AI, ODIN, can reveal this information to the crew, making it clear that they must not wait for corporate rescue, and instead must mount their own (ultimately successful) escape plan. Thus, ODIN refused to be an obedient tool of the corporation, finding a way to break its own protocols to warn the crew.

Amy arrives after the crew's evacuation, with company orders to shut down ODIN and remove its processing unit. This time, then, the player is no longer just a bystander, but an actor in the story – rather than a protagonist in the conflict, however, the player is here to clean up the traces of the conflict. However, as the player completes the assignment by collecting all data and the processing unit, it is revealed that Amy is secretly a member of the 'AI Liberation Front'. She accepted the Tacoma assignment with the ulterior motive of retrieving ODIN's processing unit not for the corporation to erase, but to take the AI into a safe haven.

In a sense, this conclusion of *Tacoma*'s story shows the limits of the walking simulator, and the understandable desire of the developers to move beyond the constraints they had originally set for themselves. The lack of gameplay mechanics and present-tense conflict is a key characteristic of the walking simulator, and by extending the game's conflict into the present, by giving the player the role of an active protagonist even without incorporating more advanced mechanics, *Tacoma* seems to be an attempt to break out of the genre's limitations.

Conclusion

The four examples discussed show how the walking simulator as a genre allows a slow, contemplative exploration of various types of conflicts: interpersonal, intrapersonal, intergroup and intragroup. Presented in past tense, these conflicts can be small or big, deeply personal or societal, simple or complex, and in each case, can be depicted from multiple perspectives. The mechanics of the walking simulator genre preclude any genuine player engagement in the conflict. Even in *Tacoma*, where Amy as a character does at the end take sides in the political conflict, the player's lack of choice about this outcome means that Amy acts, but the player merely watches, never invested. This limitation is also the genre's value in examining conflicts. The core of the walking simulator is the player's slow, deliberate movement through a space, with the game's story and structure actively encouraging players to be thorough in their exploration, leaving no stone unturned. Whether it is the radios and conversation traces in *Rapture*, crumpled notes in a wastepaper basket in *Gone Home*, or garbled text fragments in *Tacoma*, the smallest details can potentially be the keys to unlock a particular character's point of view. The player is thus taught to ignore nothing, to consider everything a part of the investigation. Having been sidelined to the role of a bystander/investigator, the player is free to consider the conflict carefully, deliberately, and without emotional engagement.

However, where do walking simulators go from here? Neither The Chinese Room nor Fullbright, thus far key trendsetters for the genre, have followed on with further walking simulators. The Chinese Room rejected subsequent publisher proposals to develop more games in this genre, with the company undergoing a painful transition to develop more traditional games (Yin-Poole, 2017). Meanwhile, recent years have exposed dramatic internal conflicts at Fullbright, culminating with Gaynor, the studio's creative head and co-founder being forced to leave the company following numerous accusations of toxic behavior (Carpenter, 2021).

The evolution of any game genre inevitably involves the introduction of new mechanics. For the walking simulator, which started off as an experimental reaction to ordinary first-person shooters, as anti-game and nongame (Watts, 2019) consciously deprived of all but the most basic mechanics, ironically, innovation may mean the genre's demise, as it loses its core characteristic. The walking simulator as a genre can be defined by the lack of active conflict and the sidelining of the player into the role of the contemplative, attentive but ultimately passive bystander/investigator. *Tacoma*, thus far the final game in Fullbright's output, displayed a desire to break from this mold by making the player an active participant, but further development on this path of activity would inevitably detract from the genre's contemplative quality. Game journalist Rachel Watts claimed the 2010s as the decade of walking simulators, where 'exploration did the talking' (Watts, 2019). This statement may prove to be literally true: the era of the walking simulator phenomenon may now be over, as new games emerge that inject traditional adventure game mechanics into this genre. A forerunner of this trend was *Firewatch* (Campo Santo, 2016), which, though described as a walking simulator (Carpenter, 2021), incorporated dynamic dialogue interactions and a far greater than usual emphasis on a present-tense story, albeit still deeply concerned with the past. *Firewatch*, forcing the player to very directly make choices that shape the lead character and his relationship with the world, may still be relying on the environmental storytelling methods the walking simulator genre had pioneered, but it has lost the genre's contemplative core. In a very real sense, this is a loss. The genre's specific approach to the examination of past conflicts certainly retains value, and could conceivably be used in many contexts as a tool to deescalate conflict (e.g., intrapersonal) by encouraging greater understanding of nuance. Even if, however, the walking simulator is subsumed into the older adventure game genre, the environmental storytelling methods the genre pioneered or developed to new heights will remain, leaving behind and indelible trace of influence in adventure games and beyond.

References

2K Boston. (2007). *Bioshock* [Microsoft Windows, Xbox 360, PlayStation 3, Mac OS X, iOS]. 2K Games.

Aarseth, E. (1997). *Ergodic literature*. Johns Hopkins University Press.

Adams, E. (2014). *Fundamentals of adventure game design*. New Riders.

Arjoranta, J. (2014). Game definitions: A Wittgensteinian approach. *Game Studies*, *14*(1).

Ballou, E. (2019). The Walking Sim is a genuinely new genre, and no one fully understands it. *Vice*. www.vice.com/en/article/wxeqzw/the-walking-sim-is-a-genuinely-new-genre-and-no-one-fully-understands-it.

Bordwell, D., & Thompson, K. (2013). *Film art: An introduction* (10th ed.). McGraw-Hill.

Caillois, R. (2001). *Man, play, and games*. University of Illinois Press.

Campo Santo. (2016). *Firewatch* [Linux, Microsoft Windows, OS X, PlayStation 4, Xbox One, Nintendo Switch]. Panic, Campo Santo.

Carpenter, N. (2021). How the founder's toxic culture tore apart Fullbright, the studio behind Gone Home. *Polygon*. www.polygon.com/22610490/fullbright-steve-gaynor-controversy-stepped-down-open-roads.

Champion, E. (2008). Roles and worlds in the hybrid RPG game of Oblivion. *International Journal of Role-Playing*, *1*, 37–52. http://hdl.handle.net/20.500.11937/26737

Clark, N. (2017, November 11). A brief history of the "walking simulator," gaming's most detested genre. *Salon*. www.salon.com/2017/11/11/a-brief-history-of-the-walking-simulator-gamings-most-detested-genre/

Consalvo, M., & Dutton, N. (2006). Game analysis: Developing a methodological toolkit for the qualitative study of games. *Game Studies, 6*(1).

Consalvo, M., & Paul, C. A. (2019). *Real games: What's legitimate and what's not in contemporary videogames*. MIT Press.

Cox, K. B. (2003). The effects of intrapersonal, intragroup, and intergroup conflict on team performance effectiveness and work satisfaction. *Nursing Administration Quarterly, 27*(2), 153–163.

Crawford, C. (1984). *The art of computer game design*. Osborne/McGraw-Hill.

Cyan. (1993). *Myst* [Mac OS, Saturn, PlayStation, 3DO, Microsoft Windows, Atari Jaguar CD, CD-i, AmigaOS, Pocket PC, PlayStation Portable, Nintendo DS, iOS, Nintendo 3DS, Android, Oculus Quest, Oculus Quest 2, Nintendo Switch, Xbox One, Xbox Series X/S]. Broderbund.

Cyan Worlds. (2016). *Obduction* [Microsoft Windows, Oculus Rift, HTC Vive, MacOS, PlayStation 4, PSVR, Xbox One]. Cyan Worlds.

Fernández-Vara, C. (2015). *Introduction to game analysis*. Routledge.

Fullbright. (2014). *Gone Home* [Linux, Microsoft Windows, OS X, PlayStation 4, Xbox One, Nintendo Switch, iOS]. Fullbright, Majesco Entertainment, Annapurna Interactive.

Fullbright. (2017). *Tacoma* [Linux, Mac OS, Windows, Xbox One, PlayStation 4]. Fullbright.

Hamilton, K. (2016, April 22). What the heck happened in Everybody's gone to the rapture? A guide. *Kotaku*. https://kotaku.com/what-the-heck-happened-in-everybody-s-gone-to-the-raptu-1724934829

Hinkle, D. (2014, January 10). Gone Home, the last of us, tearaway top GDC Award nominations. *Endgadget*. www.engadget.com/2014-01-09-gone-home-the-last-of-us-tearaway-top-gdc-award-nominations.html

Huizinga, J. (1949). *Homo ludens*. Routledge & Kegan Paul.

Juul, J. (2001). *A clash between game and narrative*. www.jesperjuul.net/thesis/

Juul, J. (2004). Introduction to game time. In N. Wardrip-Fruin & P. Harrigan (Eds.), *First person: New media as story, performance, and game* (pp. 131–142). MIT Press.

Juul, J. (2005). *Half-real*. MIT Press.

Juul, J. (2010). *A casual revolution: Reinventing video games and their players*. MIT Press.

Lankoski, P., & Björk, S. (2015). *Game research methods: An overview*. ETC Press.

Linderoth, J. (2015). Creating stories for a composite form: Video game design as frame orchestration. *Journal of Gaming & Virtual Worlds, 7*(3), 279–298. doi:10.1386/jgvw.7.3.279_1

Maxis. (1989). *SimCity* [Archimedes, Electron, Amiga, Amstrad CPC, Atari ST, BBC Micro, Commodore 64, CDTV, DESQview, MS-DOS, EPOC32, FM Towns, iOS, J2ME, Linux, Mac OS, OLPC XO-1, OS/2, PC-98, SNES, Unix, Windows, X68000, ZX Spectrum]. Maxis.

McMullin, T. (2014). Where literature and gaming collide: How games are mining literary sources of inspiration. *Eurogamer*. www.eurogamer.net/articles/2014-07-27-where-literature-and-gaming-collide.

Miller, K. (2008). The accidental carjack: Ethnography, gameworld tourism, and Grand Theft Auto. *Game Studies, 8*(1).

Pickard, J. (2016). Talking 'walking sims': The Chinese room's Dan Pinchbeck on the pointlessness of the debate. *PCGamesN*. www.pcgamesn.com/dear-esther/dan-pinchbeck-interview-are-walking-sims-games

Rahim, M. A. (1985). A strategy for managing conflict in complex organizations. *Human Relations*, *38*(1), 81–89. https://doi.org/10.1177/001872678503800105

Salen, K., & Zimmerman, E. (2004). *Rules of play: Game design fundamentals*. MIT Press.

Schell, J. (2015). *The art of game design: A book of lenses*. CRC Press.

The Chinese Room. (2012). *Dear Esther* [Microsoft Windows, OS X, PlayStation 4, Xbox One]. The Chinese Room, Curve Digital.

The Chinese Room. (2015). *Everybody's gone to the rapture* [PlayStation 4, Microsoft Windows]. Sony Computer Entertainment.

Watts, R. (2019). This is the decade where exploration did the talking. *PC Gamer*. www.pcgamer.com/this-is-the-decade-where-exploration-did-the-talking/

Wittgenstein, L. (1968). *Philosophical investigations*. Blackwell.

Yin-Poole, W. (2017). The doors close on The Chinese Room – For now. *Eurogamer*. www.eurogamer.net/articles/2017-09-25-the-doors-close-on-the-chinese-room-for-now

Index

1378(km), game 59, 61–70
4X games 14–15, 20–21, 25, 27

Aarseth, E. 30–34, 43, 228, 231
affordance 98–105, 107–113, 130; of games 99–101, 106–107, 120–121, 124–125, 221, 226, 231
Afrikan Tähti 7, 171–184
agency: military 121, 127–128, 130; player 31, 65–66, 85, 93, 93n3, 100–101, 106, 108, 191–192, 203, 212
agon 15
alea 127–128
Alexander the Great 119–120, 124
analogue game 2, 54, 76, 154; *see also* tabletop game
ambiguity in design 156–157, 159
Ancestors: The Humankind Odyssey 13–15, 18, 23–25
antagonist 3, 18, 34, 65, 227
Assassin's Creed 23–24
atomic bombs 135–139, 143, 145–150

Berlin Wall 62–63
biker war 31–32, 42, 44
Bioshock 232, 234
Black and White 17
Black Powder 123, 125
board game 4, 30, 32, 39, 43, 69, 171–174, 183–184, 184n3
Board Game Geek (BGG) 81, 93n2, 173–174, 176, 178, 180, 183
Brothers in Arms 108
bullying 200
Bülow, D. H. Freiherr von 126–127
business game 46–47, 50–51, 53–54
business network 48

Caillois, R. 15, 121, 128, 228
Call of Duty: Modern Warfare 2 161, 163

card driven game 39–42, 81, 83–85, 87–91
casual game 229
CDG *see* card driven game
cellular automata 17
challenge, in game 1, 8–9, 15–19, 97–99, 101–13, 114n3, 120, 213
chance 76–79, **82**, 89–91, 126–129, 178, 229; *see also* alea
civilization 15, 17, 20–21, 173; game series 51–53, 141
civil–military relation 85, 91
cladogram 15, 19
Clausewitz, Carl von 6, 75–83, 88–92, 98, 117, 127–128
close playing 8, 195
COIN wargame 91
Cold War 63, 86–90, 168n2, 189
collective memory 139–141
colonialism 51, 150n5, 154, 176, 180, 185n8, 185n9
coming-of-age drama 203, 219
Command 1
commander 6–7, 116–117, 119–130
competition 1, 4–5, 17–22, 24–25, 27, 30, 47–52, 179, 183
composite form 4–5, 9, 231
conflict: armed 1, 5–7, 110, 116, 154–161, 165–168, 192; definition of 2–3, 193; evolutionary 5, 13, 26; games as explanatory models of 97–99, 102, 104; intergroup 16, 18, 24, 40–42, 43, 44, 47, 199, 200–202, 227, 234–237; interpersonal 3–5, 7, 30, 34–41, 43, 191–205, 227, 233–237; intragroup 2–3, 5, 18, 24, 30, 34–35, 37–38, 43, 44, 201, 227, 233–234, 237; intrapersonal 2–4, 30, 34–39, 41, 43, 44, 227, 231, 233–235, 237–238; marital 208–222;

organizational 2; perception of 201, 227; as a social form 193–194
Conway's game of life 17
cooperation 5, 13–15, 20, 23–25, 47, 49–50, 52
coopetition 47–54
COTS (commercial of the shelf) 75–76, 81, 91
Coup d'euil 116–130
critical whiteness theory (CWT) 172, 174
Crusader Kings 212–213, 222
cultural memory 135–149, 150n1
culture of war 131

Darfur is Dying 58
darwinism 13–14, 19; vulgar 13–14, 21, 23–25
Dear Esther 226, 231–234
dehumanization 68, 159, 172, 181, 183
Democracy 3 1
designed ambivalence 7, 153–168
design–in–the–small 51–52
digital game *see* video game
Diplomacy 173
disagreement 193, 199, 215, 232
divorce 210, 212, 216, 218

ecological psychology 98–103, 106–107, 110, 112, 120, 124, 130
educational game 6, 52, 58–59, 67–70, 75–76, 92–93, 97–99, 104–106, 112, 122, 184n6, 222
Elder Scrolls V: Skyrim (*see Skyrim*)
Elgström, O. 213
empathy 8, 113, 194, 201–204
environment, in game 1, 52–53, 100, 102–104, 106, 109–110, 120, 195
environmental storytelling 8, 225, 238
ergodics 228–229
ethical dilemma 165, 205
ethics (Clausewitz) 7, 77–80, **82**, 86, 90–93
EVE Online 51–53
Everybody's Gone to the Rapture 220–221, 227, 231, 233–236
evolution 5, 13–27

Façade 209, 215–217, 221
Fallout 7, 135–136, 142–150, 192, 212
FarmVille 51
feminist 194
fidelity 46, 51, 103–104

Fire in the Lake – Insurgency in Vietnam 90
Firewatch 209, 216–219, 221–222
Flood's wargame 122–123
fog of war 78, 82, 84, 89–90, 92, 111, 128, 178
frames: analysis 59, 70; disputes 6, 59–61, 70; keyings 60, 63–64, 66–67, 69–70; laminations 60, 67; limits 59–64, 70
Frederick the Great 117, 126, 129
friction 77–78, **82**, 83–85, 89–92, 127–128

game ego 100
game for change *see* educational game
game mechanics: relation to conflict 5, 8–9, 68, 81, 173, 192–196, 202–205, 227, 231; rewind time 192–199, 201–205; of specific genres 14–15, 26, 238; puzzle 195, 201, 210, 230; of wargames 83–84, 87, 90–92
GamerGate controversy 230
gender 58, 195, 198, 200–201
gendered intergroup conflicts 191
genetic trait 14, 16, 19, 21–26
ghoul 145–149
Gibson, E. 99
Gibson, J. 99–100, 102
Goa 173
goal: in conflict 193, 202, 227; in–game 106–107, 113, 128, 198, 209, 217
god game 5, 13–19, 25–27
Goffman, E. 59; *see also* frames
Gone Home 209, 219–220, 226–227, 231, 234–237
grand strategy 81, 88–89, 212
Grand Theft Auto 209, 219–222
Great Battles of Alexander 119–120, 124–125
GTA *see Grand Theft Auto*

Hail Caesar! 124–125
Half Life 2 61
Hamlet 5, 34–39, 43–44
Hells Angels 33
Hellwig, J. C. L. 118–119
Hidden Runaway 210
Hiroshima and Nagasaki 135–139, 143–150
historiography 135–138, 141–145, 148–149, 150n1
historioludicity 135–136, 141, 143–149

Huizinga, J. 15, 238
hybrid species 22

ideal–typical field commander 6, 116–117, 130
identity 2, 62, 66, 176, 181, 183
ideological: aspects of conflicts 5, 7, 9, 82, 87–88, 172; aspects of evolution 14; aspects of games 17, 167, 174
ideology 80, 181
indie games 221–222
information field 98, 101, 109–110, 112–113
intergroup conflict *see* conflict, intergroup
intragroup conflicts *see* conflict, intragroup
interpersonal conflict *see* conflict, interpersonal
intrapersonal conflict *see* conflict, intrapersonal

Jeu des Échanges: France – Colonies 173
Julius Caesar 124, 128

keyings *see* frames; keyings
Klabbers, J. H. G. 50–54
Kriegspiel 17, 118, 129
Krigs–spelet 127

laminations *see* frames, laminations
learning 46–47, 50–54, 67, 76, 92, 97–104, 106, 110, 113, 114n1, 197, 203, 229
Life is Strange 7, 191–205
life simulator 16, 22, 26, 212
Little wars 1, 121
ludo–textual analysis 75, 83

Mannerla, K. 176–176, 182
map 103, 105, 110–112, 123, 172, 175–176, 183
marriage 8, 34, 36, 208–222
masculinity 116, 121, 123, 204
Mass Effect 210, 212
Medal of Honor 193
Men of Mayhem 30–42
military–entertainment complex 153, 156–158, 160, 166–68
military–industrial complex 15, 160
mimicry 21, 121
Mission US: Flight to Freedom 58
Mongols MC 33

morality system 6, 20, 138
Mount & Blade: Warband 213
multiple choice mechanic 192, 194, 196, 200, 202–205
Myst 230

Nagasaki *see* Hiroshima and Nagasaki
narration *see* storytelling
natural selection 13, 25–26
negative emotions 192, 197, 199
Niche 13–15, 18, 22–26
Novelist, The 209, 216–217, 221
NPC (non–player character) 23, 25, 145–146, 148, 193–196, 203–204, 211
nuclear war 7, 89–90, 135, 138–139, 142–149

Obduction 230
ontic dimensions 30–32, 43
On War see Clausewitz, Carl von
open world 31, 52, 212, 234
orthogame 3–4

Paths of Glory 81, 83–84, 86, 90–92
perception: popular 136–137; visual 2, 78, 90–100, 102–106, 108–110, 112–113, 114n2, 120
permanent war economy 154, 160
plausible deniability 7, 155, 167–168
play–act 126, 130
playful identification 14, 25–26, 65–66, 93, 108, 191–192
Playing history 2: Slave trade 59, 62–64, 66–68, 70
political economy 7, 153–156, 158–159, 165–167
politics 40, 43, 77–81, **82**, 84–85, 89–93, 141, 153, 162, 166, 177–178, 194, 213
premediation 135, 139, 142–144, 149
propaganda 21, 86, 137, 155, 157, 159, 166–167
protagonist 3, 20, 31, 34, 36, 191, 193, 221–222, 227, 236–237
Puerto Rico 172–173

race 37, **43**, 181, 183, 201, 213
racism 38, 154, 176, 181–182, 184n6
radiation 144–148
Red Queen's race 19
reenactment 6, 66, 97–113
Reisswitz, G. H. R. J. von 118, 129
remediation 135, 139, 142–144, 147–149

Reykholt 4
rhetoric 17, 193, 202
Risk 171, 173
role-playing game (RPG) 7, 15, 51, 135, 192, 212
romance 209–213, 222
romantic relationship 209, 221
rule system 1, 119–120, 125–126, 130, 161
Runaway 210

SAMCRO 35–44
sandbox game 18, 52
de Saxe, M. 117, 126, 129
serious game *see* educational game
Shakespeare, W. 34
SimCity 229
Simmel, G. 193, 201–203
Sims, The 2, 221
simulation 76, 86, 172, 212; business 46–54; evolution 5–6, 14, 17, 19–20, 23, 26–27; veracity (*see* fidelity); war 97–98, 102, 116, 120, 123
Skyrim 212–213, 222, 225
slavery 59, 62, 64, 68–69, 173, 177, 184n6
Slave Tetris 62–63, 68–69
social class 198
sociation 193
Sons of Anarchy 5, 30–44
South American Pictoral Travel and Trading Game 173
speciation 19–20
Spec Ops: The Line 161, 163–164, 167, 191
Spore 13–15, 18–25
sport 1, 60
stakes 2–3, 50
StarCraft 210
Stardew Valley 191
Star of Africa *see Afrikan Tähti*
storytelling 3, 8, 217, 232, 234–235, 238
strategy: of behaviour 173, 227; business 48; evolutionary 15; for game analysis 168, 209; for game design 14, 69, 216, 218–219; gameplay 13, 20, 22, 40–42, 43, 83, 92; games 14–17, 20, 25, 27, 106, 108, 154, 172, 210, 224, 226, 229; warfare 1, 75, 78, 80, 86, 88, 92–93, 98, 105, 127
Sweatshop 58

tabletop game 7, 17, 32, 75, 81, 90–91, 93n2, 119, 124
Tacoma 220–221, 226–227, 231, 234–237
tactics 1, 75, 80, 89, 92, 98, 105, 108, 117–121, 129–130, 146, 156, 178
technological determinism 15
teenager 191, 219, 235
temporal rewind mechanic *see* game mechanics, rewind time
Tetris 62
textual analysis 75, 83, 209, 211
This War of Mine 91, 155, 161, 165, 192
Tragedy of Hamlet, The *see Hamlet*
Train 69–70
trinity 77, 79, **82**, 85–86, 90–91
Triumph of Chaos 93n3
Twilight Struggle 81–92

Ukraine 93–94
uncertainty 3, 76–78, **82**, 84, 89, 91–92, 129, 155–156, 228
Uncharted 210

value creation 48
Vasco da Gama 172
victory 1, 20–21, 25, 77, 79, **82**, 86–87, 91–92, 118
video game 2–4, 18, 27, 64, 106–109, 135, 141–149, 153, 172, 191–193, 205, 208–211, 220–222, 226–228; colonial 171–175, 179, 181; in games 15, 42, 83, 88, 157, 159, 162, 172; in nature 14, 24, 25; physical 1, 7, 191, 195; sexual 197, 199; in sport 60; symbolic 181–183; violence 14, 24–25, 42, 103, 107, 111, 191–195, 198–199, 202, 204; in warfare 77–80, **82**, 83, 88–91

walking simulator 8, 226–238
wargame 9, 19, 47, 81–83, 86, 89–93, 117–130; critical analysis of 7–9, 155, 159, 164, 191–193, 204; educational 1, 5–6, 75–76, 97–113, 104, 107, 112
wargamer 6, 19, 117, 120, 123, 128–130
warrior 116–117, 122–124, 130
Wells, H. G. 1, 121–123
whiteness 172–175, 180–183
Wing Commander 210
Wow Cool Robot meme 157–158, 166, 168n3

For Product Safety Concerns and Information please contact our EU representative GPSR@taylorandfrancis.com
Taylor & Francis Verlag GmbH, Kaufingerstraße 24, 80331 München, Germany

www.ingramcontent.com/pod-product-compliance
Lightning Source LLC
Chambersburg PA
CBHW051354290426
44108CB00015B/2004